AF361558

New Deal, New Landscape

New Deal

Tara Mitchell Mielnik

New Landscape

The CIVILIAN CONSERVATION CORPS *and* SOUTH CAROLINA'S STATE PARKS

THE UNIVERSITY OF SOUTH CAROLINA PRESS

© 2011 University of South Carolina

Published by the University of South Carolina Press
Columbia, South Carolina 29208

www.sc.edu/uscpress

Manufactured in the United States of America

20 19 18 17 16 15 14 13 12 11
10 9 8 7 6 5 4 3 2 1

Library of Congress Cataloging-in-Publication Data
Mielnik, Tara Mitchell.
  New Deal, new landscape : the Civilian Conservation Corps and South
Carolina's state parks / Tara Mitchell Mielnik.
     p. cm.
  Includes bibliographical references and index.
  ISBN 978-1-57003-984-3 (cloth : alk. paper)
  1. Civilian Conservation Corps (U.S.)—South Carolina—History. 2. Parks—
South Carolina—History. 3. Conservation of natural resources—South
Carolina—History. I. Title.
  S932.S78M54 2011
  333.78'309757—dc23
                              2011017272

Preceeding spread and chapter opening photographs: sand ripples, © Ryan
McVay / Getty Images; rock wall detail and pine cross section, courtesy of
Pat Callahan; water ripples, © Yasuhide Fumoto / Getty Images

This book was printed on Glatfelter Natures, a recycled paper with
30 percent postconsumer waste content.

For the boys of the South Carolina CCC

And for my boys—
Mike, Mitchell, and Carson

CONTENTS

This book would not have been possible without the support and assistance of several outstanding historians who mentored me throughout the process of research and writing. I would especially like to recognize Carroll Van West, Mary Hoffschwelle, and Amy Staples at Middle Tennessee State University; Leslie Sharp, now at Georgia Tech; and J. Tracy Power of the South Carolina Department of Archives and History (SCDAH). They have all provided a great deal of encouragement and assistance in both this project and my career. Graduate school colleagues Stacey Griffin, Carole Summers Morris, Blythe Semmer, and Michael Strutt are now lifelong friends who deserve my thanks for their continued encouragement and friendship.

During the processes of research and writing, I have incurred many debts to many people. Civilian Conservation Corps (CCC) alumni and their families, especially Mr. and Mrs. I. V. Butler, Mr. and Mrs. Frank Damon, and Mr. and Mrs. Sam Blanton, all of Charleston; Mary Ann Camp, of Spartanburg; and the members of the Fort Moultrie chapter of the National Association of Civilian Conservation Corps Alumni have shared their photographs, memorabilia, and memories unselfishly with me. In Columbia, South Carolina, the following historians have provided a great deal of assistance: Karen McMullen at the South Carolina State Library, Robin Copp at the Caroliniana Library at the University of South Carolina, and Al Hester at the South Carolina Department of Parks, Recreation, and Tourism (SCPRT), who has proved himself a willing ally in all things related to researching the CCC in South Carolina. The SCPRT is the caretaker of the state parks, which are all treasures in their own right; I hope this book inspires its readers to go visit these amazing places in person.

At the SCDAH, where the bulk of the research for this project was undertaken, I have many friends and colleagues who contributed to this project, both directly and indirectly. At the risk of leaving someone out, I'd like to thank the following former and current SCDAH staffers: Tim Belshaw, Sharon Mackintosh, Wade Dorsey, Carol Crawford, Tommy "Red" Betenbaugh, Bryan Collars, Andy Chandler, Dan Elswick, Megan Brown, Elizabeth Morton Johnson, Mary

Edmonds, Ben Hornsby, and Rodger Stroup. I owe a huge debt of gratitude to J. Tracy Power, historian at the SCDAH, and his wife, Carol Thompson Power, for their friendship, encouragement, hospitality, assistance with research and editing, and use of their laptop. My editor at the University of South Carolina Press, Alex Moore, has done more than his fair share of "hand-holding" and exercised his patience beyond measure with a nervous first-time author; I am extremely grateful for the pleasure of making his acquaintance.

Claudette Stager at the Tennessee Historical Commission in Nashville provided a great deal of assistance in an early stage of this project, and ongoing encouragement. Ann Roberts, director emeritus of the Metropolitan Historical Commission in Nashville, also provided encouragement and support, and a much-needed leave of absence at a crucial stage of writing. I am grateful to both of these women for their scholarship and professional example.

Finally, I must express my thanks and, more important, my love to my family. My mother (Scarlett Pistole Stout), my grandparents (Mertie Pistole Clemons and the late Alex Pistole), my great-grandmother (the late Mary Edith Swindell), and my uncles (Larry Pistole and Neal Pistole) instilled in me a love of history and historic places from too early for me to remember. Their faith in me and love for me is unquestioned, and for that I am extremely and eternally grateful. Kitty was a constant, if disinterested, companion throughout. Mike, Mitchell, and Carson have endured many absences of mind if not body, while I was "gone to Carolina in my mind." I hope the side trips to South Carolina's state parks are happy memories for you; those trips with you were the best part of this project.

On October 24, 1929, the stock market crashed, marking the beginning of a period of American history that came to be known as the Great Depression. Throughout the country people lost their jobs, their savings, and, many believed, their future security. In South Carolina, the economy was depressed even before the stock market crash, and the crash only intensified the desperate situation in the state. Cotton prices dropped, banks failed, and city governments throughout the state went bankrupt. In the early 1930s at least seventeen counties in South Carolina had an unemployment rate of over 30 percent.

Franklin Roosevelt's New Deal came to the state in March 1933. By the end of that summer, over 400,000 South Carolinians, 25 percent of the state's population, were on relief, managed by the Federal Emergency Relief Administration (FERA). In a program tainted nationwide by favoritism, nepotism, and racism, South Carolina was the only state in which more African Americans received FERA aid than whites. One of FDR's New Deal relief programs, Emergency Conservation Work (ECW), came to the state in 1933, shortly after FDR had proposed a "civilian Conservation Corps," along with other relief programs, in March.[1] Although officially known as Emergency Conservation Work, the program retained the popular title Civilian Conservation Corps (CCC) and officially became the CCC in 1937. The program provided jobs for thousands of unemployed young men and hundreds of veterans. For their work, the men received housing, clothing, food, and payment of about a dollar a day. Of that, their families received between $22 and $25 a month in direct payment.

The CCC camps fell under the direction of the War Department and in many ways resembled army camps. These camps provided a structured environment for many young men who had never known such structure. Enrollees received educational classes at the elementary, high school, and college levels, as well as vocational instruction in typewriting, agriculture, landscaping, mechanics, electricity, and forestry, among other topics. Recreational opportunities for the young men abounded as well. Swimming, cards, and table tennis provided nightly entertainment, and movies were shown frequently. Sports teams in basketball and baseball formed and played against teams from other CCC camps or local high schools. Dances were held in the camp recreational hall with local young women, and the camp library provided both educational and recreational reading material. Camp chaplains tried to meet the young men's spiritual needs, and the young men attended worship services led by local ministers. The CCC attempted to provide an atmosphere conducive to producing fit and healthy young men for their service in "Roosevelt's Forest Army."[2]

In South Carolina as elsewhere, the CCC performed a variety of work. It promoted soil conservation by the planting of kudzu, a nonnative plant that quickly became a feature of the southern landscape. The CCC augmented necessary firefighting activities with fire prevention work, including the building of watchtowers and fire lines, and the stringing of telephone lines for faster notification of dangerous situations. It planted millions of trees in reforestation projects and nurseries throughout South Carolina and in other states. In addition, the CCC developed state and national forests, recreational areas, and parks. Prior to the work of the CCC, South Carolina had no state parks; by the end of CCC work in the state, sixteen state parks had opened, the first at Myrtle Beach in July 1936.

The work of the CCC undoubtedly changed the landscape in South Carolina, nowhere more so than in the seventeen state parks that were constructed between 1933 and 1942.[3] In addition, the CCC state parks provided the genesis of the state park system in South Carolina. By 1942, at the end of CCC construction, there were sixteen state parks open to the public, all constructed by the CCC and operated by the South Carolina Forestry Commission. Currently, there are forty-seven state parks located all over the state and operated under the authority of the South Carolina Department of Parks, Recreation, and Tourism.[4]

South Carolina's state parks are a tangible architectural legacy of an influential New Deal program. The story of the CCC in South Carolina is the story of a New Deal program that, while limited in scope and reach, was a success for the hundreds of young men who participated, and was also a success in implementing a conservation and public recreation ethic in South Carolina state government through the establishment of the state park system.

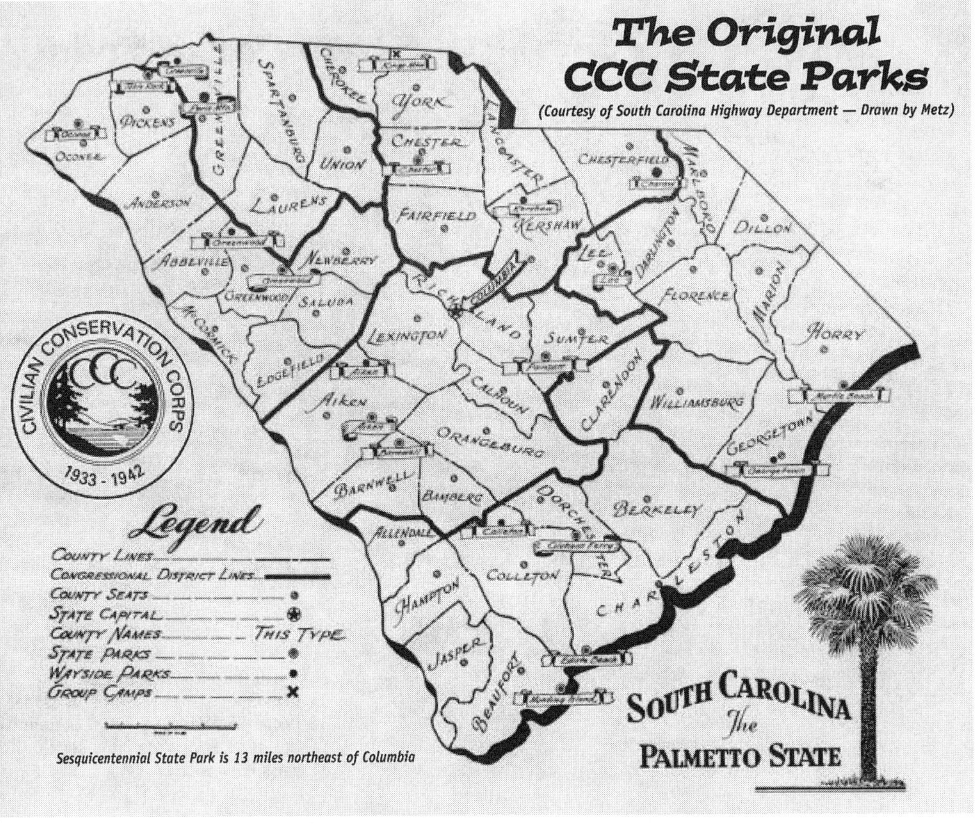

Sesquicentennial State Park is 13 miles northeast of Columbia

The Civilian Conservation Corps created the first sixteen state parks in South Carolina during the New Deal decade of the 1930s. Map originally created by Metz of the South Carolina Highway Department for the South Carolina Federal Writers' Project publication *South Carolina State Parks*, 1940. Redrawn and edited by Tim Belshaw, South Carolina Department of Archives and History. Used with permission of the artist and South Carolina Department of Archives and History

State Parks Today

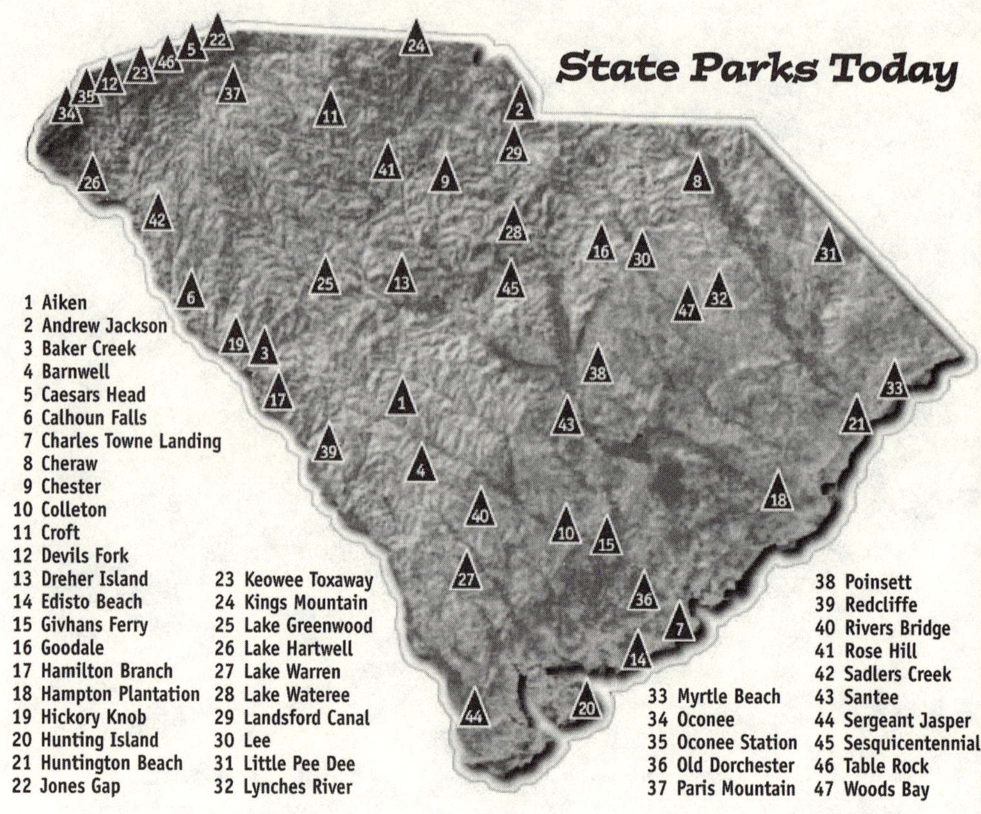

1 Aiken
2 Andrew Jackson
3 Baker Creek
4 Barnwell
5 Caesars Head
6 Calhoun Falls
7 Charles Towne Landing
8 Cheraw
9 Chester
10 Colleton
11 Croft
12 Devils Fork
13 Dreher Island
14 Edisto Beach
15 Givhans Ferry
16 Goodale
17 Hamilton Branch
18 Hampton Plantation
19 Hickory Knob
20 Hunting Island
21 Huntington Beach
22 Jones Gap

23 Keowee Toxaway
24 Kings Mountain
25 Lake Greenwood
26 Lake Hartwell
27 Lake Warren
28 Lake Wateree
29 Landsford Canal
30 Lee
31 Little Pee Dee
32 Lynches River

33 Myrtle Beach
34 Oconee
35 Oconee Station
36 Old Dorchester
37 Paris Mountain

38 Poinsett
39 Redcliffe
40 Rivers Bridge
41 Rose Hill
42 Sadlers Creek
43 Santee
44 Sergeant Jasper
45 Sesquicentennial
46 Table Rock
47 Woods Bay

As of 2010, the State of South Carolina boasted forty-seven state parks. Map created by Tim Belshaw, South Carolina Department of Archives and History. Used with permission of the artist and South Carolina Department of Archives and History

New Deal, New Landscape

CHAPTER 1

Depression and the New Deal in South Carolina

South Carolinians gathered in Columbia on the afternoon of October 24, 1929, to watch the biggest football game in the state. The Tigers of Clemson College, undefeated that year, came to town to play the Fighting Gamecocks of the University of South Carolina in a game that would all but decide the Southern Conference championship. The Clemson–South Carolina match was (and is) the state's biggest intrastate football rivalry, and Big Thursday, as the annual event was known, regularly drew several thousand fans. The year 1929 was no different, as 14,000 fans jammed the stadium at the State Fairgrounds for the contest. Clemson won, 21–14, handing the Gamecocks only their second loss of the season, and fans went home, all satisfied with a well-fought game even if not all of them were happy with the outcome.[1]

Big Thursday 1929 happened to be Black Thursday, the day the stock market took its fatal plunge and ushered in the era known as the Great Depression. The news from New York City traveled slowly to South Carolina, and when the initial shock wore off, most South Carolinians wondered what it all meant, and what it would mean to them personally. The state's economy was depressed before the crash, and few South Carolinians were investors in the stock market. But the economy quickly worsened throughout the state, as banks closed, cotton prices dropped, and mills laid off workers.

South Carolina's dependence upon cotton had pushed the state's economy into an economic downturn as early as the end of World War I, when overproduction of cotton and overextension of credit caused a sizable decline in the price of cotton. In addition, the boll weevil wreaked havoc on the cotton crop in the early 1920s, nearly devastating the crop in the state. Cotton farmers then had less cotton to sell, and what they did have sold at lower prices. Since over half of the state's workers worked in agriculture, almost exclusively in cotton, the downturn in prices and the devastation of the crop directly affected half the state's workforce. Of the other half of the workers, approximately 25 percent worked in manufacturing, primarily in the cotton mills, which also felt the brunt of the failure of the cotton crops. Workers both in the fields and in the factories had less work to do, and received less money for it.[2]

South Carolina's industrial economy consisted primarily of cotton textiles; according to historian Jack Hayes, the state's manufactured products were dominated by cotton production, with approximately 70 percent of the value of the state's manufactured products being cotton textiles. This single-industry dominance was unique to South Carolina. Competition from other domestic textile producers and the emergence of synthetic fibers in the mid-1920s, combined with the failure of the crop in South Carolina, caused a depressed textile market in the state. Textile securities dropped by half in the years between 1923 and 1929. Mill owners responded by cutting the workforce and increasing the workload or by hiring part-time workers instead of full-time workers, keeping production quotas at an unrealistic level for part-time employees. In doing so some saved their mills but created a workforce of overworked, underpaid employees who could not afford to keep their families fed and their children in school.[3]

Although the South Carolina economy was already depressed, the stock market crash plunged the state into further economic havoc. Cotton prices continued to fall and then bottomed out, dropping from a high of 38 cents a pound in 1919 to 17 cents a pound in 1920 and to less than 5 cents per pound in 1932. Land values plummeted accordingly, as did per capita income in the state, which fell from $261 in 1929 to $151 by 1933. The textile industry followed, with the average annual wage of the mill worker dropping 31 percent. The banking industry, which had suffered during the agricultural depression of the 1920s (when almost half of the state's banks closed), only worsened during the early 1930s, when even major financial institutions closed. Panic spread among depositors, who rushed the banks to withdraw savings, endangering banks that were otherwise sound.[4]

Governor Ibra Blackwood offered hollow assurances regarding the resilience of the economy and appealed to "patriotic" South Carolinians to leave their money in the state's banks. Blackwood's 1933 State of the State Address, according to historian Walter Edgar, "could have been ghost-written by Herbert Hoover," so unrealistic were its goals and expectations. State government seemed unwilling or unable to do anything: the Board of Public Welfare had ceased to exist in 1926 when then governor J. G. Richards vetoed its appropriations, and the state constitution permitted public assistance only to Confederate veterans, their widows, and faithful former slaves. The state provided no assistance to people who were blind, the aged, or dependent children until the state constitution was amended in 1937. In meeting the needs of the unemployed and the destitute, local governments were as ineffectual as the state government. In August 1930 Columbia's mayor, Lawrence B. Owens, declared that although unemployment had risen slightly, there was no crisis, and the city council refused to set up a municipal unemployment agency. In Charleston, when the People's Bank closed, the deposits for the city payroll were lost. Other cities such as Greenville, Columbia, and Florence tried to trim their budgets by cutting jobs, a technique also tried at the state level, but those local governments failed to provide assistance to the newly unemployed. The city governments of Columbia and Charleston, the University of South Carolina, and the state government resorted to paying their remaining employees in scrip. Unemployment rates climbed as textile mills and local governments laid off workers throughout the state.[5]

The urban unemployed of South Carolina found small solace in the overtures of their city governments and civic organizations. In Charleston, city trucks transported the unemployed to local farms on the outskirts of the city, where they might pick vegetables that farmers were willing to donate. A similar project in Columbia created a municipal woodyard where needy families could obtain fuel; the Woodyard Fund also provided a room and a meal for transients willing to work in the woodyard. During the Christmas season of 1930, Columbia civic groups (including the Rotarians, Lions, Kiwanis, and Knights of Columbus) collected food, toys, and clothing, and even the Ku Klux Klan (in full Klan regalia) passed out fifty baskets of food on Christmas Eve. Private charities in Columbia served more than 700,000 free meals in 1931.[6] Without garden plots or farm animals to rely upon, the urban poor were forced to rely on whatever charity was extended.

Farm families in some ways were luckier than the "city folk" in that they were more self-sufficient, at least when it came to food. Those families who owned their own farms often grew much of what they ate, owned a milk cow, and raised a few chickens to provide eggs and meat. A few pigs meant that seasoning meat was available; more pigs provided pork for meals and for bartering. But even in fairly prosperous farm families, the Depression "taught you not to wish for what you couldn't have," in the words of one South Carolinian.[7] Less than 3 percent of rural South Carolina homes had electricity, which meant that hardly anyone owned luxury items such as electric ranges, washing machines, or refrigerators, and the Depression just prolonged the lack of these luxuries. The Depression also forced many farm families to try to enter the paying workforce, when they could find transportation and a job. Fathers and older sons tried to find work in the textile mills, often with white men displacing women or African American workers, at the rate of 10 cents an hour, while older daughters or unmarried sisters looked for jobs in department stores. Younger children hired out to pick cotton in neighbors' fields.[8]

The rural poor, both black and white, were less fortunate. Sharecroppers often had no choice but to concentrate on the cash crop. If they grew gardens, the plots were small. Cows, hogs, and chickens required time and money that sharecroppers did not have. With such a meager diet, poor in nutrients and vitamins, malnutrition and disease ran rampant among the rural poor. David Kennedy, writing about the Depression era, calls southern sharecroppers "probably the poorest Americans."[9] Lorena Hickok, a journalist assigned to reporting conditions to the Roosevelt administration, described the plight of southern sharecroppers in January 1934 as "half-starved Whites and Blacks, struggling in competition for less to eat than my dog gets at home, for the privilege of living in huts that are infinitely less comfortable than his kennel." The living conditions of southern sharecroppers were so bleak that Hickok was shocked: "I just can't describe to you some of the things I've seen and heard down here these last few days. I shall never forget them—never as long as I live."[10]

While the Depression affected all South Carolinians in some way, African Americans were particularly hard hit, in both the rural and urban areas of the state. Rural blacks, like most of their white counterparts, worked as sharecroppers and tenant farmers, except there were more of them. Urban blacks usually worked in service industries as maids, porters, janitors, dishwashers, laundresses, or cooks. In the early 1930s many urban black women working as maids, laundresses, or cooks lost their jobs, as their white employers could no longer afford to employ them. Businesses in the cities felt pressure to lay off black men working as porters, waiters, dishwashers, or janitors in order to hire unemployed whites. Black-owned businesses in the cities almost disappeared during the Depression because their patrons could not afford to pay for their services.[11]

At the time of the presidential election of 1932, South Carolinians of all income levels, urban and rural, black and white, felt the ravages of the Depression. By 1932, 45 percent of South Carolina farmers were delinquent in paying taxes on their farms. That same year the *Charleston News and Courier* reported 1,400 Sumter County families were "unemployed, hungry, and practically naked," and at least two residents of Pineville and two in Beaufort died of starvation.[12] Meals, when available, became more and more monotonous, as fewer and fewer families could afford delicacies such as seasoning meats, ice, or sugar. Mothers and wives mended clothing and shoes, and then mended them again. "New" clothes were most often fashioned out of old clothes or flour or feed sacks. "Visiting" and going to church became the most popular spare-time activities, replacing going to the movies. Children dropped out of school to look for work, because they did not have clothes to wear or were so malnourished or sick they were unable to attend. Families who had once felt financially secure found themselves forced to cash in life insurance policies, to bring older children home from college, or to move in with relatives.[13]

Columbia's central location in the state and its role as a transportation hub made it a stopping point for hundreds of transients looking for any type of work, including sharecroppers, unemployed mill workers, and some unemployed professionals. Temporary quarters were found for some of these transients at the Young Men's Christian Association (YMCA), Camp Jackson, or the county jail, but the city could not, or would not, provide for them all. At least 100 people lived in boxes and abandoned cars at the Columbia city dump in 1932. In 1935 Columbia mayor Lawrence B. Owens was quoted as saying: "They don't worry about themselves, so I stopped worrying about them."[14]

South Carolina voted overwhelmingly Democratic in the 1920s and 1930s, and the state's senators, representatives, and Governor Blackwood provided a strong base of support for Franklin Roosevelt in 1931 and 1932. South Carolina refused to listen to Herbert Hoover's hollow promises of "prosperity just around the corner," and the state gave Roosevelt his widest margin of victory in any state, with 98 percent of the vote. South Carolina's junior senator, James F. Byrnes, emerged as a close confidant of the new president, a leader of the New Deal, and South Carolina's most influential senator on the national stage since John C. Calhoun.[15]

The state's support for Roosevelt paid off immediately during the president's first hundred days. According Walter Edgar, "Given the scope of economic distress in South Carolina, almost all New Deal legislation had an impact on the lives of its citizens."[16] The Emergency Relief Act provided the states with grants to assist their needy citizens, administered under the Federal Emergency Relief Administration (FERA). The South Carolina Emergency Relief Administration (SCERA) began operation in June 1933 under the directorship of Malcolm Miller. The grant money, administered at the county level, was used to provide jobs, food, clothing, and direct money for the needy, and it provided thousands of South Carolinians with subsistence, if not comfort. However, the administration of SCERA was a "nightmare," due primarily to the absence of a state welfare agency before the creation of SCERA. FERA director Harry Hopkins and the federal government expected the states to match the federal money in most cases, often at a ratio of three dollars for every federal dollar; the fact that Hopkins required South Carolina to match only 2 percent of the total FERA funds spent within the state is partially indicative of the desperate situation in which South Carolina found itself. With no state welfare program to serve as an institutional foundation, South Carolina's state and local governments were required to create a large, complex administrative agency from scratch, resulting in untrained personnel working for little pay, described in one account as "conscientious, hardworking, sincere, and incompetent."[17] Whatever the difficulties, SCERA provided some sort of relief to approximately 25 percent of the state's population, and South Carolina was the only state in which African Americans received more FERA aid than whites.[18]

SCERA money provided jobs in farming, construction, and public works for men but also provided opportunities for women in the forms of sewing rooms, day nurseries, and public libraries, as well as working with a school lunch program that provided hot meals for over 100,000 South Carolina children in 1934. Women also assisted county home demonstration agents in training rural families in canning and preserving fruits and vegetables and in making clothes. As important as the work program was to the relief of South Carolinians, SCERA's direct relief, in the form of food and clothing, was even more important. SCERA workers planted vegetable gardens in each county to provide food, while over 100,000 head of cattle came to state slaughterhouses from the drought-stricken Midwest, alleviating the plight of midwestern farmers while at the same time providing beef for malnourished Carolinians. With the assistance of FERA, SCERA distributed more than 14 million pounds of meat (in addition to the beef), 3.5 million pounds of flour, and 2.7 million pounds of potatoes, as well as butter, lard, rice, cheese, milk, sugar, and fruits between 1933 and 1935.[19]

Roosevelt never intended FERA and SCERA to be permanent relief measures, only immediate, stopgap attempts to alleviate some of the devastation wrought on South Carolinians. More lasting relief came through other New Deal agencies, such as the Agricultural Adjustment Administration, the Social Security Administration, the Works Progress Administration (WPA), and the Public Works Administration (PWA). These New Deal agencies generally were more successful than others in providing long-term relief. Other agencies, most notably the National Recovery Administration (NRA), also attempted to provide long-term relief, and while not usually judged as a success, the NRA did provide limited relief to South Carolina's mill workers. Together, these programs provided economic relief to a variety of South Carolinians, reaching whites and blacks, young and old, men and women, urban and rural residents, professionals and laborers, and the educated and the uneducated alike.

Agricultural Adjustment Act (AAA)

South Carolina's farmers may have been some of the last to hear the news of the Great Depression; according to them, the economy had been depressed for a long time prior to 1929. In 1933 both cotton and tobacco were selling for less than the cost of production, prompting South Carolina congressmen, as well as those from North Carolina and Georgia, to approach Secretary of Agriculture Henry Wallace for assistance. Wallace responded with a plan setting guaranteed minimum prices for both cotton and tobacco, the foundation of the Agricultural Adjustment Act (AAA). Passage of this plan led to increased support of Roosevelt and the New Deal among the farming population. During Roosevelt's first hundred days, March to June 1933, Congress passed the AAA, creating the Agricultural Adjustment Administration (also known as the AAA), which asked farmers producing seven basic commodities (including cotton and tobacco) to take land out of cultivation in exchange for payment from the secretary of agriculture. South Carolina farm owners almost unanimously voiced approval of the plan and began signing contracts to plow under parts of their existing crops and to leave segments of land fallow in future years.[20]

Although the AAA provided a great deal of assistance to the struggling farmers of the state by the end of the 1930s, it did not end the economic struggle of many farming families; the war years of the early 1940s later brought the desired economic boon to South Carolina farmers, not the New Deal. In addition, the AAA did little to relieve the drastic situation of South Carolina sharecroppers and tenant farmers, who rarely saw the benefits the AAA provided to farm owners. Their only protection under the AAA was a clause that provided that they would be allowed to continue to live in their homes and work the land, even if the landowner cut his or her overall production as required.[21]

Tenant farmers were to receive parity payments through the AAA, a system that worked marginally well. Very few complaints about the system were reported, likely owing more to the tenuous relationship tenant farmers had with the landowners than to the success of parity payments. Although originally designed to provide direct payment to tenants, South Carolina senator Ellison "Cotton Ed" Smith prevented this type of direct relief: "You can't do this to my niggers, paying checks to them. They don't know what to do with the money. The money should come to me. I'll take care of them. They're mine."[22] This was just one instance when the issue of race prevented economic relief from reaching the population in which it had the potential to do the most good. It was up to other New Deal programs to provide relief to the rural South Carolina population. The federal administration had to find more creative ways to provide relief for the poorest of the South Carolina population, especially the large African American population. Programs like the Rural Electrification Administration, the Soil Conservation Service, the Farm Credit Administration, and the Resettlement Administration provided additional assistance to South Carolina's farmers.

Rural Electrification Administration (REA)

Although the public had been advocating the extension of electricity to rural areas since about 1920, the public utilities in the state had deemed it too expensive to run lines to outlying areas (in reality, most of the state), and the state government simply could not afford to conduct the needed studies or run the lines by itself. But extending electricity to rural areas was a priority throughout mostly rural South Carolina, and in 1932 the legislature created a new division of the Railroad Commission to investigate the state's electrical industry. The Utilities Division of the Railroad Commission worked with the University of South Carolina's Department of Electrical Engineering to produce a statewide survey of potential electricity customers along state highways. The resulting study led to the passage of a bill designed to extend electrical services to farms situated on state highways, providing electricity to 11,000 homes. The South Carolina Rural Electrification Act of 1933 had one main catch: the money had to come from the federal government.[23]

While South Carolina pursued providing farmers with electricity, at least on paper, the federal government, building on lessons learned through the experience of the Tennessee Valley Authority (TVA) in providing electricity to rural southerners, assisted in this effort. Beginning in 1935 the Rural Electrification Administration (REA) provided the federal financing required to extend electrical power to those in rural areas, who received electricity with great enthusiasm. South Carolina's rural landowners were quick to install electric lights and buy radios and electric irons when electricity became available. By 1940 almost 15 percent of South Carolina farmers had electricity, up from less than 3 percent in 1934. As the quality of life improved as a result of electricity, so did farm production: for example, egg production increased by 30 percent through keeping poultry buildings lit at night (perhaps keeping the chickens awake to continue to lay), and milk production increased by 5 to 15 percent at some farms.[24] Aside from the small gains in egg and milk production, the REA did not directly affect most South Carolinians' pocketbooks, but it did improve the quality of life for many rural residents, enabling them to enjoy evening hours together while listening to news and radio programs.

Soil Conservation Service (SCS)

The Soil Conservation Service (SCS) began as the Soil Erosion Service in the Department of the Interior, but in 1935 Roosevelt transferred it to the Department of Agriculture. The SCS worked to educate farmers about methods of soil conservation. South Carolina's farmland was badly eroded; in fourteen counties at least half of the farmland was so eroded it was classified as useless. With labor provided by the Civilian Conservation Corps (CCC), the SCS taught farmers the benefits of terracing, cover cropping, and reforestation. By 1936 five demonstration projects were under way in South Carolina, with 95 percent of farmers in the project area following prescribed SCS practices, and over 90 percent of farmers living in a twenty-five-mile radius received instruction through SCS projects. Farmers and CCC young men planted over 700,000 acres of South Carolina land with soil-conserving crops and grasses and implemented soil conservation measures on more than 75 percent of the state's total cropland.[25]

Farm Credit Administration (FCA)

The Farm Credit Administration (FCA) lent money to farm owners to refinance farm mortgages and to assist in buying seed, livestock, and equipment. The FCA provided over $61 million in assistance to South Carolina farm owners but did not give direct assistance to sharecroppers or tenant farmers. SCERA's Rural Rehabilitation Division, however, did provide sharecroppers and tenants with similar loans for farm equipment, livestock, seed, and fertilizer. The Rural Rehabilitation Division, and later the Resettlement Administration (RA) and the Farm Security Administration (FSA), worked to relocate farmers living and working on submarginal land to more productive land, while teaching the relocated families additional skills to increase their self-sufficiency. These programs eventually established six resettlement projects in South Carolina, providing some 460 families with new farmland. Resettlement provided a new start for black as well as white tenant farming families, although in segregated projects. Although ambitious, the resettlement program was plagued by mismanagement from the start. In addition, most resettlement farms in the state were designed to provide only a semblance of self-reliance; in actuality, the farms were too small to successfully raise cash crops such as cotton and tobacco. However, resettlement provided some individual families with a higher standard of living, better land for farming, and greater education and opportunity for increased self-sufficiency.[26]

National Recovery Administration (NRA)

Federal relief programs also impacted industrial and commercial activities in South Carolina. The National Industrial Recovery Act (NIRA) and its National Recovery Administration (NRA) brought federal assistance to mill workers, although not without some backlash from the mill owners. Federal programs guaranteed a minimum wage, established a forty-hour workweek, and abolished child labor. These initiatives raised the standard of living for mill workers and their families and significantly improved their quality of life. South Carolina textile workers wholeheartedly endorsed the NRA. One such worker, Henry Coyle, of Gaffney, wrote the president: "I want you to know that I am for you in this most wonderful undertaking. . . . My faith is in you my heart with you and I am for you sink or swim."[27]

Despite the positive impact the NRA had on many South Carolina mill hands, the federal requirement of a minimum wage for textile workers negatively impacted the state's black mill workers. Instead of paying black operatives the same minimum wage prescribed for whites, mill owners simply laid off their black employees, choosing to cut costs or employ more whites in those positions. Historian Paul Lofton calls the NRA "the one New Deal program that had a basically negative effect on South Carolina blacks."[28]

Federal collective bargaining provisions rang hollow in South Carolina. Textile unions found it difficult to unionize in South Carolina, and striking workers faced state governmental opposition in meeting their demands. The failure of the 1934 general textile strike left many mill workers in South Carolina, as elsewhere, frustrated with the unionizing experience.[29] Mill owners and management felt threatened by the new federal regulations as well as foreign competition, until Congress, pressured by Senator Byrnes in 1936, increased the tariffs on imported textiles. Textile orders then increased to the point that South Carolina mills had to refuse incoming orders, until demand fell off with the 1937 recession. After the recession, the cotton and textile market in the state did not recover fully until the 1940s, during World War II.[30]

Social Security

The minimum wage for workers was just one part of the federal strategy to increase consumer spending. Just as important was Social Security, which increased the buying power of the elderly. Social Security changed the expectations of aging South Carolinians. South Carolina was one of only six states that did not have a pension plan for seniors by the mid-1930s and one of fourteen lacking aid for people who were blind, and only South Carolina and Georgia had failed to provide assistance to dependent children. With the advent of Social Security at the national level, the state government had to act to amend the state constitution to provide assistance for these groups. The requisite 1937 amendments provided aid for the aged, those who were blind, and dependent children. That same year the legislature passed the Public Welfare Act, which created a permanent department to administer Social Security programs as well as other welfare, insurance, health, and unemployment compensation programs. However beneficial the early Social Security program in the state, a large number of the population was overlooked. Farm and domestic workers were not eligible for the program, leaving out most African Americans and women, and the state's poorest citizens.[31]

FERA and SCERA had provided some initial direct relief to the most needy of South Carolinians in the early 1930s, and Social Security generally provided for children and the aged. But a large segment of South Carolina's population—the middle class—needed some sort of assistance as well. FERA and SCERA met immediate needs such as food and clothing, but at the same time demonstrated the need to provide work relief for the middle class, and the New Deal institutionalized these programs through the WPA and PWA, which found jobs for skilled and unskilled manual workers as well as white collar employees. Both programs had similar objectives, to provide work relief while making a lasting impact on public infrastructure. The WPA concentrated efforts on projects with a budget of less than $25,000, while the PWA primarily handled larger projects. Both agencies addressed a variety of needs in South Carolina and performed projects that left lasting benefits in the state.

Works Progress Administration (WPA)

The WPA assisted the state government with projects aimed at improving infrastructure, education, and the arts. The agency changed the landscape of the state through road projects, improving the highway system and the quality of farm-to-market roads. WPA projects increased the number of miles of the state highway system by over 50 percent, from 6,000 to over 9,600 between 1933 and 1941. WPA educational work "contributed to the development of the educational facilities of the state unparalleled in its history," according to a 1938 state appraisal committee. The agency built or improved over 2,000 schools for white and black students, provided literacy training for children and adults, built facilities for state colleges, and provided training and counseling for teens and young adults through the National Youth Administration (NYA). The NYA was one of the most successful WPA programs nationally, and became its own agency in 1939.[32]

The WPA provided opportunities for South Carolina's blacks as well as whites, probably more equally than most other New Deal programs. The WPA paid workers at the same rate regardless of race. This policy drew criticism from many whites desiring work on WPA projects, and from white employers who began losing workers to higher paid jobs with the agency. White contractors in Greenville and elsewhere required black laborers to provide a "kickback" of their WPA wages in return for hiring them for jobs. While the WPA paid the same rates for whites and blacks, for the most part the WPA, as with many other New Deal programs, limited work opportunities for blacks to manual labor positions. Professional blacks in Columbia, including Dr. Robert Mance and educator and activist Modjeska Monteith Simkins, protested the limited possibilities for South Carolina's African Americans. WPA officials responded by creating professional positions in Columbia. Professional blacks worked for the WPA as teachers in adult and nursery schools and in health projects. While the WPA provided for black professionals in the state capitol, it is likely that this project was the only one of its kind in the state.[33]

The WPA's Women's and Professional Division provided work for women, especially those who were single heads-of-households or who had spouses who were unable to work. Many of these projects were derivatives of projects initially begun under FERA and included sewing rooms, libraries, housekeeping or medical programs, and land beautification projects. Women also found work through other WPA divisions, especially working with the educational programs in classrooms, lunchrooms, or children's health programs. These programs were more than "make-work"; they provided women with much-needed employment as well as assisted children, who were direct beneficiaries of some of the programs. The School Lunch Program in South Carolina operated through the assistance of local advisory councils, who assisted the federal government's work by obtaining additional food. South Carolina had the second-largest WPA school lunch program in the country, feeding over 77,000 schoolchildren daily and recording an average weight gain of three to eight pounds per child over the first five weeks of the program.[34]

Professional women as well as men found work through the programs of the WPA's Professional Division, such as the Federal Writers' Project and the Federal Artists' Project. Writers, historians, journalists, musicians, and artists found the Depression particularly hostile to their professions; they welcomed the opportunity to use their specialized training and talents.[35] The South Carolina Writers' Project, under the direction of Mabel Montgomery and Louise Jones DuBose, found work for writers, researchers, editors, and typists. While the Writers' Project produced some twenty-three publications, including the massive *South Carolina: A Guide to the Palmetto State*, *Palmetto Pioneers: Six Stories of Early South Carolinians*, and *South Carolina State Parks*, the Writers' Project also employed historians, including Anne K. Gregorie, the first woman Ph.D. in history from the University of South Carolina. Under Gregorie's leadership, historians began locating, transcribing, and preserving public records in all forty-six South Carolina counties, as well as some church records and private manuscript collections. The project, however, ignored records from black churches and manumission records. Although overall a successful project, in several counties local court clerks put the WPA workers in clerical positions, rather than allowing them to work on the records project. The state director closed the projects in at least two counties when the local clerks refused to cooperate. The Historic Records Survey, now a part of the South Carolina Department of Archives and History, is still used daily by historians and genealogists alike. The Federal Writers' Project in South Carolina also collected narratives of

African Americans who were former slaves, recognizing the historical value of their life stories.[36]

Other tangible benefits of the New Deal came through the Federal Artists Project (FAP). Musicians and artists in the employ of the WPA provided instruction to children and adults alike who were interested in music or art; South Carolina requested a massive teacher increase as a result of the popularity of the music classes throughout the state. The WPA also operated art galleries in Greenville, Columbia, Florence, Walterboro, and Beaufort.[37] One early WPA project involved the reconstruction of a Charleston landmark, the Dock Street Theater. This building project delighted Charleston's historic preservation community, which previously had been ambivalent at best about New Deal projects. Artists employed by the FAP created scenery for the theater's second grand opening gala, and WPA administrator Harry Hopkins presented the key to the theater to Charleston mayor Burnet Maybank. The Dock Street Theater was Charleston's first, but not the only, WPA historic preservation project; when the city sustained tornado damage in September 1938, Hopkins made $500,000 available for building repairs, including to the historic City Market and City Hall. Mayor Maybank's support of Roosevelt and friendship with Hopkins helped to ensure the infusion of WPA money into Charleston.[38]

Related to the arts projects conducted through the WPA, the Treasury Department contracted with artists across the country to provide murals and sculptures in courthouses and post offices throughout South Carolina. Vermont artist Stefan Hirsch's 1938 mural for the Federal Courthouse in Aiken caused a highly publicized controversy; when the mural was unveiled, the dark-skinned central figure, "Justice," caused an uproar among local white residents and the judge in whose courtroom the painting was installed. The Treasury Department tried to broker a compromise in which Hirsch would lighten the skin tone of the female figure, but Hirsch refused. The federal judge, Frank Myers, covered the objectionable painting with a curtain while court was in session.[39] This controversy serves as a reminder that although most New Deal projects were welcomed throughout South Carolina, there was some criticism and even hostility when projects did not go as initially planned. Often, if not always, race played a role in projects, in terms of pay scale, availability, and type of work, or even in the subject matter—or paint color—of a painting.

The WPA provided work relief for a large number of skilled workers, including educators, medical personnel, artists, and writers, as well as assisting state government in projects that would have otherwise been unaffordable, such as infrastructure improvements in highways and schools. Another New Deal program, the PWA, concentrated on federal property within the state and also assisted in funding for other nonfederal projects.

Public Works Administration (PWA)

The PWA, established at the beginning of the New Deal, worked on repair and construction of federal property within the state and funded nonfederal projects through a grant-loan system. The government also funded slum clearance and housing projects through the PWA. In South Carolina, the PWA spent almost $36 million from 1933 to 1939, which resulted in several projects that, in the words of historian Jack Hayes, "literally changed the face of the Palmetto State" through the construction of highways, schools, courthouses, hospitals, post offices, a shipyard, and two massive hydroelectric projects as well as housing projects in Charleston and Columbia and, later, in Greenville and Spartanburg.[40] The largest PWA projects in South Carolina were the federal Charleston Navy Yard and the two nonfederal hydroelectric projects, Buzzard Roost and Santee-Cooper. The Charleston Navy Yard dated to 1901 but had fallen into disrepair, and by the early 1930s it employed only 400 workers. In 1933 navy officials recommended closing the Navy Yard, to the dismay of Mayor Maybank and Senator James Byrnes. Byrnes's influence helped save the Navy Yard, directing additional federal work to Charleston, and later that same year, the first PWA project began with the construction of the gunboat *Charleston.* Following the construction of the *Charleston,* the PWA constructed other boats and ships at the Charleston Navy Yard. The Navy Yard employed some 1,600 workers as shipbuilders, while other projects there provided an additional 1,700 workers on the repair and maintenance of the facilities and the construction of a new hospital and officers' quarters.[41]

The PWA also constructed hydroelectric projects throughout the state, which met with some controversy from the privately held power utilities. However, as the private companies proved unable or unwilling to extend electrical power to the most rural parts of the state, the federal projects received more acclaim than hostility. The Buzzard Roost project in the upstate and the much larger Santee-Cooper project in the midstate and low country provided much-needed electrical power to much of the state. Initially designed as a private enterprise, the federal government refused to grant PWA money to South Carolina for a private project, instead requiring the state to set up a state public service authority to oversee the project and thereby enabling it to qualify for PWA funds. The state legislation, modeled after the emerging federal TVA, provided for improved navigation, reclamation of swampland, reforestation, and hydroelectric power through the construction of dams, canals, and power plants. The Santee-Cooper project alone was the largest, most expensive PWA project on the East Coast. Besides providing hydroelectric power across South Carolina, Santee-Cooper employed over 16,000 workers, created two lakes, drained swamps, and indirectly improved health through the eradication of malaria in a five-county area. In addition, the creation of impound lakes at both Buzzard Roost and Santee-Cooper expanded recreational opportunities in hunting, boating, and fishing, and further impacted the changing landscape in the state.[42] The site for Greenwood State Park was selected in 1938 for its location in part because of the lakefront created by Buzzard Roost. The Santee-Cooper project also indirectly created an additional New Deal–related state park in the late 1940s, Santee State Park, in Orangeburg County, to take full advantage of the growing recreational opportunities provided on Lake Marion.

The legacy of the New Deal in South Carolina is mixed, as it is elsewhere. The previous narrative highlights both some of the failures and successes of a variety of New Deal programs in the state. Agencies such as the Agricultural Adjustment Administration failed to provide adequately for the rural poor, while the NRA improved the lot of textile workers only marginally, at best. Many New Deal programs in South Carolina, as in other states, were fraught with racism, incompetence, or corruption. Other programs, such as the WPA, provided limited opportunities for previously marginalized sections of the population, including women and African Americans. However small the gains or few the opportunities, these opportunities were indeed improvements over the situations for many in South Carolina prior to the New Deal.

There is no question that the New Deal changed South Carolina's landscape, from the rural landscape to the built environment of the cities. The Agricultural Adjustment Administration, the RA, and the SCS transformed the way South Carolinians farmed their land, introducing terracing, crop rotations, and other farming techniques that changed the farm landscape. The REA added electrical lines to the landscape. WPA projects improved roads and added everything from school buildings to art projects to many small-town environments, while also reconstructing historic buildings such as Charleston's Dock Street Theater. The PWA did a great deal to change the state's landscape through its public buildings, roads, housing projects, and, of course, the lakes, dams, power plants, and resulting recreational facilities of Santee-Cooper. These visual legacies should remind South Carolinians and visitors of the impact of the New Deal within the state.

Another New Deal program, the CCC, assisted in the creation of a new landscape for South Carolina through its work in forestry, fire prevention, soil conservation, and the construction of state parks. The CCC employed South Carolina's young men, white and black, and provided them with jobs, education, and vocational training. The CCC's work changed the state in many ways. The building of fire towers across the state and the implementation of soil conservation projects such as terracing and the planting of kudzu permanently altered the countryside, while providing jobs and homes to thousands of young men. Most obviously, the CCC state parks dramatically altered the landscape, with the construction of buildings, lakes, roads, and smaller recreational facilities, and the planting of thousands of trees throughout the state. No CCC project has been more lasting than the seventeen state parks constructed with CCC labor, and, along with Santee-Cooper, these state parks are perhaps the most visible and tangible New Deal legacy in South Carolina.

CHAPTER 2

Emergency Conservation Work and the Civilian Conservation Corps

An Administrative Overview of the Civilian Conservation Corps

When Franklin D. Roosevelt was inaugurated as president on March 4, 1933, he instituted a period of reform so sweeping it has become known as the "Hundred Days' War." Roosevelt's inaugural address compared the economic crisis at hand with one of war, and he stated that he intended to meet the crisis as he would any other enemy. South Carolinian James F. Byrnes, a longtime friend of Roosevelt's, played a large role in Roosevelt's administration, assisting in much of the "Hundred Days" legislation, and in the process steered a great deal of New Deal benefits to his home state.[1] With such immediate responses to the exigencies of the Great Depression as a bank holiday, the slashing of federal salaries, a farm bill, and an end to Prohibition, Roosevelt quickly turned the mood of the country from "depressed" to "relieved," in more ways than one.

During his first week in office, at a White House press conference, Roosevelt proposed conservation-related employment. Less than a week later, Roosevelt asked four cabinet members, including the secretaries of war, the interior, agriculture, and labor, to coordinate an informal meeting to plan the organization of the relief plan closest to his heart, the creation of a civilian group made up of unemployed young men to work for land and forest conservation across the United States.[2] After working closely with a joint committee from the Senate and House, President Roosevelt signed the bill that officially created Emergency Conservation Work (ECW) on March 31, 1933, although the program retained its more popular moniker, the Civilian Conservation Corps (CCC).[3]

On April 5, 1933, with Executive Order 6101, Roosevelt appointed widely respected labor leader Robert Fechner (1876–1939) to oversee ECW. Fechner, born in Tennessee and raised in Georgia, had joined a machinist union local at age sixteen and, at the time of his appointment, had served for twenty years as an executive officer of the International Association of Machinists. He also had lectured on labor relations at prestigious universities, such as Dartmouth, Brown, and Harvard, and had worked on Roosevelt's presidential campaign.

Although Fechner's appointment as director of ECW could be viewed as a political reward, his selection also mollified labor leaders who were concerned with several ECW provisions.[4] Fechner proved to be a capable and controversial leader, and he remained director until his death in December 1939. Although Fechner was the "director," the CCC was Roosevelt's pet project, and many early decisions were ultimately left up to the president. Decisions such as where to place camps often languished on Roosevelt's desk until he had time to get to them. CCC historian John Salmond has noted that Roosevelt's "genuine interest in the Corps cannot be doubted; yet by insisting that he approve personally every single camp site, the President greatly limited Fechner's authority and geared the pace of the work to his own availability."[5]

Executive Order 6101 also created an advisory council consisting of representatives from the Departments of War, Agriculture, the Interior, and Labor, the four cabinet offices that Roosevelt had initially consulted when drafting working plans for the CCC. Each cabinet department was responsible for overseeing a separate responsibility in the creation and operation of the CCC. The Department of Labor selected the enrollees, and the War Department operated the camps, while the Departments of Agriculture and the Interior were charged with supervising the work projects. The executive order appropriated money for the payroll, supplies, and equipment needed to carry out the work of ECW. Such cross-agency cooperation was not unheard of; President Calvin Coolidge had organized the National Conference on Outdoor Recreation in 1924, calling upon his secretaries of agriculture, commerce, the interior, labor, and war to discuss "country recreation" for the American people.[6]

At first, CCC enrollment was limited to the segment of the population that Roosevelt most wished to reach with the CCC, unemployed, single men aged eighteen to twenty-five. The army, charged with camp operation and initial training of the enrollees, accepted the first enrollees on April 7, 1933, and the first camp, Camp Roosevelt, was established in Luray, Virginia, on April 17. Roosevelt's interest in seeing the program work is evident in that within less than two weeks of issuing the executive order, the CCC was a working agency, with enrollees and at least one working camp. Less than a month later, ECW was extended, more specifically not only to white men but to African American men, Native American men, and veterans, primarily of the First World War. For the most part women were excluded from ECW and, later, the CCC, except in a few instances as clerical staff at regional levels and as teachers in camps.[7]

On April 21 the *State* newspaper in Columbia announced that South Carolina's quota for CCC enrollment would be 3,500 initially, and that interested men should make application to their local relief officer and be prepared to come to Columbia to the recruiting office. By April 23 the *State* reported that some 8,000 applications for the 3,500 estimated spots had been received, but that it was "doubtful whether there will be any projects in this state." Alan Johnstone, South Carolina's director of relief work, requested at least seven CCC camps for South Carolina, in order to keep at least half of South Carolina's enrollees in the state.[8]

In addition to the initial national allotment of 250,000 "junior enrollees," the Labor Department hired 25,000 local experienced men (LEMs) to assist with the training of the young men in forestry, field work, handicrafts, and trades. The hiring of the LEMs served another purpose as well. It provided employment to unemployed loggers, foresters, and woodsmen at civil service rates of pay, further ameliorating the fears of organized (and unorganized) labor that the CCC would take jobs away from skilled and semiskilled workers.[9]

Roosevelt charged the War Department with administering and governing the training and day-to-day life of the enrollees in the CCC camps. The role of the War Department caused the most controversy during the establishment of the CCC, and many of the CCC's early critics commented upon its resemblance to the military work and youth camps in Europe, most notably in Adolf Hitler's Germany. During congressional hearings in March 1933, William Green, president of the American Federation of Labor, argued that the CCC legislation "smacks of fascism, of Hitlerism, of a form of Sovietism."[10] In 1935 an article in the *Nation* recommended moving the primary administrative duties from the War Department to the United States Forest Service (USFS), in order to prevent the CCC camps from becoming "similar to the labor camps of Germany, which make a deliberate effort to bring about a mingling of classes on a footing of equality," which appeared to many as an early sign of Communism.[11] CCC officials continually battled this perception, claiming that similarities to European work camps were more coincidental than anything.

Several contemporary writers acknowledged that both the European and American models of youth employment drew inspiration from American philosopher William James, who had proposed conscripted youth doing manual labor for public service—in his words "an army enlisted against Nature"—as early as 1906.[12] Others claimed that the CCC was modeled in part on the work of the International Voluntary Service for Peace (IVS), an international volunteer organization that worked in Europe following World War I. At the same time, President Roosevelt claimed that he had never read James's essay, and failed to acknowledge any European antecedents for his CCC, instead pointing toward his programs in New York while governor and his work with the fledgling Boy Scouts of America as the genesis of the CCC.[13] Although some

Americans had worked with the IVS in the early 1920s and had observed such organizations as the National Union of Swiss Students and the German Free Corps, CCC promoters and Roosevelt's allies claimed that the European camps did not provide direct models for Roosevelt's CCC. South Carolina senator James Byrnes visited a Hitler youth camp in Germany in 1937 and later recalled: "The guide spoke of the benefits to the country of promoting an organization in which boys from every class and every corner of Germany could learn to work together. His sentiments were not dissimilar from those expressed to me by President Roosevelt. What made the end product so different was the fanatical hero worship of the Leader and the encouragement of militarism which figured so largely in the German camps and was conspicuously absent in our program."[14] Writing in 1942, sociologists Kenneth Holland and Frank Ernest Hill played down any similarities to German work camps: "It is important to realize the essentially American character of the CCC even in its earliest stages. Of equal importance to note is the relative completeness and even the relative superiority of [the CCC] as it began its life."[15] As international tensions increased through the 1930s, comparisons to anything German became less and less favorable, but the CCC's connection to the War Department became more important.

In addition to early public concern over the role of the War Department in the CCC, War Department officials worried that these new responsibilities would limit other army activities by placing additional pressures on army officers. These fears were well-founded; all but two army schools were closed, and their faculties and student officers were reassigned to CCC work. Of the almost 10,000 regular army officers on duty at the CCC's founding in 1933, over half were used on full-time CCC duty. Colonel Duncan Major of the General Staff Corps and Secretary of War George Dern protested the War Department's involvement to trusted Roosevelt aide Louis Howe and to the president himself. When Roosevelt assured them that the War Department was the best agency for the job, Major found himself on the CCC's advisory board and as such wielded considerable power and influence. All of Fechner's directives to the camp passed through military channels. The War Department called up and appointed reserve officers to serve with the CCC without contacting Fechner. The army's chief of finance served as the CCC's fiscal officer, allocating some 90 percent of CCC funds. Fechner's staff, in contrast, was small, and the director had to depend on the authority and efficiency of the army to carry out many of the president's wishes in regard to the CCC.[16]

The army, conceding to the president's wishes, began organizing CCC camps the only way it knew how—the army way. Camps were organized with 200-man companies, divided into sections and subsections (known as platoons and squadrons in military terms), supervised by leaders and assistant leaders. Although the military terms for these junior officers were "platoon sergeants" and "squadron leaders," the CCC retained the civilian terms "leader" and "assistant leader" as titles for promoted enrollees. A regular army officer commanded each company of 200 men, and four enlisted men were assigned to each camp as first sergeant, supply sergeant, mess sergeant, and cook.[17]

War Department officers and personnel were unprepared for such a rapid and large-scale mobilization, and throughout 1933 the War Department's handling of its new CCC responsibilities was generally haphazard. But the army's experience in handling and training large groups of men made induction and camp life run fairly efficiently. By keeping organization centralized and granting wide latitude to area commanders and camp commanders, the army was able to mobilize, train, and manage large numbers of men in a relatively short period of time.

Charged with the supply, administration, medical care, sanitation, and welfare of the 250,000 young men Roosevelt planned for the CCC, the War Department divided the country into nine geographically distinct corps areas, each commanded by a major general. South Carolina fell into the Fourth District, along with Louisiana, Mississippi, Alabama, Georgia, Florida, North Carolina, and Tennessee.[18] Each company received a permanent number, with the third digit from the right identifying its home corps' area of origin, and the next two digits indicating its order of formation.[19] For example, in South Carolina, Company 409 was the ninth company organized in the Fourth District. However, some companies were organized in one corps area but served in another, depending on where work projects were needed. At least five companies organized at Fort Dix, New Jersey, served in South Carolina early in the life of the CCC, with company numbers 1201, 1205, 1206, 1207, and 1221.

Camps were also identified by project number, with a letter signifying the assigned project type, and a number. "F" stood for forestry projects on federal land, "SCS" for Soil Conservation Service, "NP" for National Park (including national monuments, military parks, and historical parks), and "SP" for state park, for example. Increasing confusion in tracing CCC company histories lies with companies moving from location to location, and assigned to different projects. While the company number remained with the CCC company, the project number remained with the project. Companies also received unofficial pet names, often derived from a geographical location or local hero; in South Carolina, Company 445 near Cheraw, working on project SP-1—Cheraw State Park—in 1933 named itself Camp Jeff Davis. Companies 5465 (SP-5) and 5466 (SP-6) worked simultaneously on Table Rock State Park, and both called their camps Camp Table Rock. Camp names such as Francis Marion, William

Moultrie, and Peter Horry stayed with the camp location, regardless of project number or company. Additionally, throughout the life of the CCC, enrollees were shuffled between companies and projects as needed; even contemporary enrollee accounts noted that "the membership of a CCC company is constantly changing."[20] CCC alumni often describe themselves as being a part of the camp "SP-1" or by camp name, rather than the company, making their company's place and time of service often difficult to trace.[21]

The War Department also worried about the public's perception of the army and feared that the public would equate service in the CCC with that of the army, and sought to distinguish between service in the two organizations. When Strom Thurmond, then a South Carolina judge, offered to dismiss theft charges against two teenage boys if they enlisted in the army, enrolled in the CCC, or obtained "reliable" jobs, the army's immediate response was that only young men of "good character" were allowed to enlist in the army but made no reference to the character of young men entering the CCC.[22] Instead of poor public relations, however, War Department officials noticed that the public perception of the army improved in part as a result of its work with the CCC. Morale among junior officers serving with the CCC improved as well. These unexpected developments convinced the War Department that although President Roosevelt was requiring the department to undertake CCC work, it could also be a valuable endeavor for the military.

Training and education were a part of the CCC from very early in its inception. Almost from the beginning Fechner expressed his belief that the CCC was an ideal opportunity to educate and train a group of young men who were largely undereducated and, in many cases, illiterate. Education Commissioner George Zook supported Fechner's attempts to provide educational opportunities for the young men of the CCC. However, CCC educational programming met with a great deal of resistance from the War Department and, in particular, from Colonel Duncan Major. Since the army maintained control over the camps and did not want to interfere with working hours, initially the educational program was offered only at night, and attendance was voluntary.[23]

Clarence Marsh, of the University of Buffalo, was appointed educational director of ECW on December 29, 1933, and following the lead of other New Deal relief programs, Marsh used this opportunity to put to work unemployed teachers and university graduates. Developing an appropriate curriculum proved challenging as a result of the variety of educational experience of both the enrollees and the newly appointed camp educational advisers, and the lack of materials, time, and support from camp supervisors. In addition, camp commanders determined what types of classes could be taught at the individual camp level.[24] Early classes offered in 1934 at Company 442 (P-56) in Berkeley County, South

Carolina, included "graded school work as well as some college instruction" and classes in "radio, social dancing, first aid, typing, shorthand, bookkeeping, boxing, swimming, life-saving, and academic subjects."[25] In other camps, the educational program was forced to focus on the literacy problem. Company 4468 near Barnwell echoed this problem when they reported in July 1936 that when twenty-nine new enrollees arrived at their camp, "this was an unusual group because every man in it was able to sign for the clothing and equipment issued to him," indicating that this had not been the case in groups of previous new enrollees.[26]

Because of the lack of support on all levels of the program, Marsh resigned in frustration in 1935. Howard Oxley, a former educational adviser to the Liberian government, replaced Marsh; Oxley stayed until the CCC was disbanded in 1942. Under Oxley's direction the CCC educational program became much more formal and standardized. Oxley outlined nine specific goals of the CCC educational program: the elimination of illiteracy, the removal of deficiencies in common school subjects, on-the-job training, general vocational training, cultural and general education, health and safety education, character and citizenship training, and employment assistance. Company 445 (SP-1) at Cheraw echoed these goals of the educational program at the camp level, stating in their camp newspaper that "education in the CCC has very definite and specific objectives, organized and administered to meet clearly defined ends," and listed five objectives, including citizenship, training in fundamentals ("reading, writing, and number work"), vocational training, health and safety, and leisure-time activities. This combination of both academic and vocational training apparently appeared more practical and thus more attractive to both the enrollees and the army leadership, and camp educational programs became more formalized. By November 1937 each camp was required to provide enrollees a building for educational and vocational classes, and a compulsory educational program replaced the voluntary nature of the educational program. The more formalized program and the building erected specifically for educational purposes improved the morale of camp educational advisers, and the enrollees themselves took the educational program more seriously.[27]

Although Fechner championed the educational program, he understood that education was secondary to employment, and that the CCC "is a work centered organization and not a substitute for high schools and colleges."[28] Camp educational advisers were often poorly trained, little money was provided for books or supplies, and the young men themselves were often less than motivated to attend classes or study outside of class. As CCC historian John Salmond observed, "academic courses were of limited practical value to youths who would almost certainly lead non-academic lives."[29] Inadequate funding and support for the CCC educational program affected the programming at the individual camp level. The *Pinopolian*, the camp newsletter for Company 442, serving in Moncks Corner, South Carolina, reported how a lack of funding affected their camp building as well as their educational program. Although in January 1935 more permanent buildings had replaced the temporary tent camp that had served as housing, the newsletter reported that "the little ten by eighteen feet room used by the Educational Department is being hampered due to lack of room. However, the 'midget' room, or library, reading room, printing office, workshop, lecture hall, classroom, and Education Private Office has been given a very appropriate desk and reading table along with the general improvement scheme. The desk and table can not be used due to lack of assembling room."[30] It appears the irony of the situation was not lost on the enrollees editing the camp newsletter.

Both enrollees and the army accepted the vocational education more readily than general academics. Officials offered vocational classes that related directly to CCC work, such as classes in truck driving, mechanics, equipment maintenance and repair, landscaping, surveying, carpentry, forestry, and wildlife conservation, as well as classes that related more indirectly to the administration and day-to-day operation of the camps, such as typing and office skills, accounting, and cooking and baking. In addition, some classes doubled as recreational activities. Some enrollees became "special reporters" to local newspapers; Columbia's the *State* included several columns highlighting individual CCC camps throughout the state. In other cases journalism classes gave enrollees opportunities to produce a camp newspaper while also providing interested enrollees an opportunity to explore reporting, writing stories, and newspaper production; in South Carolina approximately sixty CCC companies produced camp newspapers. Often these camp newsletters contained an editorial from either the commanding officer or the educational adviser extolling the opportunities of the educational programming and exhorting the enrollees to attend classes.

Both the vocational and more recreational types of classes met with approval of the advisory committee, as they contributed directly to the CCC's mission or, in the case of recreational classes, were offered only during "free time." Enrollees were encouraged to take classes that improved their work and that would introduce them to fields in which they might pursue full-time employment after they left the CCC. However, even these types of vocational classes met with later criticism, as CCC historian John Salmond wondered if "one can legitimately question whether instruction in digging ditches and building dams was fitting the enrollee for life in an increasingly urbanized society."[31]

According to Salmond, "education must be counted one of the less successful fields of CCC endeavor," due to the lack of commitment to the educational program at all levels of CCC administration.[32] The CCC's educational program faced a dearth of support on both the camp level and at the highest administrative levels. Like many other New Deal programs, the CCC's educational program had results at individual levels: by 1937, 35,000 illiterate young men had been taught to read and write, more than 1,000 had received high school diplomas, and almost forty college degrees had been awarded to CCC men at the halfway point of its existence. During the year 1938–39, over 8,000 additional enrollees learned to read and write, and over 700 received scholarships to attend college.[33]

While the Labor Department was responsible for enrollee recruitment and selection and the War Department trained enrollees, governed their daily lives, and educated them, the Departments of Agriculture and the Interior supervised the CCC's various projects. Agriculture managed approximately 75 percent of all CCC work, and more than half of these agriculture projects were under the direction of the USFS. Interior supervised its projects through the National Park Service (NPS), the Bureau of Indian Affairs, the Bureau of Land Reclamation, the Soil Erosion Service, and other bureaus. After 1935 the federal soil erosion program was transferred to the Department of Agriculture, under the Soil Conservation Service (SCS), and related CCC projects were likewise transferred.[34]

The NPS was given direction of park development, especially the improvement of existing national and state parks and the development of new parks. NPS director Horace Albright appointed Chief Forester John D. Coffman as supervisor of CCC work in the national parks. Albright also appointed the chief planner, Conrad L. Wirth, as supervisor of CCC work in state parks. In 1936 Albright's successor, Arno B. Cammerer, consolidated administration of the CCC programs under Wirth.[35]

The CCC's work with the USFS and the NPS dramatically changed the professionals who worked under the auspices of the Departments of Agriculture and the Interior. Only three landscape architects had worked with the USFS since its inception in 1905; when the CCC began in 1933 there were no landscape architects working for the USFS, and only ten working for the NPS. By the fall of 1933 over 1,400 CCC camps were working under the USFS or the NPS, and the NPS established a policy to hire one landscape architect for each camp. According to landscape architect Phoebe Cutler, the NPS and the USFS "had begun the hunt which was to propel the profession of landscape architecture out of obscurity."[36] Indeed, the USFS and the NPS were hiring landscape architects even before they graduated from college; NPS recruiter William Carnes boasted that the NPS employed 400 landscape architects, while the American Society of Landscape Architects (ASLA) listed only 284 members.

Approximately 90 percent of people in the landscaping profession worked for the government.[37]

The rise in employment opportunities for landscape architects and other landscaping professionals caused a rise in interest in pursuing a professional degree in landscape-related fields; new programs sprang up in colleges around the country, especially west of the Mississippi River, where the greatest numbers of national parks and forests provided the greatest demand for landscape professionals. The types of projects landscape architects were working on also changed, from private estates to park roads, trails, and facilities. Darcy Bonnet, the regional landscape architect for California's CCC projects, observed, "Most landscape architects hadn't messed around with public recreation."[38] Thus CCC work provided these professionals with a new avenue in which to exercise their expertise.

Similar to the controversy over the army's role in the CCC, controversy also arose surrounding the relationship between the NPS and the CCC. Most concerns came from within the NPS. Many park superintendents and other NPS professionals were uncertain about putting numerous boys and young men to work in the existing parks, and feared that the predicted labor glut would result in the overdevelopment of parks and in losses of cultural and natural resources. For example, near Memphis, Tennessee, as a CCC crew cleared land for construction, it stumbled across a major Mississippian period site at Shelby Bluffs State Park. Luckily the archaeological significance of that site was recognized, and park development continued elsewhere. To counteract these fears, the NPS developed a project review system, in which all proposed CCC park work was to be reviewed at the Washington office by landscape architects, historians, archaeologists, and wildlife experts.[39] Although this review allowed the Washington professionals a chance to assess a project's potential impact on existing natural, cultural, and historic resources, it also added additional administrative steps to a program that was awash in bureaucratic complexity.

When his contemporaries complained that the CCC administration was too unwieldy to work efficiently, Roosevelt replied, "Oh that doesn't matter. The Army and the Forestry Service will really run the show. The Secretary of Labor will select the men and make the rules and Fechner will 'go along' and give everybody satisfaction and confidence."[40] With the CCC's administrative duties divided up over four cabinet departments, then further subdivided within those departments, and with the involvement of other governmental agencies, it is apparent that the bureaucracy involved in running the CCC was an organizational nightmare. Added to the federal levels of bureaucracy were the divisions at the corps district, state, and local levels—with the state and local relief boards; state forestry, agricultural, and parks departments; and state and local political officials often weighing in on decisions with their own opinions and preferences. However complicated, Roosevelt, Fechner, and the many others made it work for thousands of young men, and for thousands of acres of American land.

As the 1930s ended, the CCC was at its lowest point. With Fechner's death on December 31, 1939, the CCC lost its most vocal supporter after the president. By 1940 economic relief was no longer as pressing an issue, as more opportunities became available for the young men for whom the CCC had been designed. As the number of enrollees decreased, camps were closed and projects left uncompleted, and as hostilities in Europe and the Far East continued to intensify, pressures from within the United States began suggesting using the CCC as a military training camp for future soldiers. Representative James Richards, a congressman from Lancaster County, South Carolina, and a World War I veteran and a Roosevelt ally, proposed legislation that would require six hours of military training a week for CCC enrollees, the first of nine bills introduced between 1939 and 1941 that would have further militarized the CCC. For the most part, however, the War Department was opposed to the idea of adding military training to the CCC, believing that such training should be given priority to men who were planning to be career soldiers. In addition, the War Department wanted to avoid the appearance of a large-scale military mobilization among CCC men. General George C. Marshall, the army chief of staff and a former CCC commander, was also opposed to adding additional military training to the CCC, although he did agree that noncombatant training would be an asset to the CCC.[41]

South Carolina senator James F. Byrnes introduced an amendment to the 1940–41 Relief Appropriations bill providing for noncombatant training in the CCC, with limited support from the Federal Security Agency, the War Department, and the White House. General George C. Marshall testified before the Senate Appropriations Committee, listing the benefits such training would have, from allowing the CCC to provide specialized training in fields that could be important to the army to its emphasis on engineers' and cooks' roles. Byrnes's amendment passed with little opposition, and in 1941 fifteen minutes of marching and fifteen additional minutes of calisthenics were added to the daily routine of the CCC. At the same time, federal funding for the CCC was decreasing, causing the states either to close camps or take on additional state appropriations for funding projects.[42]

The improving economy and ever-intensifying European hostilities provided a prelude to the demise of the CCC, as well as other New Deal programs. The 1941–42 appropriations bill created a congressional joint committee to examine all federal agencies and to propose elimination of those not essential to the war effort. Following the bombing of Pearl Harbor on December 7, 1941, and the subsequent entry of the United States into war, the committee recommended the abolition of the CCC no later than July 1, 1942. Roosevelt tried to save his beloved conservation program and rallied support from even the War Department, but by April 1942 public opinion also favored closing the CCC. In early May 1942 Roosevelt asked Congress to appropriate funding to keep 150 CCC camps in operation during 1942 and 1943. In June 1942 the House voted 158 to 151 not to approve funding for the continuance of the CCC, and the Senate voted 32 to 32, with 32 abstentions. With no further funding, the CCC simply ceased operations at the end of the legislative session.[43]

The rather abrupt end of the CCC caused a myriad of bureaucratic problems at the local level, as enrollees scrambled to finish projects where possible, and commanding officers wrote letters of recommendation for these young men both for employment and for military service. In South Carolina, as elsewhere, company numbers dwindled, as young men left camp for the military or for other employment, and were not replaced, leading to poor morale in camp. Thomas Rutledge, project superintendent for Company 4480 at Hunting Island in Beaufort County, reported eight enrollees deserted the island in a rowboat in January 1941 rather than being transferred to the West Coast. By October 1941 the company had declined to eighty-three total, with forty available for "technical agency" work.[44] R. A. Walker, the assistant state forester in charge of state parks, wrote to the NPS that "our development plans will be very seriously affected" by the loss of federal funding; these plans were most notable in the slow development of the planned segregated state parks in Greenwood and Beaufort counties. Additional correspondence between Walker and the Regional Director Thomas J. Allen in March 1942 reveals a lack of communication regarding camp closures during this period. Allen apologizes to Walker for not informing him of the imminent closure of the camps at Greenwood and Hunting Island: "due to the recent numerous camp abandonments and the placing of the CCC on an all-out defense program, it has been impossible to keep the park authorities advised in advance of camp movements and abandonments."[45]

Although the CCC lasted only nine years, it was one of the most popular and successful New Deal programs of the 1930s. Several studies of the New Deal and the CCC rely upon statistics, such as the number of young men who enlisted or the number of acres of land reclaimed, to judge the impact of the CCC. Perhaps a better way to judge the successes of the CCC is to examine the letters and writings of the young men who served in the CCC, and to talk with the men they became, letting their stories of the lessons learned in the CCC and how that experience changed their lives speak to the achievements of the program. Another is to view the CCC projects that remain all over the country, in places like the Great Smoky Mountains or Yosemite National Park, lakes and dams such as Deer Creek Dam in Utah, and the hundreds of state parks across the country. Men who served in the South Carolina CCC have left similar built reminders all over the state, as well as individual narratives of what life was like as an enrollee the South Carolina CCC. Both their personal reminiscences and their constructed landscapes are their legacies to the Palmetto State.

"A good set of boys here and I like it fine"

Life in the South Carolina Civilian Conservation Corps

Intended to put to work a large segment of unemployed American men, President Roosevelt also designed the Civilian Conservation Corps (CCC) to make use of the virtues of America's young men—their strength, their vitality, and their hunger for employment. In addition to providing employment for this segment of the population, the CCC assisted the families of the enrollees by requiring that part of the enrollee's pay be sent home for support. Money was spent in the local communities where the camps were located, providing indirect stimulation to the local economies. Most important, Roosevelt hoped to use the CCC to preserve the outdoor environment he loved and to foster this love of the outdoors in a new generation of American men. Reclaiming America's youth and America's land were Roosevelt's dual goals for the CCC. According to an early study of the CCC, Roosevelt believed that "more important than material gains will be the moral and spiritual value of such work."[1]

Relatively little is known about the individual daily life of the young men enrolled in the CCC camps. Many of the historical studies of the CCC are primarily bureaucratic or celebratory in nature, focusing on the accomplishments of the CCC as a whole, rather than the individual experience of the enrollees. More recent studies have examined the social impact of the program on the enrollees, including physical, educational, and social development. Although some CCC studies mention the firsthand experiences of the enrollees and a few books have been privately published that record the memoirs of the men who served in the CCC, few of these men preserved their letters or diaries written during their time of service, and most of these primary sources, if they exist, are hidden in boxes in attics or basements. Camp newspapers, written and published by the CCC enrollees, have often shared the same fate, although some copies can be found in local or regional archives, and many have been preserved on microfiche at the Center for Research Libraries in Chicago.[2] Camp records, as noted by Frank Holland, an educational adviser in the corps, "were incomplete. . . . Very little record-keeping [was] maintained at the camp level, where the opportunity to record the lives of the men would have been greatest,"[3] and indeed, there is sometimes a disconnect between the recorded activities of individual companies at the federal level and at the state level, where apparently decision making was rapid and subject to change depending on the needs of various projects. The memories of those who served are the best link to describing the daily lives of these young men, both the work they did and the educational and recreational opportunities afforded by the CCC. This chapter examines the daily lives of these CCC men, often in their own words, in an attempt to better understand the perspectives of the enrollees as they experienced the program and benefited from it. Understanding the daily life and experience of the young men of the CCC is essential in understanding the legacy they left in the built environment and in the establishment of the state park system in South Carolina.

Although the CCC was comprised of a diverse group of young men and older veterans, most of the enrollees were white and native born. In 1940 the typical CCC enrollee was a white male seventeen to eighteen years old who weighed 145 pounds, was five feet eight inches tall, and had an eighth-grade education. Only 9 percent of enrollees were African American, a result of an unwritten quota system that restricted the opportunities for young black men.[4] Other minorities participated in the CCC, including Native Americans, Mexican, Chinese, Japanese, and Filipino Americans; these other ethnic groups were found mostly in the camps located on the West Coast. In the South the CCC consisted primarily of young native-born white men, mostly of Scots-Irish descent, with a larger percentage of African Americans than in the rest of the country, but a percentage that was far less than the percentage of blacks in the region's general population.[5]

These young men joined the CCC for many reasons, although unemployment and a desire to assist their families ranked at the top of the list. In a survey conducted near the end of the CCC's work, Kenneth Holland and Frank Ernest Hill found that 77.5 percent of enrollees surveyed said they had joined "to help their families," with 62 percent stating that was their chief reason for signing up. Other reasons given included "had nothing to do"; "to get away from home"; "family wanted boy to go"; and "friends were going."[6] The CCC provided a sense of stability and purpose for young men searching for work and a way to help their families, while at the same time decreasing their dependency on their families. Two South Carolinians who were teenagers in the early 1930s remember distinctly the effects that the Depression had upon their family life and employment. Wilbert Bernshouse of Sumter, South Carolina, recalls that as a teenager in 1932, he worked part-time at a furniture store, and most of his earnings "went to the family which wasn't much at ten cents an hour." Bernshouse's father had gone to New Jersey to look for work, while his mother "did cooking and catering."[7] James Dawkins, who worked near Darlington as a laborer for the State Highway Department after his high school graduation in 1931, remembers that his wages had been cut to 10 cents an hour and that he was only allowed to report to work three days a week by 1934.[8] Both Bernshouse and Dawkins joined the CCC in a search for meaningful work and as a way to supplement their families' incomes.

Enrollees initially went to an army base for their induction period, which in some ways resembled early basic training for the military. Most South Carolina enrollees found themselves at Fort Moultrie in South Carolina or Fort McPherson in Georgia, although early recruits were sent to Fort Benning, also in Georgia. A few companies that served in South Carolina came from Fort Bragg (North Carolina) or Screven (Georgia), and five companies working in South Carolina had been organized at Fort Dix (New Jersey). The induction period lasted, on the average, about two weeks. During this time enrollees received physical examinations, vaccinations, and information about what would be expected of them in the camp.

Potential South Carolina enrollees were directed to travel to one of the state's assembling points in Columbia, Charleston, Greenville, and Spartanburg. South Carolina's first group of enrollees were conditioned at Fort Moultrie during the first two weeks of May 1933, with an advance group of fifty leaving Fort Moultrie on May 17 to set up the state's first CCC camp, in Oconee County. Five hundred enrollees gathered in Columbia on May 17 and 18, 1933, for physical examinations prior to being sent to Fort Benning for a two-week conditioning stay before being assigned to CCC camps. The first 250 to leave from Columbia gathered on the steps of the statehouse for a group photo printed in the *State* newspaper of Columbia. Four hundred other recruits left Spartanburg on May 20 for Fort Moultrie, 250 from Charleston to Fort Moultrie on May 23, and 450 from Greenville on May 24 and 25 to Fort McPherson. An additional 250 left Columbia on May 28, following a musical program performed by the University of South Carolina band at the statehouse grounds in their honor. By the end of May South Carolina's quota of 3,500 was almost filled, including a group of 200 African Americans who enrolled in Columbia on May 31 and left for Fort Benning on June 1, 1933. South Carolina's director of relief, Alan Johnstone, received a telegram from Washington in the first week of June congratulating the state on being one of the first states to achieve completing its enrollment quota.[9]

In a letter to his mother on May 19, 1933, Wilbert Bernshouse wrote about his induction experience at Fort Benning, after having traveled from Sumter to Columbia, and then by train to Fort Benning:

We got off [the train] at headquarters and carried our baggage over a mile across camp to a group of tents (What a walk). We were given a mess kit,

2 army blankets, 4 sheets, a matress tick, 2 towels, and a mosquito net. At 11 AM Sumter time or 10 AM Columbus, GA time, we were given breakfast and was it good! Hominy, chipped beef, bread, butter, an apple, milk, apple butter, coffee, post toasties, and all you wanted of everything. We rested around our tents till 4 PM and marched to the hospital, a building 2 or 3 times larger than ours and a good mile away. There was over 20 MDs and each examined for a different thing. At the end was 2 Drs vaccinating and giving typhoid shots. I took mine, steped off and dog if I didn't faint right there. I was alright in a minute but I sure did hate [that]. When we got back from the exams we were put in companies and sworn in for 6 months. We carried our baggage another half mile to the tent we will occupy for the next 2 week or more and then went to supper which was just as good as breakfast. Everybodies arm is sore and we are not doing anything today. We are to stay in a quaranteened area till our 3rd typhoid shot.[10]

Even after fainting and in quarantine with a sore arm, Bernshouse concluded his letter, "There seems to be a good set of boys here and I like it fine."[11] Bernshouse's induction experience was not unique. Sam Blanton remembered that when he joined the CCC in 1933, during his induction at Fort Moultrie, "one man grabbed [my] right arm and another the left and gave me shots. Boy! I was sore the next day."[12] Frank Wardlaw, reporting to the *State*, gave an account of one poor soul from Columbia who did not move quickly enough through the vaccination line, and received two typhoid shots instead of one: "Needless to say he was a very sick man the next day."[13]

Local newspapers reported the induction experiences of local boys, often to the amusement of family and friends back home. Gene Milligan, a member of Company 421, attended induction at Fort McPherson. He reported to the *State* that a day in conditioning camp consisted of breakfast at 6:30 A.M., drilling and hiking for three hours, dinner at 11:30, and supper at 4:30. "After supper, the fun begins," according to Milligan, "the guys start pulling jokes on one another." Induction also saw its share of regional rivalries, as Milligan reported that the enrollees from South Carolina and Georgia often boxed or wrestled, and that the South Carolina boys had all "won or drawn over the Georgia guys." Frank Wardlaw reported similar experiences from Company 1408, conditioning at Fort Benning: "Enough sleep, food, work, and amusement is provided to keep even the most discontented of souls happy. . . . The only thing that can be depended upon is that [the day] will be utterly different from the preceeding [*sic*] days." Wardlaw also reported on regional rivalries, including the tale of a brazen Columbia youth who claimed he could beat "any lousy so-and-so from Georgia," until he discovered that his challenger happened to be a first cousin from across the state line and the potential fight turned into a joyful reunion.

R. A. Conard, at Fort McPherson, summed up the induction experience for the newspaper: "Oh, it's hell—but it's great!"[14]

The induction experience seemed similar in different years and location. The *State* reported on recruits near Effingham spending a weekend in July 1934 searching for "elusive objects such as anvil oil, left-handed monkey wrenches, bugle keys and other intangible assets" before being "sent to the woods for more intensive training."[15] Harlan Crook, a CCC enrollee from Mississippi, remembered that in 1934, during his induction at Fort McClellan, Alabama, "we were given shots and vaccinations. We were there for three weeks of conditioning. We exercised, we ran, we picked up rocks and carried them across a little creek one day and carried them back across the next day." George Cmar, who traveled from Philadelphia to New York in 1933 to sign up, recalled his induction at Fort Dix as "shots—inspection—shots—uniform issued. Learned a lot about making catsup [and] drilling. Then we got word we were being shipped to camp in a place called Withersbee, South Carolina. Big disappointment!" Cmar described his group of fellow enrollees in Company 1204 as "a bunch of conscripts from the East Side. . . . Puerto Ricans, Cubans, Italians, some Irish, and ME. Man, what a tough-looking bunch!" Other South Carolina companies organized at Fort Dix included Company 1221 at Luray and Company 1207 at Awendaw, north of Charleston in the Francis Marion National Forest. The last names of enrollees there demonstrate that they most likely were not South Carolina natives, either. Enrollees named Prinz, Sanchez, Schwimmer, Mastramatteo, Tarwaski, Pulcinello, and Dvorsky put out a camp newspaper at Awendaw called the *Ditch Diggers Digest* in the summer of 1935; at Withersbee, enrollees named Yablonsky, Germanio, Barba, and Cambangola joined George Cmar as leaders in various positions.[16] Apparently the "culture shock" of these young men from the big city being sent to rural South Carolina was not as traumatic as in other locales, as there is no evidence of any real trouble at these South Carolina camps. Comparatively, two incidents at Shenandoah National Park have been chronicled by Patrick Clancy, who recounts that two CCC camps had trouble when "Yankee" CCC recruits from Pennsylvania were placed in camp with native Virginians.[17]

Along with the vaccinations, the uniforms remained in the minds of the men as one of the "highlights" of their induction period. Only after swapping with other new enrollees did the young men find uniforms that fit correctly. James Dawkins, who enrolled in the summer of 1934, recalled that "you took what they handed you and if you got a fairly good fit, you were fortunate. We swapped around however, and managed eventually to obtain clothing that came very close to fitting." At Fort Benning, Durwood Stinson received a pair of pants with a forty-six-inch waist, quite a shock for the eighteen-year-old who weighed ninety-eight pounds. He remembered that "another CCC man who weighed 170 pounds and me put the pants on over our civilian pants. We buttoned the Army issue pants and with me standing on his shoes walked down the company street."[18] Frank Wardlaw, also at Fort Benning, claimed that the army "seems to have a standard size man and if you don't happen to conform to his measurement it is just too bad."[19] These ill-fitting clothes were a common experience (and complaint) of new CCC enrollees all over the country, and many of them modified not only the sizes but the styles of the uniforms to better suit their size and taste.[20]

Roosevelt's goal of providing for young American men was not limited to finding jobs, but in creating men from boys. The CCC met these goals both psychologically and physically. Having a job and providing support for their families helped these young men mature psychologically, while the physical nature of the work and the "three squares" a day meant that enrollees gained muscle and kept physically fit. Durwood Stinson was only admitted to the CCC on his third attempt to enroll. During his first two attempts, Stinson was told he was malnourished, weighing in at only ninety-two and ninety-four pounds. On his third try, prior to weigh-in, he ate "two hamburgers, two hot dogs, four bananas, and drank a pint of milk and two glasses of water" in order to make the scales read "a little over 98 pounds." Thirteen months later, he weighed 135 pounds, a testament to the power of the hard work and healthy food provided in the CCC.[21] In their study of CCC enrollees, Holland and Hill report that at discharge, the "average enrollee" had grown approximately a half an inch and gained between ten and thirteen pounds.[22] At least three contemporary scholars have examined the physical impact that the work of the CCC had on young men throughout the country.[23]

During the induction period, these young men met other enrollees about their age, but from different places and walks of life. Some came from working-class, urban backgrounds; others sought work away from the family farm. For many, these few weeks of induction were the first of an extended stay away from their homes and families and an immense learning experience. After induction, the young men were placed into companies of approximately 200 and sent to the sites where they would set up camp for six months and perform their work.

The induction period and first few weeks of CCC camp life were new experiences for many enrollees, regardless of background. During induction at the army forts, many of the rural boys experienced modern conveniences to which they were unaccustomed, but these same rural boys felt more at home at camp, while the more urban enrollees were as unfamiliar with the untamed terrain and wildlife as the rural boys had been with running water and toilets. Both sets of new experiences fostered teasing, jokes, and pranks.

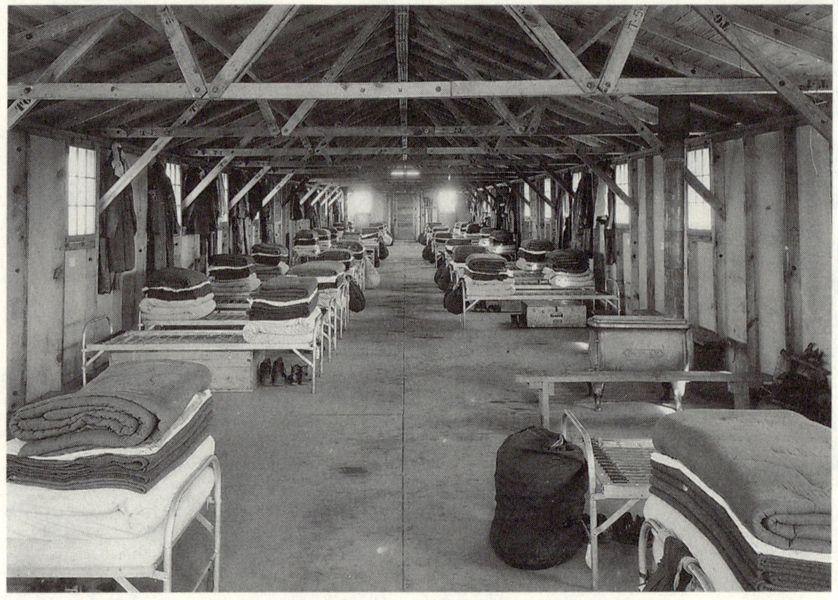

Interior view of the barracks of Company 1417, Camp SCS-11, near Rodman. Photograph courtesy of South Carolina Department of Parks, Recreation, and Tourism, George Buell Collection

CCC alumni remember some of the "endless pranks" that were played at camp, including making "Shadow Soup" as a remedy for laziness. "Shadow Soup" consisted of a pot of boiling water, over which a piece of meat was passed, letting only the shadow fall into the pot. After a steady diet of this special soup, shirkers were ready to return to duty in order to receive a more substantial meal. Although most pranks were good-natured, others were more spiteful, but usually aimed at "rookies," slackers, or boys who did not abide by camp norms. One example is the "fishing trip" one young man experienced with the boys of Company 486 in Mississippi, where he was stripped down and scrubbed with "GI soap and two scrub brushes." The young man evidently learned the lesson the rest of the camp was trying to teach him, as enrollee Harlan Crook remembered that "after that, no matter how cold it might be, he took a shower in the morning and also after coming in from work." Frank Wardlaw, reporting from Company 1408 while at Fort Benning, told of one method enrollees used to prevent pushing, shoving, and passing in the mess line: allowing a six-foot-four enrollee named Eargle to be first in line, and he would control those who would try to pass. Company 441 at Greer, South Carolina, published a list of "good advice" and camp norms for new enrollees who joined their camp in October 1937:

> Obey your superiors. (This might include most everyone at least until you find out Who's Who.)
>
> Make up your bed and keep the floor around it clean.
>
> Be on time for mess.
>
> Wash, and comb your hair before meals.
>
> Become interested in some of the camp activities.
>
> Write home at least once a week.
>
> Make lots of good friends and then stick by them.
>
> Be quiet when coming in late.
>
> Respect your officers.
>
> Put in an honest days work.
>
> Respect the rights of the people in town. (After all, they were here first.)[24]

Enrollees could avoid being on the wrong end of camp pranks and jokes or more serious trouble by adhering to camp rules, both the official rules and the more unofficial ones set by the enrollees themselves.

Camp life was not all fun and games. The CCC meant to provide work for these young men, and work they did. Many different types of employment opportunities within the CCC were available, and the young men were placed in areas where they demonstrated natural aptitude. Enrollees varied in the amount and quality of education they had received. Although some had graduated from high school or even attended college, many more had only eighth-grade or lower educational experiences, and some were illiterate. Illiterate or poorly educated men were required to take some literacy classes while in the CCC. The better-educated men often received jobs of higher responsibility, such as running the camp canteen (where candy, cigarettes, and other "nonessentials" could be purchased) or mess hall, serving in the Camp Overhead as leaders or assistant leaders, or serving as an administrative assistant to the camp officers. The Camp Overhead was best described in one of the South Carolina camp newsletters, written to inform the "folks back home" about life in the CCC camp: "The Camp Overhead is made of enrollees who, in the opinion of camp officials, are capable of successfully overseeing the directing of the various lines of duty. These young men don't necessarily have to have an education, but

Myrtle Beach State Park, unidentified camp personnel, no date. Photograph courtesy of South Carolina Department of Archives and History

dependable authority in the position for which he receives his rating. . . . The Overhead, or enrollee camp directors, are held responsible for any misdemeanor. Their actions are considered as an example and are closely followed by respectful enrollees."[25]

Frank Damon, who had graduated from Charleston High School, received an office job as company clerk, in part because he had taken typing classes in high school. Damon also served as editor of the camp newsletter, the *Cherokean*. Other CCC jobs included driving trucks and emergency vehicles, assisting in the dispensary and sick hall, and preparing meals. However, most men worked "in the field," clearing brush, planting trees, fighting fires, building roads and fire towers, and the like, doing the jobs for which the CCC had been founded. Many CCC men remember their jobs, most with a great sense of pride, and see the remaining structures such as the fire towers and park buildings as a testament to their hard work.[26]

A typical day for a CCC enrollee began with a bugle call at 5:30 A.M., followed by exercises and the raising of the American flag. Enrollees straightened their barracks for a morning inspection and went to breakfast, usually a hearty meal. One camp's breakfast menu included fried eggs, oatmeal, milk, hot biscuits, syrup, stewed prunes, and fried potatoes. At around 7:45 a roll call was held. Then enrollees loaded up on trucks to be taken to their work sites, and work began around 8:00 each morning. The day's work could consist of a variety of projects. In South Carolina, companies assigned to the State Forestry

Commission engaged in forestry and conservation work, such as road building, tree planting, tree cutting, fire fighting, or stringing telephone wires for fire prevention; other forestry projects could include gathering pinecones for seed, surveying timber, or building fire towers or other structures. A half-hour to hour lunch break was given on-site, with another truck bringing the meals, usually sandwiches, to the enrollees. Then it was back to work, until four o'clock in the afternoon, when the enrollees loaded back into trucks to be taken back to camp. Sometimes camp maintenance was performed in the afternoons, and the men were expected to shower and dress for mail call and supper at 5:00 or 5:15. Evenings were usually left free for recreational games, going into town twice a week, crafts, reading, or classes, although by the end of the CCC illiterate enrollees were required to attend literacy classes. "Lights out" was expected by 10:00 P.M., with little protest, as the next day would begin early with hard work.[27]

CCC alumnus Wilbert Bernshouse remembers one job of gathering pinecones near McClellanville, South Carolina, to provide seed for a CCC nursery in October 1933: "We climbed the tall trees with climbing spurs and pushed the green cones off with a long stick. The cones were carried to Wedgefield and spread over the floor of an old house to dry."[28] Bernshouse also worked building fire towers near Sampit and Conway, as well as in the CCC Forestry Nursery at Georgetown. George Cmar, the young enrollee from Pennsylvania who ended up in Berkeley County, South Carolina, in 1933, learned to grade land for

Table Rock State Park, Pickens, four CCC enrollees training in furniture construction. Enrollees Harold Willis, Raymond Fulmer, Luther McCrary, and George Carter show off their table and stools, 25 January 1938. Photograph courtesy of South Carolina Department of Archives and History

Company 445, Cooks and KPs in front of the mess hall, named Marshall Hall, April 10, 1934. George Marshall was the commanding officer at Fort Moultrie in the early 1930s. The back of the photograph states that H. B. Floyd (back row, second from right) was "senior steward [and] operated the mess. A very capable young man." Photograph courtesy of South Carolina Department of Parks, Recreation, and Tourism, George Buell Collection

roads, camps, and a ball field; dynamite stumps; run a bulldozer; cut ditches; and erect a fire tower. Cmar remembers the fire tower as a job to be proud of: "Man, that was a job! Bolting and riveting in the wind. And, sure enough, we put it up. Man, we city folks were proud!!"[29]

Cmar also remembered fighting fires "all over Berkeley County. At times we were up to our chests in water, sometimes frozen stiff and wet." Company 441 at Parr Shoals fought forest fires in Fairfield County in June 1933, garnering praise from their camp officers and county officials. Fighting fires and fire prevention were some of the most important jobs for the CCC, but also some of the most trying. Willis Felix Cox, serving in the Smoky Mountains of North Carolina, and later near Liberty, South Carolina, found many of his enrollees went absent without leave (AWOL) when expected to fight fires. As leader, he restricted them to camp upon their return and put them to work cleaning out septic tanks. According to Cox, most decided that perhaps fighting fires was not as demanding as previously thought.[30]

Sometimes enrollees had to fight fires of their own making as well. While working at Kings Mountain National Military Park near York, enrollees John

Brumby and Clyde McGee sounded a fire alarm at four o'clock one Sunday morning in 1935, when a fire erupted from a lantern they had been using while trying to fill a truck's gas tank. The district newsletter reported, "the only damage reported was to McGee's throat from yelling so loud in giving the alarm."[31] Although dealing with these types of emergencies often were not the primary job of the enrollees, they quickly learned to be prepared for any emergency.

Besides fighting fires, South Carolina's CCC enrollees were often ready to respond to other emergencies. In the summer of 1937 fifty enrollees from Company 4487, an African American company stationed near Anderson, offered to give blood to a needy local man; enrollee Malverse Singleton was selected to donate a pint of blood. Company 441 in Greer proved their claim that they were "willing to help at any time" when those junior enrollees assisted victims in a car accident outside of their camp in September 1937, and nine men volunteered to give blood for a transfusion to one of the victims. The next year twelve enrollees from Company 441 volunteered when a blood drive was undertaken to assist a local woman who needed blood. Company 441 also journeyed from Greer to Tryon, North Carolina, to aid in the search for a missing hunter. The CCC enrollees found the missing man, dead from an apparent heart attack, and headquarters gave permission for the CCC camp to accept the $50 reward. Enrollees at other camps were also called upon to assist in finding missing people, including a "lost Negro man" and a three-year-old child at Myrtle Beach State Park in the summer of 1935.[32] With these necessary activities, enrollees not only learned about manual labor but also learned how to deal with emergency situations.

CCC officers and camp leaders were very aware that "all work and no play" would be a very unhealthy way to run the camps, and ample recreational and educational opportunities were provided for the relaxation, entertainment, and edification of the young men in the camps. Organized sports, such as basketball and baseball, were among the most popular recreational outlets. Organized musical and singing groups attracted participation as well. Other, more spontaneous, diversions included playing cards, checkers, or dominoes; swimming in nearby lakes or rivers; and reading. Enrollees made trips "into town" weekly, for shopping, movies, dancing, dates with local young women, or visiting bars and playing pool. These diverse recreational opportunities are some of the CCC alumni's fondest memories of their time at camp. For the most part local citizens welcomed the CCC camps and their enrollees, who provided a much-needed boost to the local economy with the camp purchases and the enrollees' $5 per month allowance, which was often spent in local shops or at the local movie theater. John Genes worked as an ambulance driver and apprentice plumber both at Fort Moultrie and in Company 445 near Cheraw, South Carolina, and recalled going into town to the Star Theater, selling his shoes for a quarter to obtain admission. Frank Damon recalls that while he served in the CCC near Cheraw, South Carolina, the townspeople invited the enrollees to their homes for parties and dinners, and the enrollees reciprocated with dances and picnics at camp.[33] In these ways the CCC camps tried to develop good relationships with the local residents, and as recreational areas developed, the local residents began using the facilities and appreciating the work of the enrollees.

Organized sports were among the most popular recreational activities among the young men in the CCC, and South Carolina's CCC men were no exception. Camps organized teams that played against teams from other CCC camps and local high schools. Camp teams are prominently displayed in various camp and district yearbooks, and were well outfitted with matching uniforms and proper equipment, usually paid for out of the money made in the camp canteen. Company 442, stationed at Moncks Corner in the winter of 1934–35, shared the basketball gymnasium at Berkeley High School with the local high school students. The coaching staff of the high school assisted the CCC team in practices, and both high school and CCC games were played in the gym.[34]

Several South Carolina enrollees excelled at the sports opportunities offered in the CCC and worked to create recreational facilities in their camps. Enrollees

Company 439, Camp F-1, Walhalla, baseball team. Front row (l-r): Martin Baguire(?), Earl Tuck, Hoyt Kyle, Bill Robinson, E. E. "Spec" Jamison, Harold Jones, unknown. Back row (l-r): Tom Stribling, Nat Price, Coleman Harrison, J.T. Gary, —— Malone, unknown, unknown, —— Boggs, J.Y. Stribling. Photograph courtesy of South Carolina Department of Parks, Recreation, and Tourism

of Company 445, while building Cheraw State Park, constructed a clay tennis court, baseball diamond, horseshoe courts, a basketball court, and a volleyball court for their own use at camp by working in their "off hours." Ellison Jamison received a medal and commendation from CCC officials for his achievements on the baseball field. While serving with the Supply Company at Fort Moultrie, Samuel Blanton played both basketball and baseball, and "helped District I win two championships in basketball." At least one enrollee, Frank Wells, left Company 421 at Poinsett State Park to attend the University of South Carolina on a football scholarship, and John Jamison left Company 4479 at Kings Mountain State Park in 1939, signing a minor league baseball contract in North Carolina. Individual sports were also popular, especially at state park facilities being constructed; enrollees enjoyed swimming in both lakes and swimming pools, and golf during their time at camp.[35]

Two of Samuel Blanton's clearest memories of his time in the CCC involve trips he made to play baseball with his company. After a game with the camp at Withersbee, South Carolina, he and his teammates were headed back to Fort Moultrie when they "came across a wagon loaded with corn whisky [*sic*]. The colored man jumped off the wagon and we stopped and took 8 or 10 gallons. The truck went around a few curves in the snake-like road and a man was sitting in the middle of the road with a shotgun. He said, 'All I want is my liquor, I don't want to hurt anyone' so we passed it out of the truck."[36] Blanton also remembered playing baseball at a camp near Stokes, South Carolina, and meeting three young women who drove up in a Model A Ford Roadster. Later he and another enrollee went on a double date with two of the women, and he married one of them in 1937.[37]

As should be expected with a group of young men, women were often the focus of much attention, much of it found throughout the camp newsletters in "gossip columns" and jokes pages. Camp dances provided opportunities to meet local women. Frank Damon, serving with Company 445 while building Cheraw State Park, recalls that the dances in the camp recreational hall "were so great that in order for people outside of the camp to attend they had to present the invitation we sent them. We had well-known bands and everybody had a ball at our dances." One of the local young women who received an invitation to the Cheraw dances later became Frank's wife, Weta.[38] Other women were less memorable. Wilbert Bernshouse recorded in his "Autobiography" that while in the CCC, he "double dated with another friend in an old house in town. I don't remember the girls but we did make cocoa."[39]

In addition to sports and dating, the CCC enrollees found other ways to occupy their spare time. The camp recreation hall often hosted shows, plays, and dances, both for the enrollees and, at times, for local residents. Frank Damon and Harry Kugley, along with two Cheraw young women, produced a live "radio show" that was "broadcast" to the rest of Company 445 at the recreation building in 1935. That fall, enrollees building Edisto Beach State Park hosted a Stunt Night, and those at Barnwell had an Amateur Night. Recreational tournaments in pool, Ping-Pong, checkers, and dominoes were held, with many enrollees participating in these events. At Cheraw, the tournament winners received prizes of canteen coupon books and a carton of cigarettes. Listening to radio programs was also a popular activity, as it was for many people around the country. Company 4479's paper, the *Mountaineer*, reported in October 1938 that the company had experienced a "mild sensation" when a radio program was interrupted to report a meteor had fallen in New Jersey and aliens from Mars had landed in the United States, concluding that "we expect we were not the only ones who were taken in" by Orson Welles's initial production of H. G. Wells's *War of the Worlds*.[40]

John Genes, who had hiked from Bennettsville, South Carolina, to Charleston to join the CCC, recalls his time in camp at Kingstree, South Carolina: "We told tall tales, played jokes on each other, played cards, checkers, and listened to guitar music. We would meet local people and be friendly with them, they were mostly farm families. In season, we went to corn husking, peanut boiling, candy pulling parties and wood chopping contests. The person who chopped the most wood won a 25 cent box of candy; which some girl always got and the poor boy was left with nothing, but a quick kiss."[41] Although enrollees lived and worked at the CCC camp, many of them participated in community life as well, through sports, shopping, and movies in town; friendships with local teens (especially girls); and in other community events.

Company 440 served in the South Carolina upcountry, building Paris Mountain State Park in the late 1930s. William Taylor, a member of the camp, remembers the CCC more like summer camp than a work experience: "In 1939–1940 the swimming area and concession stand, bath house all were alive and well with young people having a good time all through the summer. There was a juke box playing the music of Tommy Dorsey's, 'In the Mood,' 'Chattanooga Choo Choo,' and other artists and tunes to dance by."[42] Taylor also remembered driving into the nearby city of Greenville to "spend our $5," the monthly allowance each young man received after the majority of his wages had been sent home to his family. Historian James Steely has commented that the CCC's resemblance to the popular summer camp experience of the 1920s "offered a comforting model for parents of younger CCC enrollees, even if they lacked the means for such higher-class rituals."[43] Indeed, most South Carolina CCC alumni remember their time in the CCC as a cross between summer camp and high school or college.

Company 1408, SP-4, Myrtle Beach State Park. Photograph courtesy of South Carolina Department of Parks, Recreation, and Tourism, George Buell Collection

CCC enrollees played hard, but the work was hard, too, especially for some of the young men who were unaccustomed to outdoor work or were used to living by their own rules. Some tried to shirk their duties by playing sick or going AWOL for a brief time. Camp doctors frequently "cured the sick" by dosing them with castor oil. These shirkers were often subject to derision by their fellow enrollees, such as the column that appeared in Company 4468's camp paper, the *Bugle,* entitled "Sick, Lame, and Lazy." Raymond Paul, assigned to build a road and causeway at Hunting Island State Park in Beaufort County, remembers trying to "goof off" by hiding out in the woods with several other men one day, but they "worried about being caught and the mosquitoes nearly ate us up. We decided that we would rather work than hide out."[44] Camp leaders punished others who "goofed off" by restricting them to camp on weekends, or assigning additional and less desirable camp jobs, like latrine duties or KP duty in the mess hall.[45]

Although illness was given as an excuse to shirk work, enrollees sometimes were sick or injured, and epidemics in camp were an occasional occurrence. Colonel George Buell, adjutant over District I at Fort Moultrie, kept reports listing the number of men in the camp infirmary each week, and the various camp newsletters contain several articles reporting on the condition of men in the hospital or welcoming them back to service. The *State* newspaper in Columbia reported a measles outbreak at Fort Benning, with five companies, including Company 1408 from South Carolina, placed under two-week quarantine.[46] In December 1934 Company 442 in Berkeley County had sixty enrollees confined to bed with the flu, after spending the early part of the winter in tent camps. Most of the sick were housed in the camp's Recreation Hall, although eighteen had been hospitalized at the Naval Hospital in Charleston. Due to the epidemic, "camp activities are practically paralyzed. No lectures, movies, or sermons are to be permitted. Classes may be abandoned." Evidently most of the sick were back at work soon after, for by January 24, 1935, the camp newsletter reported that forty-eight new huts had replaced the "uncomfortable tents and inadequate quarters," and lectures resumed by February 26, when the enrollees were treated to a lecture by a Miss Matheson of the Women's Christian Temperance Union (WCTU). Several boys were confined for several weeks in a "mumps ward" at Oconee in the winter of 1937–38. Most often, sick enrollees were treated at camp, in a "sick ward" or "dispensary," although sometimes more serious illnesses or injuries required them to be hospitalized at a local hospital, such as enrollee H. Grayson, who dislocated his shoulder during a touch football game at Clover in October 1935. Sadly, occasionally sick enrollees or others associated with the camps died, leaving the other enrollees to contemplate the shortness of life. Camp newspapers from South Carolina have memorial columns with short obituaries of enrollees who died of meningitis, pneumonia, and, in at least one case, a truck accident while on duty.[47]

Although sickness, whether real or imagined, sometimes caused enrollees to miss work, more serious offenses—especially desertion, stealing, and alcohol problems—were met with serious forms of discipline, including formal admonitions and reprimands, additional work assignments, forfeiture of pay, and reduction to lower ranks for those men who had been promoted to leaders or assistant leaders. Jonathan Hodgin recalled that while working in Chester County, a local farmer complained that the CCC boys were stealing his watermelons. The commanding officer informed the enrollees that the watermelons had been poisoned to kill crows, and that anyone who had eaten those watermelons should report to the infirmary immediately. Hodgin remembered that "every one of us lit down there and they got us. They made every one of us work in the kitchen to 12 o'clock every night for two weeks."[48] Often, creative disciplinary measures were required to deal with the more petty offenses.

In the most serious of offenses, administrative discharges or dishonorable discharges were options, as was legal action. Most disciplinary problems in the CCC appear to stem from the "culture shock" experienced by many of these young men: a large number of young men away from their homes and families for the first time found themselves with new freedoms and new temptations. These new situations manifested themselves in problems with liquor consumption in the post-Prohibition New Deal era, and in absences without leave, usually in homesick boys stationed within walking or driving distance from home.

South Carolina CCC camps were not immune from these types of offenses. At Fort Moultrie, George Buell and J. G. McMeekin posted the following list of rules for CCC enrollees, along with the admonition that "offenders . . . found guilty will be dishonorably discharged":

Any member or members of this organization

Found drinking, drunk, indicating that he has been drinking, or having intoxicating liquors or narcotics in his possession will be dismissed.

Any man lying, stealing, or making a false official statement will be dismissed.

Any man guilty of insubordination to the commissioned personnel, the duly appointed leaders and assistant leaders, or the forestry personnel will be dismissed.

Any man refusing to work will be dismissed.

Any man AWOL seven (7) days or more (desertion) will be discharged.

Any man contracting venereal disease will be discharged.

Any man guilty of continued or serious misconduct, or unwillingness to abide by the rules and regulations prescribed for the Civilian Conservation Corps by those in responsible charge will be discharged.[49]

Colonel Buell's weekly reports detail several of these types of offenses, reporting raids on local bootleggers, the discharge of at least one enrollee for "physical disability (venereal disease)," and warrants being taken out for an enrollee accused of stealing government property and going AWOL. One unnamed enrollee from Company 4468, near Barnwell, was hitchhiking home (whether he was AWOL or on leave is unclear) when he and two other hitchhikers he met on the road were picked up by the police and held on suspicion of robbery and murder that occurred in Georgia. The three young men escaped from jail, but the CCC enrollee was quickly recaptured. The other two were also soon recaptured in North Carolina, where they confessed to the crime and exonerated the CCC enrollee, who was returned to camp and admonished for his choice in traveling companions. His story made its way to the camp newsletter as a cautionary tale for other enrollees as well.[50]

Work was hard, and recreational periods were fun for the young men in the CCC, but there was trouble in the camps at times. CCC officials tried to keep enrollees busy, and I. V. Butler, who served both in Louisiana and in California, claimed that there was not any trouble in his assigned camps because "too many activities [were] going on and everyone had something to do."[51] When trouble did arise, however, it often had to do with liquor. Frank Damon reports that while he served with Company 445, "now and then one of the boys would come in drunk and would be loud and the commanding officer would have to restrict him to camp."[52] Three members of Company 445 were arrested for being "drunk and disorderly" at Fort Moultrie following a Halloween celebration in 1933 and were summarily discharged from the CCC.[53] Enrollees were not the only problem at Fort Moultrie, for on December 23 and 30, 1933, Colonel Buell reported that a forestry foreman and an army private stationed in the Cheraw camp had both caused problems with drinking in the camp, setting a poor example for the enrollees. Buell requested that the forestry man and the private and his family be removed from the camp; although "no direct trouble has been experienced with [the private] himself . . . his wife and worthless son are the centers of the trouble."[54] The *Pinopolian,* the newsletter of Company 442, reported in January 1935 that two men had been given administrative discharges because of desertion, even after expressing their desire to remain in the CCC. According to the *Pinopolian,* "this makes six boys discharged since January 1, 1935, the other four being given like discharges due to their drunken condition and disorderly conduct." Another boy was discharged in February for a second offense of "serious misconduct."[55] Most of the time the most serious offenses committed by South Carolina CCC enrollees were alcohol-related and were minor offenses compared with the trouble found in CCC camps in some other states, including in Florida and Virginia.[56]

Many CCC alumni credit the CCC with giving them training that served their future employment or military service. James Timmons, who learned how to string telephone wire, left the CCC in the summer of 1938 and took a job as a lineman with South Carolina Electric and Gas for over thirty years. Beverly Gleason, given the job of mechanic helper in 1936, so quickly learned the job that he was promoted out of the CCC as an enrollee and hired on as a civilian mechanic a year later, at quadruple the salary. Gleason later transferred to the Charleston Navy Yard, where he retired after thirty years. The Charleston Navy Yard also employed enrollee John Genes, who had worked as an ambulance driver and plumber at Cheraw and Fort Moultrie. Others, like Walter Gunter, who served at Poinsett State Park, used their CCC training in the military. Many recall meeting lifelong friends, and even their wives, while CCC enrollees. Still others, like Durwood Stinson, identify their CCC experience with "becoming a man," both figuratively and literally. Several South Carolina alumni point proudly to the state parks as one of the CCC's most notable achievements. Most CCC alumni describe their experience in similarly glowing terms: "wonderful years [that] were thoroughly enjoyed"; "I am very grateful . . . and thank the Good Lord for giving me that opportunity"; "I loved all the months of my CCC life"; and as "the best thing that ever happened to me."[57]

However joyously most accounts of life in the CCC are remembered, it should be noted that there were obviously those young men who were dissatisfied with their experience. In their 1940 study of the CCC, Holland and Hill found that between 1933 and 1940, approximately 500,000 men out of the 2,750,000 CCC men enrolled, or 20 percent, had deserted the corps or had been discharged for disciplinary reasons. These figures demonstrate that although CCC alumni seemingly almost universally remember their experiences in the corps as "the best thing that ever happened," not all enrollees enjoyed their CCC experience.[58] The vast majority of those dissatisfied enrollees have chosen not to join in the alumni activities that so many other alumni have participated in, and, for the most part, their voices have almost disappeared from the historical record.

Although most young men in the CCC in South Carolina had similar experiences, two groups of men had unique experiences in the CCC: African Americans and World War I veterans, both of whom successfully participated in the program, although in a segregated fashion. Both veterans and African Americans found themselves isolated in segregated camps, in companies with not just a number but also a letter designation—V for veterans, and C for "Colored."

In the late summer of 1935 CCC Company 4475 moved to Wedgefield, near Sumter, South Carolina, to continue work on the state park that had been begun by Company 421. The CCC had constructed recreational facilities and a lake at Poinsett State Park, and during the summer the public began using the recreational facilities provided at Poinsett even before the park officially opened. However, when Company 4475, consisting of 200 African American young men, primarily from South Carolina, moved to the Poinsett area, white Sumter residents refused to share the lake and park facilities with the young men who were building them. This incident from Poinsett State Park demonstrates the disparate experience of African American enrollees in South Carolina's CCC; while receiving much-needed work, training, and educational opportunities through the program, they still faced segregation, discrimination, and often hostility. The CCC could not overcome those obstacles.

Segregation and discrimination were not new experiences to young black South Carolinians, but many African Americans had hoped that the CCC would provide better opportunities than what they experienced previously. The incident involving the young black men at Poinsett echoed a larger issue in the CCC: how to deal with enrollees who did not fit the standard profile, such as African Americans, other racial or ethnic minorities, or older men interested in CCC work. Although the CCC would not solve the problems of racism for African Americans and other ethnic minorities, the program provided much-needed work and economic assistance to these previously marginalized groups and included African Americans, other minorities, and older men who were veterans of the First World War. In South Carolina, both African Americans and veterans enrolled in the CCC, and while the program was successful in providing employment, these enrollees met with challenges based on their race or age. For the most part both of these groups made the best of the situation, and they contributed to the development of South Carolina's state parks through their work as well.

The initial enrollment of men in ECW, and later the CCC, was to be limited to unmarried young men, ages eighteen to twenty-five. Selection based on these criteria began on April 6, 1933, and enrollees began training with the army the next day. However, CCC enrollment quickly grew to reflect a more diverse cross-section of the American public, and CCC work was extended to reach many different American men. Barely a month had passed from the beginnings of ECW when white men, African American men, Native American men, and veterans all enrolled in "Roosevelt's Forest Army." In most cases, separate camps were created to serve the diverse needs of these groups and to maintain the segregated society of the times. These different camps were distinguished by different titles: "Juniors" for the young, white, single men; "Colored" for young African American men; "Veterans" for the army veterans; and "Indian" for the Native American men.

While ECW provided employment for men of a variety of ethnic backgrounds and even ages, ECW afforded very little opportunity for women of any age or ethnicity, other than as secretaries or nurses in the district offices or hospitals. These few positions were limited to women with a certain amount of education and training. With the beginning of the CCC in 1933, Eleanor Roosevelt enthusiastically supported the program and the opportunities it would provide for young men and pressed for a similar opportunity for unemployed young women. Secretary of Labor Frances Perkins, the first woman cabinet member, joined the First Lady in these efforts. Primarily resulting from the demands and leadership from Eleanor Roosevelt and Perkins, an experimental camp for women opened in June 1933 in New York State. While the camp capacity was 360, only about seventy-five women were admitted in its first two weeks. Women had to be "without resources" and between the ages of eighteen and thirty-five to join, according to the requirements set by New York's Emergency Relief Administration.[59]

A few other camps followed the example set in New York. These "She-She-She" camps, as they quickly became known, were operated by the Works Progress Administration's National Youth Administration (NYA), rather than ECW. The women's camps focused first on literacy and then on vocational training, while providing a healthy diet and much-needed medical care for the few weeks the women were allowed to remain in the program. As in the male CCC camps, provisions were made for women of different ethnic backgrounds, and included white, African American, and Native American women, although the women had to be unmarried and childless to participate. While the CCC boys signed up for six-month terms and received $30 a month in wages, women received only a maximum of $5 a month for an eight-week enrollment period, along with room and board. Although Eleanor Roosevelt was frustrated by the discrimination between the opportunities offered to young men and young women in similar residential camps, her "She-She-She" camps provided some social and economic relief to over 8,500 young women during the mid-1930s, before being eliminated by Congress in 1937. The ninety camps included two in South Carolina, at Kingstree and Orangeburg.[60] For the most part, however, women's participation in CCC-type work was limited to secretarial or nursing positions, although young women found somewhat similar opportunities through work in the NYA.

Other minority groups, including Hispanic Americans and Native Americans, sought to participate in ECW. Hispanics were not regarded as "special enrollees" (as were the "Colored" and "Veteran" statuses), and they served in ethnically integrated camps, primarily in the Southwest.[61] While Hispanics were integrated into the camp structure of the CCC, veterans, Native Americans, and African Americans were housed primarily in separate camps, segregated on the basis of age, ethnicity, or race.

Over the course of the CCC, 85,000 Native Americans enrolled in the program, working on 200 reservations in twenty-three states. Unlike other CCC camps, the Native Americans employed with the CCC were housed in family camps, rather than in militarily structured camps, and their work largely focused upon projects dedicated to preserving sites important to their own culture. In addition, they were taught industrial skills in order to widen their chances for gainful employment outside of the CCC. Directors in the Department of the Interior's Bureau of Indian Affairs cooperated with the CCC's Indian Division, and both saw great benefit in extending conservation work to Native Americans;

reservations were in need of soil conservation and reforestation as much as the rest of the country, and Native Americans were in need of employment as much as the rest of the population.[62]

On May 6, 1933, Veterans Administration administrator Frank T. Hines wrote to President Roosevelt to ask that veterans of World War I be allowed to serve in ECW. Roosevelt agreed that ECW would be an excellent way to assist these veterans, and on May 11 Roosevelt issued Executive Order 6129, authorizing initial enrollment of 25,000 veterans, with no limits on age or marital status. The Veterans Administration would be responsible for selecting veteran enrollees, on a state quota basis. Although the administration gave some consideration to integrating the veterans into regular camps, Frank Persons with the Labor Department overruled this idea, wanting to lessen the military atmosphere of the regular camps as much as possible. Veterans found themselves grouped together in special camps, and, for many, this provided an opportunity to reconnect with other men who had shared similar experiences during World War I.[63]

In 1933 the average age of World War I veterans was forty, and some were in poor mental or physical health as a direct result of their wartime experiences. The CCC provided these veterans with an opportunity to reconnect with other veterans who had shared similar experiences, as well as providing this segment of the population with much-needed economic relief. CCC historian John Salmond provides an excellent capsule of what CCC life was like for the veterans who served in the camps: "They were housed in separate camps and performed regular conservation work, modified to suit their age and physical condition. They benefited from the education and medical programs. To many veterans, the CCC became a rehabilitation center, a place where they could regain health and self-respect. Here they received a second chance, an opportunity to gain the knowledge, skill, or confidence they needed to earn a decent living."[64] Because of their work in the CCC camps, World War I veterans again felt useful and believed that their government cared about them.

In South Carolina, throughout June 1933 veterans of the First World War enrolled in the CCC, along with one Spanish-American War veteran, and were sent to Fort Moultrie for conditioning. South Carolina's initial veterans' quota was 350, and the state attempted to fill the quota throughout June, encouraging interested veterans to apply at the veterans' hospital in Columbia and promising work in reforestation camps in their home state. The *State* newspaper in Columbia proudly reported that by June 26, South Carolina had filled the state's allotment. The men departed for Fort Moultrie from Greenville, Columbia, Florence, and Charleston at the end of the month. A typical veteran camp was found in South Carolina's Company 2413; in 1934 these enrollees averaged forty-one years of age, and 90 percent of them had overseas military service.[65]

Many of the veterans were glad to once again have a job and some income to support their families, and they enjoyed the opportunity to reconnect with other veterans. However, the veterans' experience in the CCC was not always a pleasant one. In the camps, these former military men found themselves once again under army command; in some cases their commanding officer was a much younger man, with little to no actual combat experience, although ideally mature officers with overseas service commanded the veterans' camps. The veterans, unlike the CCC juniors, had wives and children as their dependents at home, and their money was, in most cases, the only income that their family received. Their families counted on the $25 a month allotment. Such was the case of one South Carolina woman, who wrote to the governor after an unsuccessful attempt to claim her husband's monthly allotment after he had left the CCC for another job with the Public Works Administration (PWA). On December 4, 1935, Mrs. Edward James wrote:

Dear Governor,

I am writing you to see if you can advise me on how to get my allotment and my husband's pay from the CCC. He enrolled in the CCC Aug. 26 1935 an[d] was honorably discharged Sept. 30, 1935 and I haven't received my allotment or his pay either and I have wrote to every one I know to try and get it. I have wrote several letters to the commanding officer at CCC-SC SP 6 Pickens County, SC where he was stationed at and I can't even get an answer from him. I have also wrote to the Veterans Administration Facility at Columbia and to Atlanta where his discharge came from. I have been two months trying to get it and haven't got it yet and I am in great need of it. My husband is on the PWA and we can't hardly make it. We have five children and trying to keep four in school and they all need shoes and clothes. I have been depending on this money to get them all shoes and clothes. If I don't soon get it I guess I will have to stop them from school. So the only one I knew left to write to was you and I feel sure you will get it straightened out so I can get my money. I certainly will appreciate all you can do for me and please let me hear from you at once.

Yours sincerely, Mrs. Edward J. James, Simpsonville, SC[66]

The letter was forwarded to H. A. Smith, state forester in charge of CCC Forest Service and state park projects. Smith then wrote to Norman House, project superintendent at Table Rock State Park, to investigate the claim. It appears

Table Rock State Park, Pickens, Veteran CCC enrollees of Company 2434, "ready for the day's grind," May 18, 1936. Photograph courtesy of South Carolina Department of Archives and History

that Edward James was inadvertently assigned a "no pay due" status at the end of his service in the CCC. House and Smith "straightened out" the matter, and the James family was paid $22.50 in either December 1935 or January 1936.[67]

Getting paid was apparently not the only problem for veterans of Companies 2434 and 2435 stationed at Table Rock State Park in the fall and winter of 1935. Finding appropriate work for the veterans was not always easy. Weather conditions and undisclosed "unfortunate experiences with personnel" slowed the work at Table Rock in late 1935. Roosevelt adviser Louis Howe received a telegram that was forwarded to South Carolina CCC officials regarding the treatment of veterans and their working conditions: "We Veterans stationed Pickens, South Carolina, find the time of work beginning 7:35 until 11:50 and from 12:50 until 3:50 a mighty long time for we old VFW veterans to stand on feet. We have palpitation of the heart, post hernia operation varicose veins and our nerves are wrecked. Would appreciate sitting down a couple minutes every hour to catch our breath. We are willing to do our bit as we did in '17 and '18."[68]

The regional officer, H. E. Weatherwax, sent a copy of the telegram to the camp supervisor in January 1936, suggesting that a three-, five-, or ten-minute rest period for these "older men" be implemented every hour to hour and a half.[69] Two junior camps replaced the veteran camps stationed at Table Rock State Park later that year.[70]

Other than direct participation in the Veteran CCC camps, some South Carolina veterans found work in regular CCC camps. Paul Hartley, of Chesterfield

County, South Carolina, worked with Company 445 near Cheraw. Hired as one of the local experienced men (LEMs), he assisted with the building of Cheraw State Park. Several years older than the enrollees with whom he worked, Hartley received the respect of the younger enrollees, who wrote an article about his war service in their camp newsletter. The article highlighted Hartley's medals—including his Purple Heart, the Medal Militaire, and the Croix de Guerre—and a letter of commendation for his service from King George. Hartley's service certainly impressed the young CCC enrollees at Cheraw, and they were pleased to be able to honor his service to the country during war and during peace.[71] Several commanding officers had also seen military action during World War I.

ECW provided for separate camps for the war veterans and the younger enrollees, and also provided separate camps for African Americans. While the bill creating ECW was being discussed in Congress in late March 1933, Oscar DePriest, a Republican congressman from Illinois and the only African American serving in the House of Representatives, proposed an amendment that stated "that in employing citizens for the purposes of this Act no discrimination shall be made on account of race, color, or creed."[72] Although the nondiscriminatory amendment extended CCC opportunities to African Americans, it did not question segregated camps, which quickly became the norm for most African Americans serving in the CCC. Although the law creating ECW prohibited racial discrimination in enrollment, the letter of the law was not followed in the early weeks and months of ECW. Although the program was fast-tracked by President Roosevelt and enrollment proceeded rapidly in the spring of 1933, African American enrollment lagged vastly behind that of white enrollment, especially in the South. Southern selection agents were reluctant to begin enrolling blacks, especially when so many white youths needed employment.[73]

Although the initial memorandum to the state selection agents had called for selection of enrollees "in accordance with the spirit of American government and American ideals of fair play," and that there would be "no discrimination on account of race, creed, color, or politics," the actualities of selection were largely based upon the prejudices of the state and local selection officials. Director Fechner, himself a southerner, was hesitant to question local norms, and when blacks were enrolled, they found themselves in segregated camps. From the beginning Fechner maintained that he was committed to segregated camps. Fechner also stipulated that black enrollees should only work in camps in their home state as practical (but this practice was not always followed). Although not a written policy until 1939, Fechner appeared satisfied with a quota of African American enrollment approaching 10 percent of total enrollment, but in 1933 African American enrollment was barely over 5 percent. The percentages varied widely; Mississippi's African American enrollment was less than 2 percent of total enrollment, and North Carolina's approached 9 percent, while South Carolina's African American enrollment surpassed 35 percent. South Carolina's ratio of African American to white enrollees matched more closely the ratio of the state's general population (45 percent African American) than any other southern state.[74]

When African Americans enrolled in the CCC, they found themselves facing a microcosm of the larger segregated society. In some states the small African American population limited enrollment to such a small number that whites and blacks served in the same camps. There African Americans found themselves in segregated barracks and serving in low-status positions such as cooks in the mess hall. However, the vast majority of black CCC enrollees served in segregated camps, designated as "Colored" in official records. Director Fechner issued a directive in the summer of 1935 ordering the "complete segregation of colored and white enrollees. . . . Only in those states where the colored strength is too low to form a company unit will mixing of colored men in white units be permitted."[75] After visiting integrated camps in California, Fechner remained committed to "deintegration" of the camps in part as a result of "unfortunate relationships that existed in some of the camps where there was a mixture of white and negro enrollees" and the "vigorous resentment shown by some communities."[76] When the National Association for the Advancement of Colored People (NAACP) complained to both Fechner and Roosevelt, Fechner responded that "segregation is not discrimination," and Roosevelt failed to take a stand against the CCC director's position, calling it "political dynamite."[77]

Discrimination in the CCC began at the induction center. A 1935 article in the NAACP's publication *Crisis* gave one young man's account of his time in the CCC. Luther Wandall recalled that at his induction at Fort Dix, New Jersey, white young men were processed before the African Americans, and blacks received the picked-over uniforms, bedding, and tents. Army officials he identified as "Southern" were alternately offended and amused by the presence of blacks, either making offensive comments to and about the black enrollees or giving them pennies for singing and dancing. Wandall was assigned to a camp made up of African Americans, but with white officers in command, and sent to work on a park in the Upper South (Colonial National Monument in Virginia). Although he experienced "Jim Crow" in the CCC, this young African American could conclude in 1935 that "on the whole, I was gratified rather than disappointed with the CCC. . . . As job and an experience, for a man who has no work, I can heartily recommend it."[78] Although he experienced the typical racial discrimination during his CCC experience, Wandall's article indicated that he enjoyed his time spent in the CCC.

In addition to the segregated camps, African Americans experienced discrimination in the CCC in other ways, especially in leadership positions. The failure to appoint black officers to command African American camps came under fire from the NAACP and other African American organizations. In 1934 Director of Education Howard Oxley appointed twenty-four blacks as camp educational advisers, and pressed General George Mosely, commander of the Fourth Corps area in the Southeast (including South Carolina), to place an African American educational adviser in each of the "Colored" CCC camps. Mosely declined to do so, believing that in the Fourth Corps area at least, only white educational advisers could effectively deal with the local education officials, who were almost all white.[79]

Much as she had advocated CCC-type camps for women, First Lady Eleanor Roosevelt also supported the extension of New Deal benefits, including the CCC, to African Americans across the country. While most of President Roosevelt's advisers had not supported her "She-She-She" camps, several New Dealers joined her in promoting extension of the various New Deal programs to all Americans, regardless of race. With the support of Eleanor Roosevelt, Harry Hopkins of FERA, Secretary of the Interior Ickes, and Frank Persons in the Labor Department, the CCC almost doubled its African American membership, from less than 6 percent prior to 1936 to 9.9 percent that year and up to 11 percent by 1938, where it held steady. The numbers of African Americans in supervisory capacities also increased slightly in Roosevelt's second term nationally.[80]

For the most part supervisory officials in CCC camps remained white, especially in the South. In her 1940 sociological study of South Carolina CCC camps, Edna Kennerly found that all commanding officers of CCC camps operating in South Carolina in 1939–40 were white, as were the project superintendents. Kennerly found that, contrary to the earlier opinion of General Mosely, in most "Colored" camps the educational advisers were black. All of the enrollees serving as leaders and assistant leaders in those camps were African American. Kennerly concluded her analysis of the "Negro Program" in South Carolina's CCC by stating "the education, health, recreation, and religious programs carried on are similar to those practiced in the white camps."[81] However, the educational program for African Americans often reflected the stereotypes of the day; historian Robert Waller points to the example of Company 4465 receiving a twelve-lesson course limited to domestic service jobs such as waiter, porter, cook, and gardener, with those completing the course receiving job recommendations.[82] Although segregated by race, black CCC enrollees generally received the same camp experience as their white counterparts; however, their relationships with the local community were not always as cordial as those reported by white CCC participants.

Camp newsletters published by the African American camps in South Carolina and the CCC yearbooks verify that, for the most part, African American camps and junior white camps were very similar in structure, organization, and administration. Photographs and articles from these publications demonstrate that enrollees in both white and African American camps formed sports teams and musical groups, attended religious meetings and educational classes, and dated local girls of their own race. Young African American men from Company 5418 serving in Charleston County formed the Withersbee Quartet, a musical group that performed for other CCC camps around the state as well as on a radio program broadcast from Charleston. The work program for both camps was similar as well. In South Carolina, African American camps worked on State Park, Biological Survey, National Forest, Soil Conservation, and State Forest projects, and many of them received training and worked for the first time in skilled labor positions. However, in the annual district yearbooks, as in the rest of CCC organization, segregation prevailed, with the African American camps being pushed consistently to the back of the books, following the listings of all of the white camps, regardless of company number.[83]

Camp newsletters from African American camps serving in South Carolina focused on making the most of the opportunities given by the CCC. Company 5419, a forestry camp near Awendaw, produced a monthly newsletter throughout 1936, describing their work program, including the building of the Wando and Buck Hall fire towers. Similarly Company 4487, Camp SCS-15 near Anderson, also put out a monthly newsletter. Their first edition, January 1937, provides biographical information for Company Commander Captain Dewey Herrin, Camp Educational Adviser (CEA) Clarence Ross, and Chaplain Hal Keller. Later issues contained autobiographical profiles of several enrollees, all of which concluded that their CCC experiences had better prepared them for future life. Haskel Hare, writing in March 1937 after three years in the CCC, concluded that being exposed to so many different kinds of men gave him the opportunity and courage "to compete with and orientate myself with any group of personalities in life." Ernest Coney, writing in February 1938, told of his childhood in a single-parent home, listening to the "old people's horrible tales of slavery," and he had entered the CCC to "do good for myself and my mother," a refrain echoed by Howard New and others who wrote similar articles. T. V. Nash wrote a lengthy editorial in the August 1937 *Hi-De-Hi-De-Ho*, summing up his experience in the CCC and extolling the several things he had learned in twenty months in camp, including obedience, physical fitness, leadership skills, musical training, sportsmanship, and academic education, concluding that "I must say that the CCC is one of the greatest helps to the United States and her citizens. It helps us all Physically-Mentally-Morally."[84]

African American enrollees in Company 4465 (Camp F-100), near Clinton, pose for the camera on top of the root cellar and refrigerator built below ground, ca. 1935. Photograph courtesy of South Carolina Department of Parks, Recreation, and Tourism, Frank Damon/ George Buell Collection

The newsletters at South Carolina's African American camps all gave great attention to the educational programs offered in camp, primarily in the achievements in literacy but also in preparation for future employment. Company 4470 reported in November 1935 that in one class, thirty men were being taught to write their names in order to sign for payroll, then they would go back and use their names to learn their letters, and from there, learn reading, writing, and spelling. Company 4487 in Anderson reported that although the largest class was in "the three R's," secondary education classes as well as courses in first aid, agriculture, woodworking, and poultry production were offered, and proudly announced that the Educational Program under CEA Clarence Ross received a perfect rating in its inspection at the end of 1937. A Miss Cowan, home economics teacher from Anderson, gave a demonstration on table manners in November 1937.

Placing African American CCC companies proved to be as problematic as enrolling African Americans had been. Many local communities complained about having African American camps located nearby. Although the reasons varied from location to location, they followed a general trend. Complaints received in the director's office feared an increase in social disorder and drunkenness, a bad influence on the youth of the community, and the safety of white women. The complaints and fears were not limited to the South; Fechner received letters from people in Pennsylvania, Washington, D.C., Indiana, Texas, and California, among other states, voicing their concerns about African American camps in their vicinities. Fechner complained that "there is hardly a locality in this country that looks favorably or even with indifference on the location of a Negro camp in their vicinity," although he noted that there was far less protest about African American camps in the South than in other regions.[85]

As a response to the racist fears across the nation, Fechner issued a directive that African American enrollees were to serve in their home state as much as possible, in campsites selected by the state's governor. The "Colored" camps in South Carolina bear out this order, with the district yearbook for 1938 noting that almost all of the enrollees were South Carolina natives, and those who were not South Carolinians were fellow southerners from Georgia, Alabama, or North Carolina. For example, Company 4470–C was made up of African Americans mainly from South Carolina, with others from North Carolina and Alabama.[86]

However, African American camps were sometimes not even welcome in their home state; the earlier-described episode at Poinsett State Park in Sumter, South Carolina, involved both an African American camp and a veterans' camp. In the fall of 1935 Company 4475–C replaced the original camp, whose members had been working on Poinsett State Park. Although the park had not officially opened to the public, Sumter citizens were using the lake for swimming, and protested the loss of the swimming facilities to African American CCC enrollees. Several meetings were set up between State Forestry Commission officials and local townspeople to deal with the issue, and although local leaders agreed that the camp was necessary to complete the work at Poinsett, they expressed their wish that the park be kept open for the exclusive use of local residents. Due to the public outcry, the black enrollees were prohibited from using the lake for swimming during recreational periods and were only allowed on the state park grounds during work hours. These enrollees also experienced other hostilities from the local citizens, such as name-calling when they went into town.[87]

After only three months at Poinsett, Company 4475 was transferred to Chester County in November 1935, where the company completed most of the construction of Chester State Park between November 1935 and February 1937. Superintendent F. H. Murray had reported that "our company of Negro workers have proven satisfactory. They are easily controlled and have given no trouble in the community."[88] When, in February 1936, the state forester submitted an application for retention of a CCC camp to continue work on Poinsett State

Park, he noted, "Colored companies are not always acceptable to people in locality of camp. Sufficient notice of intention to occupy this camp with colored company should be given to allow us to contact local people."[89] Company 2413, made up of veterans, transferred to Poinsett from their work at Givhans Ferry State Park near Charleston in February 1936, and by the end of March completed a large number of landscaping projects, continued work on the incomplete bathhouse, and built two overnight cabins.[90]

A more serious racial incident involved white CCC enrollees stationed near Fort Jackson in Columbia, separate from but adjacent to African American soldiers training at the newly reorganized camp. Both the enrollees and soldiers used nearby Washington Lake as a recreational swimming facility, and on April 20, 1941, white enrollees "dunked" a black soldier who was trying to use the diving platform. Official records indicate that the black soldier was apparently a known "troublemaker," which may have simply meant that he was unwilling to stick to the racial status quo. The attempt at integrating the diving platform and the subsequent "dunking" resulted in a more serious fight between blacks and whites, with rock throwing and name-calling, which then escalated as the incident became more widely known at Fort Jackson. Although both groups were confined to their quarters, later that day white soldiers from the Georgia National Guard stationed at Fort Jackson armed themselves and attempted to breach the "colored area" before military police intervened. Two hours later some 400 whites, most members of the 121st Regiment of the Thirtieth Infantry Division, resumed the attempt on the black soldiers, resulting in a shooting into the barracks before military police could once again restore order. Although the larger violence began in what could have been viewed as a minor incident involving CCC enrollees and escalated into a melee between soldiers of different races at Fort Jackson, post authorities focused local newspapers' attention on the disagreement between CCC enrollees and black soldiers, not on the larger violence between white soldiers and black soldiers, in an attempt to avoid any negative publicity featuring the newly reopened Fort Jackson. An investigative board studied the incident and made several recommendations, including designating the lake for use of African American soldiers only and instituting classes in race relations at Fort Jackson. Not until June did a reporter writing for the *Pittsburgh Courier* reveal the larger violence beyond the incident with the CCC, and by then the investigation had been completed and closed. The incident was one of several similar episodes of racial tension on military bases that spring, especially throughout the South, as the U.S. military reorganized in anticipation of entry into World War II, and black and white soldiers found themselves in closer contact than had been experienced previously.[91] No indication of the response of the commanding officer for the CCC camp has been found, but it is logical to believe that the white officer over the CCC camp would have supported the desire of the army officer to deflect negative attention from Fort Jackson, and thus likely he kept silent regarding the issue, at least in the press.

In South Carolina, the number of young African American men who benefited from the CCC numbered over 2,000, and at least nine of the almost sixty CCC companies that served in the state were made up of African American enrollees, primarily from within the state. In addition to the African American young men and their families who directly benefited from CCC work, scores of other black South Carolinians benefited from the creation of state parks. Although the parks were segregated and facilities were not equal, South Carolina and federal authorities at the time recognized the necessity of providing parks and recreational facilities for the state's African Americans. Racially based segregation was mandated by law in 1930s South Carolina, but the State Forestry Commission desired to reach the African American population, which accounted for 45 percent of the total population in the state during that decade, and to provide parks for blacks' enjoyment. "Colored areas" were in the plans for Hunting Island and Greenwood, although both parks were still in the development stages, and segregated recreational areas had been developed at the Sand Hills project, administered by the Soil Conservation Service (SCS). The SCS had also developed a similar recreational area for African Americans, known as Mill Creek, at the Poinsett Land Use Project, adjacent to Poinsett State Park. Although the Forestry Commission continually asked for additional funding to increase the number of state parks available for African Americans, the state legislature seemed even less enthusiastic about funding black park facilities. In addition, the Forestry Commission often used what little funding was available for state parks for maintaining and improving white facilities rather than acquiring or developing additional facilities for blacks.[92] These limited provisions provided a small opening to African American participation in the state park system, and the Forestry Commission provided six segregated areas for African Americans through the 1950s. South Carolina's state parks integrated in the mid-1960s, after protracted legal challenges.[93]

Although Fechner and Roosevelt chose not to challenge the accepted segregated society of the American South in the 1930s, African Americans did benefit in limited ways from the New Deal, and the CCC was no exception. At least one South Carolina historian has argued that the New Deal experience taught the state's African American population valuable lessons in "determination, unity, and ingenuity" that later led to the state's movement toward desegregation in the 1950s.[94] Another has noted that while "New Deal programs invariably discriminated against black Carolinians . . . the New Deal was a mixed blessing for [them]," ultimately perpetuating a system of inequity for the state's

African Americans while at the same time ensuring that the relief programs of the New Deal, including the CCC, extended to the state's blacks.[95] A more recent study of the New Deal in South Carolina echoes the "mixed-blessing" sentiment, but argues that the New Deal in South Carolina provided opportunities for the state's African American population that otherwise would have remained closed. According to Jack Hayes, "the New Deal fostered activism, organization, and political awareness among black Carolinians," and that while the gains for African Americans were not immediate during the Depression decade, the New Deal "spawned hope" for South Carolina's blacks.[96]

At first praised for successes in providing jobs for blacks, then castigated for not doing more to enhance the quality and equality of life for African Americans, the CCC and the New Deal should be recognized as successful but limited programs that helped numerous African Americans but failed to reach later goals of desegregation and equal treatment, and should be judged in context of the times. In South Carolina, more than any other southern state, a number of African American young men participated in the CCC, finding jobs and room and board when their options were even more limited than those of their white counterparts. Although not immune to the pervasive racism that permeated southern society, these young men received vital job training and an income for their families, and in most cases their work garnered praise from their superior officers. Regardless of the limitations of the program, for those African American young men who participated in the CCC, the program provided them with opportunities they most likely would not have found otherwise, especially in the highly segregated South.

The young men, both black and white, who enrolled in the CCC lived life much as any other young men would. They attended classes, played sports, dated and danced, played practical jokes on one another, and, of course, worked hard. They formed lasting friendships with one another that have continued for over fifty years. CCC men and Depression-era scholars alike have drawn comparisons of life in the CCC to summer camp, high school, or college, and these comparisons are not accidental. The CCC provided a similar experience that young men would have obtained if they had had the opportunities to attended summer camp, high school, or college, in that they received some sort of education in a variety of subjects, on-the-job training, and the opportunity to explore vocations and avocations of interest to them. For many of these young men, the CCC was the only opportunity they had, and they made the most of it. The lasting friendships made in the CCC appear to be as strong, if not stronger, than the bonds of college fraternities, and the life lessons learned while in the CCC have proven for many to be more valuable than a high school or college degree. Through their work the young men who enrolled in the CCC left lasting testaments to their life and work in the 1930s, in the national and state parks they developed across the country. The development of the state park system in South Carolina is one example of the legacy left by the men of the CCC. In addition to providing jobs for many of South Carolina's young men, the CCC, through its work in the establishment of South Carolina's state park system, institutionalized recreational opportunities for all South Carolinians.

CHAPTER 4

Building Opportunity

Tourism, Forestry, and State Parks in South Carolina

Prior to 1934 South Carolina had no state parks. Although the State Forestry Commission had made plans for the development of state parks as early as 1931, land for parks was only to be obtained "when areas are made available through gifts," and by the early 1930s no land gifts had been made to the state for park development.[1] State park development in the United States largely dates to 1921, when several dozen conservation-minded individuals, led by National Park Service (NPS) director Stephen Mather, met in Des Moines, Iowa, and founded the National Conference on State Parks. At the time of this meeting twenty-nine states had no parks, and seven others had only one park. The activists were appalled at these numbers, and their National Conference on State Parks proclaimed that outdoor recreation was a basic human need. The group announced that its purpose was "to urge upon our governments, local, county, state, and national, the acquisition of additional land and water areas suitable for recreation, for the study of natural history and its scientific aspects, and the preservation of wild life, as a form of the conservation of our natural resources; until there shall be public parks, forests, and preserves within easy access of all the citizens of every state and territory of the United States."[2] This first meeting of the National Conference on State Parks established lofty goals for the states, and Mather promised the assistance of the NPS in meeting these goals. The NPS recommended six types of park development to the states, and through the decade of the 1920s progress was made in a variety of degrees in a handful of states.

A second national conference provided additional impetus to the creation of state parks when, in 1924, President Calvin Coolidge convened the National Conference on Outdoor Recreation. Sponsored by the National Recreation Association (NRA), the National Conference on Outdoor Recreation assembled twenty-eight national organizations and several state organizations that pointed to the growing need for recreational areas for Americans, both adults and children. As the amount of leisure time increased, either through federally mandated shorter workweeks, child labor laws, or free time gained through unemployment, state and federal governments searched to provide structured activities for adults and children to fill their nonworking hours. Coolidge's conference emphasized the creation of a national cooperative association of national, state, and local recreation groups to form national policy regarding recreation.[3]

By the early 1930s a few states, primarily in the Midwest, had established strong state park systems. Then recreation and park development took center stage in Franklin D. Roosevelt's ambitious goals for a New Deal in America. New Deal programs such as the Works Progress Administration (WPA), and more indirectly, the Civilian Conservation Corps (CCC), mark the first time the federal government took a fiscal interest in the recreational needs of its citizens through the establishment of city parks and playgrounds with controlled and structured play areas, and the establishment of additional national parks and new state parks. The WPA focused on direct recreational facilities such as playgrounds and athletic fields, but for the most part, and especially in South Carolina, state parks were a product of the CCC.[4]

As viewed by reformers, state parks provided an ideal cure for several different ills spawned by the Great Depression. Through the work of the CCC, creating state parks would provide work for many young men who had no other job prospects, as well as pumping additional dollars into the local economy through the purchase of provisions for the CCC enrollees and materials needed in CCC camps. The state park would also provide cheap outlets for the growing number of Americans interested in tourism, while providing structured camping and recreational facilities for those travelers.

Motor tourism was an expanding business in the first three decades of the twentieth century. Historian Warren James Belasco has noted that "prior to World War II, Americans used their cars primarily for recreational purposes," and autocamping provided a vacation alternative for middle-class Americans. Between 1910 and 1920 car ownership in America increased sixteenfold; over eight million cars were registered in 1920. In six years car ownership doubled again; by 1926, 19.2 million cars were being driven on American roads.[5]

These American car owners discovered that one way to "get away from it all" was to pack the car and drive. Sleeping in the car, or in a makeshift tent pitched next to the car, was a viable alternative to spending money in high-class hotels, and autocamping appealed not only to the lower and middle classes but also to the adventurous elite, who praised the concept in travel journals and magazine columns. In the years between 1910 and 1920 these motor tourists camped wherever it was convenient: by the side of the road, in a farmer's field, near an orchard or stream, or in a schoolyard. But by the 1920s, as car ownership and the number of motor tourists increased, so did the need to better monitor the campers' activities. Rather than camping wherever, whenever, autocampers needed specific sites at which to camp, lending a sense of security for both the surrounding community and the campers themselves. This bourgeoning group of potential consumers also drove the newly expanding tourism industry. Municipal governments and business owners banded together to provide free campsites for motor tourists, seeing a single solution to both the problems and the possibilities that tourist-campers offered. Businessmen and chambers of commerce assisted communities in setting up municipal camps, and drew boosters from other civic organizations. When hotel owners complained that municipal campsites threatened the hotel business, campground operators and other local businessmen disagreed, arguing that this new group of tourists would not stay in hotels anyway, and that as potential customers of other businesses, their needs should be met. Waterloo, Wisconsin, established the first free municipal campground in 1920. The typical small-town camp offered potable water, privies, electric lights, wood or gas stoves, a central kitchen facility, a lounge or clubhouse, bathing or shower facilities, and laundry tubs. Belasco notes that the free campground "was the first roadside institution designed to balance public order, private profit, and tourist comfort."[6]

These free municipal tourist campsites catered both to families in search of "freedom" and impoverished travelers and hoboes, whose presence discouraged family camping. In addition, maintenance costs quickly forced towns to abandon their free camps in favor of collecting fees for cars and people, while at the same time attracting more desirable types of campers. This new method of making money attracted entrepreneurs, and by 1925 the campground industry was born, with some privately owned campsites even providing cabins for those travelers who wanted more privacy. By 1930 imposed fees, registration requirements, time limits for camping, and police supervision replaced the free municipal campground. The attitude of local governmental authorities operating campgrounds later influenced state and national parks in setting up their controlled camping areas.[7] Seeing the benefits to the local economy a state park could provide them, the citizens and local government in Cheraw, South Carolina, banded together in such a way in pursuit of South Carolina's first state park, along Highway 1, one of the state's busiest highways.

As tourist courts and campsites opened at places along major thoroughfares, Americans with moderate incomes could find places for recreation and enjoyment. These low-rent shelters represented, in the words of landscape architectural historian Phoebe Cutler, "the democratization of summer vacation."[8] The lure of these tourists of more modest means also meant additional dollars to local communities who could boast about the added values of a state park in their vicinity. Many communities around the country, as in Cheraw, soon worked together in search of support for state parks in their region, echoing the sentiments of the municipal campground boosters. Communities across South Carolina, especially those located along U.S. Highways 1 and 17, provided stops for later "snowbirds" en route to the coastal communities in South Carolina, Georgia, and Florida, and sought to provide accommodations for those travelers "just passing through."

Automobile tourism in South Carolina followed a similar path in the early twentieth century, although tourism in the state had an older history. Aiken and Camden had attracted "horse people" and other wealthy Yankees who came for extended visits since the 1880s. The natural formations at Table Rock Mountain in the upstate attracted visitors throughout the nineteenth century, and the Table Rock Hotel, first opened in 1845, developed as a summer resort during the 1870s, but it had been largely abandoned by 1910 because of access issues. Charleston had promoted itself as a tourist destination since at least 1912, and as automobile ownership increased, so did tourism in the Holy City. Entrepreneurs there built the Fort Sumter Hotel on city-donated land in 1923; the Francis Marion Hotel followed the next year. The emerging development community in Charleston often clashed with the emerging preservation community, as one attempted to provide comforts for tourists while the other attempted to save the very buildings attracting the tourists. By 1929 approximately 47,000 tourists, most from out of state, visited Charleston annually, although this number declined sharply during the Depression. Across the state, developers such as Greenville mill owner John T. Woodside built tourist hotels in Greenville and Myrtle Beach, and elsewhere in the mountains and along the coast during the 1920s. Myrtle Beach's Ocean Forest Hotel boasted a ten-story tower, more than 200 rooms, and an indoor pool upon its opening in 1930, in a town with a population of 500.[9]

As the Depression deepened in the early part of the 1930s, travel and tourism opportunities for most families dwindled, but gas was cheap, as were roadside camp accommodations. In contrast to luxury hotels such as the Woodside developments in Greenville and Myrtle Beach, which went bankrupt for lack of visitors during the 1930s, autocamping provided a vacation outlet that most Americans could still afford. The rise in travelers and campers, many of whom were accustomed to staying in more posh surroundings, in turn caused a demand for a rise in standards for roadside accommodations. Contemporary tourism trade journals noted "one of the few oases of the depression, this business has thrived on hard times and limited purchasing power."[10] South Carolinians viewed tourism as a potentially profitable business even during the Depression decade; the Columbia Chamber of Commerce investigated the possibility of building horseracing tracks and horse-jumping courses in 1934, in an attempt to "get some excellent people to winter at Columbia," as they had traditionally wintered in Aiken and Camden. Although the Ocean Forest resort was bankrupt by 1933, several businesses actually opened in Myrtle Beach during the first years of the Depression, including restaurants, liquor stores, drugstores, and the Broadway Theater, Myrtle Beach's first movie theater.[11]

Despite some success in Myrtle Beach and the growing coastal communities, throughout most of Depression-era South Carolina, the number of the state's residents who could afford recreational opportunities for their families dwindled. The South Carolina Forestry Commission recognized the opportunity state parks would present to alleviate the "social dislocation" present in the state. State parks would provide "areas where families can find rest and relaxation . . . where they can absorb the principles of forest conservation."[12] Following the creation of the CCC in 1933, and the CCC's work in the national park system, state officials began to see the wisdom of putting young men to work creating parks and recreational areas for residents and tourists alike. In 1934 the South Carolina legislature gave the State Forestry Commission the responsibility for the creation and maintenance of a state park system, following the donation of over 700 acres to the state for a park by the citizens of Chesterfield County. Soon after, a camp of 200 CCC enrollees was at work near Cheraw, creating Cheraw State Park.[13]

Beginning with the work at the park near Cheraw, the CCC provided the genesis of the state park system in South Carolina. Using CCC labor, industrial skills provided by local experienced men (LEMs), and professional assistance from the NPS, the CCC built sixteen state parks and six wayside parks between 1934 and 1942 in South Carolina.[14] From the original CCC parks, the South Carolina park system has grown to over forty-five state parks, showcasing the state's natural and historical treasures to residents and tourists alike.

Unlike some state and national parks in other areas, South Carolina's original state parks developed primarily on land that had been overworked and denuded to the point that it was unusable for farming, South Carolina's most profitable venture. By 1934 eight million acres of the state's nineteen million acres had been farmed to the point that they were so badly worn out, they were declared otherwise destroyed.[15] Where other parks were developed on land highly prized for its scenic beauty and natural state, many of South Carolina's parks were developed on land that seemingly had no other use and was being reclaimed to provide recreational facilities for the state's residents. Land reclamation, as well as recreation, was one of the major goals of South Carolina's state park program. Some state parks, such as Aiken and Cheraw, were constructed at "entry points" into the state, from the north and west. Other South Carolina state parks highlighted the state's natural and historical features, as well as made use of land not suitable for farming, from the Native American sacred site at Table Rock in the mountainous upstate to the beaches at Myrtle Beach, Edisto, and Hunting Island.

The work throughout the 1930s of the CCC in South Carolina's state parks undoubtedly changed the public landscape of the state. In addition to clearing overgrowth, planting seedling trees and kudzu, and building roads and bridges, the CCC constructed hiking and nature trails; campsites; swimming pools; amphitheaters; dams and lakes; buildings of all sizes, from lodges to cabins; and smaller but important recreational structures such as picnic shelters, water fountains, and fireplaces. Although highly touted as presenting South Carolina's best natural areas, these early state parks were, for the most part, created landscapes, strictly guided by NPS guidelines.

In response to the rapid development of parks across the nation as a result of Emergency Conservation Work (ECW), the NPS published *Park Structures and Facilities* in 1935, to serve as a textbook for the training of CCC workers and to provide a handbook for design and construction of "safe, convenient, and beneficial" structures for parks. *Park Structures and Facilities* became so popular for work in national and state parks that it was expanded into a three-volume edition in 1938, called *Park and Recreation Structures*.[16] Although park structures demonstrated some variety in style and construction, depending upon the area in which they were built, most CCC-built state and national park buildings bear a strong resemblance to one another, and have all been classified as "NPS rustic architecture," or, less formally, "parkitecture."

Albert Good, the author of both books, defined "rustic" as an architectural style that "through the use of native materials in proper scale . . . gives the feeling of having been executed by pioneer craftsmen with limited hand tools. It thus achieves sympathy with natural surrounds and the past."[17] Good and the NPS advocated the use of native materials, not because of their innate "nativeness" but because of their character-creating features. The use of locally available natural materials like wood and stone meant that construction material would be easily accessible, and that the local experienced men would likely be skilled in handling these materials. In South Carolina, this emphasis on native materials took several different forms, such as the coquina rock at Poinsett State Park, cypress along the coast, pine in the inland parks, and one of the most unusual uses of native materials, sand concrete at Sesquicentennial State Park in Columbia, a technique pioneered at this park.

Additionally, many of South Carolina's parks sought to imitate local architectural styles, or imitate historic styles of the region. As Cutler states, "A fusion of nostalgia and economics propagated Government Rustic," and this held true in South Carolina as well as throughout the country.[18] Kings Mountain showcases several park buildings imitating log construction, while the coastal and lowcountry CCC camps touted their "colonial" buildings in camp newsletters.

Using "pioneer" methods and materials as NPS advocated provided additional opportunities for manual labor for the CCC enrollees. Why use machines or machine-made products when hand tools and manual labor could employ so many more young men? The CCC enrollees received a vocational education through their work, even if the construction practices they learned were quickly disappearing in favor of mass production. CCC workers at Hunting Island earned the nickname of "mudpuppy" as they hand-built the causeway from the mainland to the island; mud was dipped out by the bucketful, rather than bringing in heavy equipment rapidly gaining favor in other construction industries in the 1930s. "Rustic" described both the style as well as the construction techniques the NPS often practiced in South Carolina and throughout the country in the 1930s.

According to architectural historian Linda Flint McClelland, Albert Good did not approve of the word "rustic" in defining the architectural style being practiced in state and national parks of the 1930s, and hoped that a better term would evolve. But the rustic style as practiced by the NPS architects and their counterparts in state parks had evolved from already-established forms in the national parks, as seen in the 1903 Old Faithful Inn; the New Deal "rustic" style was not new to the NPS. Despite the style's antecedents and Good's misgivings about the word, the term "rustic" (also "Government Rustic" or "NPS Rustic") has come to be the identifying stylistic term when discussing park architecture, especially as practiced by the CCC in the 1930s.[19]

In the East particularly, other federal agencies, including the Federal Emergency Relief Administration (FERA), the Resettlement Administration (RA), the Works Progress Administration (WPA), the Tennessee Valley Authority (TVA), and the United States Forestry Service (USFS), banded together to alter the landscape with the assistance of labor provided by the CCC. In South Carolina, these cooperative efforts are best seen in the development of state forests and especially in the development of Recreational Demonstration Areas (RDAs), in conjunction with the state parks.

The majority of CCC camps fell under the jurisdiction of the USFS, and forest protection was the primary objective of the CCC. Protective measures undertaken included forest fire prevention and disease and insect control in national and state forests. Preventative measures were taken as well, including stringing telephone lines to provide a method of communicating hazardous conditions, and the building of trails, roads, and fire towers in order to provide protection. USFS CCC camps also conducted forest improvement activities, including timber-type surveys, seedling nurseries, and reforestation. Other types of ground-cover projects included the planting of kudzu, an activity that changed the landscape throughout the Southeast.[20]

Although the USFS controlled the largest number of work projects for the CCC nationally, in Forest Service Region 8, or the Southern Region, only about half of CCC projects were forestry related. The NPS and the TVA supervised the majority of the Southern Region's projects. The USFS worked on South Carolina's national forests, including the Sumter National Forest, the Francis Marion National Forest, the South Carolina portion of the Nantahala National Forest (now part of the Sumter National Forest in Oconee County), and the Wambaw National Forest (now part of the Francis Marion National Forest in Charleston County). The U.S. government purchased additional lands (the Enoree Purchase Unit in Newberry County and the Long Cane Purchase Unit near Bradley) in 1934; these lands, along with the South Carolina portion of the Nantahala National Forest, became part of the Sumter National Forest in 1936. Most of these lands were former cotton farms that had been eroded through continuous use for over 100 years. As the lands had declined in profitable cultivation, they had been used for hardwood and pine production, which accelerated the depletion of the land. By the mid-1920s much of the land that had been used for farming had been abandoned. The federal programs allowing for lumber companies and other owners of nonproductive land to sell their lands for CCC and federal use helped meet Roosevelt's objectives of environmental employment. In the Enoree and Long Cane Purchase units, the CCC built fire towers, roads, nurseries, a fish hatchery, and trails; many of these features are still present.[21] South Carolina's CCC camps under jurisdiction of the USFS working on state forestland also built what were first termed "forestry parks" but soon became established as state parks at Aiken, Oconee, Lee, and Paris Mountain.

Joseph Kircher, regional forest director for Region 8, also established a unique fire control program for subsistence farmers in South Carolina. Kircher offered small farmers a salary and farmland adjacent to lookout towers in exchange for helping take care of the land and operating the towers. Farmers had to qualify by having previous farming experience, livestock, and dependents. The CCC assisted with this program by constructing the fire towers and roads, and through providing labor for construction of outbuildings on the newly acquired parcels of land.[22]

Forestry work also provided a good deal of usable vocational education for CCC enrollees. By 1936, 15,000 young men had worked in state and national forests and on privately held forestlands, primarily in fire control and prevention, but also in reforestation, thinning, and land-improvement activities. Their interest in forestry work, and their foresight in seeing that forestry could become a career, led the South Carolina Forestry Commission and State Forester H. A. Smith to publish a book for use in educational classes on the fundamentals of forestry. Topics studied included types of trees in South Carolina, forestry economics, forest management, and reforestation.[23] Forestry activities were one of the most important areas where vocational education immediately improved the work of the CCC.

Roosevelt's twin goals of the CCC were to put to good use marginalized American land and marginalized American youth. In addition, the development of recreational facilities on otherwise submarginal land would provide opportunities that many in the American public would find unobtainable elsewhere as a result of their financial situations. The development of RDAs met all of these needs successfully. By 1938 more than 10,000 people nationally had received employment through FERA, the WPA, or the CCC in relation to RDA development, and over 352,800 acres of land had been placed under development. Visitation numbers in the completed areas in 1937 topped one million days of daytime use, and 100,000 days of use by overnight campers.[24]

RDAs were developed as model campgrounds for people who were poor, people with disabilities, and otherwise underprivileged segments of the American population. Originally a project of the RA and FERA, the NPS quickly became involved, as did the CCC. Across the country, forty-six RDAs were created in eighteen states, mostly east of the Mississippi River. Four types of RDAs were developed: vacation areas, waysides (developed only in Virginia and South Carolina), land added to existing national parks and monuments, and recreational areas adjacent to state scenic areas. The NPS quickly warmed to the RDA project, and Director Arno Cammerer described the RDAs in 1937 as "a unique form of land use increasingly valuable to the American people, affording outlets for out-of-door recreation accessible to congested populations, and retiring from agricultural use unarable lands of no economic worth."[25] After development, RDAs were to be turned over to the states, and twenty-nine of them became state parks. Other RDAs became waysides along the Blue Ridge Parkway or joined existing national parks or monuments. Two original RDAs remain in the national park system. One is Prince William Forest Park in Virginia. The other, Catoctin Mountain Park in Maryland, later became the presidential retreat now known as Camp David. In South Carolina, RDAs developed at Cheraw and at Kings Mountain are now part of the state park system. Six wayside RDAs were also developed in South Carolina; one of these is now Colleton State Park.[26]

Visiting historic sites has long been the focus of the American tourist, and the NPS had just undertaken the care of several of the nation's most historic sites during the Hoover administration, including the development of the George Washington Memorial Parkway and Colonial National Monument. With the advent of a variety of New Deal programs that influenced NPS work nationwide, these new initiatives changed the face of the NPS, transforming the agency from a primarily environmental agency to one concerned with historic preservation and with the recreational activities of Americans. The passage of the Historic Sites Act in 1935 provided for an increased official governmental role in historic preservation, administered by the NPS. New Deal programs such as FERA, the Civil Works Administration (CWA), the WPA, and of course ECW and the CCC provided much-needed funds and manpower to the NPS. This infusion of funds and labor provided the NPS with the ability to carry out projects that had been previously planned but postponed as a result of lack of funding, as well as giving it additional projects in the area of state and local park developments across the nation.[27]

The activities of the CCC in South Carolina provided many new opportunities for a variety of South Carolinians, not just the CCC enrollees. Through their various accomplishments with the USFS, the NPS, and other programs, the CCC enrollees reclaimed and improved marginal land, developed recreational areas, and provided impoverished farmers with alternative places to farm and new jobs in fire prevention. Tourists and travelers found new places to camp, and tourist-related business increased in communities near state and national forests and state and national parks and RDAs. Young men received jobs, a place to live, an education, and money to aid their families. Nowhere in South Carolina are these benefits more evident than in the development of the first state parks, which formed the infrastructure for the state park system that continues to contribute to South Carolina's tourism economy.

CHAPTER 5

Conservation and Commemoration

South Carolina's Recreational Demonstration Areas, Cheraw, Colleton, and Kings Mountain

While the work of the Civilian Conservation Corps (CCC) was primarily responsible for the physical construction of South Carolina's state parks, its work also allowed the National Park Service (NPS) to use its experience in park planning to reclaim overworked lands for park areas through a program known as Recreational Demonstration Areas (RDAs). These RDAs represent the ideas and ideals of the New Deal's emphasis on outdoor recreation, especially extended to the economically disadvantaged population. NPS planners and New Deal idealists believed that cooperative recreation (where groups of people found organized recreational activities) and the exposure to nature and the outdoors could better American lives, both physically and psychologically. Based on these beliefs, state parks and RDAs were often designed to bring people together in the outdoors, with communal recreation areas such as large picnic shelters, playing fields, bathhouses, swimming facilities, and group camping areas.[1]

NPS officials hoped that these proposed recreational areas would meet different needs. Architectural historian Linda Flint McClelland has identified four areas in which the NPS sought to develop RDAs: 1,500–2,000 acres located near major population centers; 20–50 acres along principal highways, where motorists could rest and picnic in the outdoors; extensions to national parks and monuments developed for recreation; and extensions to state parks or scenic areas for recreational use.[2] By 1936 forty-six projects had begun in twenty-four states. South Carolina was the only state to have two RDAs, including a new park near Cheraw and one adjacent to the national military park at Kings Mountain. In addition to these two RDAs, the NPS also established prototype wayside parks in Virginia and South Carolina. The larger RDAs proved more popular, and only thirteen wayside parks were established, including six in South Carolina. The wayside established near Walterboro in Colleton County, South Carolina, became Colleton State Park.[3]

Cheraw Recreational Demonstration Area / Cheraw State Park

With the creation of Emergency Conservation Work (ECW) in South Carolina in 1933, citizens of the state quickly saw the benefits of putting young men to work in their communities. Although particularly hard-hit by the Depression, people in the Pee Dee region in northeast South Carolina immediately responded to the founding of the CCC. Believing that the creation of a state park would attract tourists to the area and provide much-needed economic relief in the form of government contracts with local merchants and suppliers, the citizens of Cheraw and Chesterfield County partnered to raise funds for purchasing land for the construction of a state park near Cheraw.

In January 1934 Larry Sharpe, a landscape architect with the NPS, met with L. C. Wannamaker, a Cheraw attorney, about the possibilities of developing land near Cheraw as a park. Wannamaker took Sharpe to a location near U.S. Highway 1, believing that it would be the most likely area in the region for park development. According to Wannamaker, Sharpe "fell in love" with what became Cheraw State Park and advocated that Wannamaker seek approval for development of a park at this location.[4]

Officially, the federal government permitted ECW to develop parks only on federally owned land or on land owned by other agencies cooperating with the federal government, not on private land, except in specific instances regarding specific forestry projects on large tracts of private forestlands. In January 1934 ECW director Robert Fechner wrote South Carolina governor Burnet Maybank outlining this policy: "no projects shall be undertaken in lands or interests in lands, other than those belonging to or under the jurisdiction of the United States, unless adequate provisions are made by the cooperating agencies (State Forestry Commission) for the maintenance, operation, and utilization of such projects after completion."[5] In order to use CCC enrollees to develop a state park in Chesterfield County, the state had to acquire the land. State Forester H. A. Smith visited Cheraw to assess the feasibility of building a park on the land that Wannamaker had shown to Sharpe, but he was less impressed than Sharpe had been and stated that he believed the area did not have enough population to warrant the creation of a state park.[6] Not easily discouraged, Wannamaker and several other Cheraw businessmen met in early February with H. L. Tilghman and B. S. Meeks, the chair and vice-chair, respectively, of the State Forestry Commission in hopes of promoting their proposed state park. Tilghman suggested that the Cheraw citizens set up a commission to raise money and provide some maintenance for the land until Washington approved the project. Five Cheraw citizens were appointed to the Park Commission: W. P. Smith (who was also the president of the Cheraw Kiwanis Club), Dr. G. A.

Bunch, H. L. Powe, Mrs. H. H. Anderson, and Mrs. Edwin Malloy, wife of a cotton merchant and part owner of the Cheraw Yarn Mills.[7]

State Forester Smith had cited the area's relatively low population among his concerns regarding a state park in Chesterfield County. The county population was 34,000 in the 1930 census, and the six-county Pee Dee region had a population of only 221,400, a mere 13 percent of the total state population. What the Cheraw population lacked in numbers, it made up for with enthusiasm. Undaunted, the citizens of Cheraw began a fund-raising drive to raise money for the purchase of land to donate to the state for the purpose of developing a state park. Under the leadership of Wannamaker and J. H. Ramseur, over $5,300 was raised in less than a month's time, with contributions from local businesses and individuals. Even Cheraw schoolchildren joined the effort, with nickel and dime contributions placed on deposit with a local bank. When presented with such obvious interest in a state park from the local people, State Forester Smith relented and gave his approval for the potential development of a state park at Cheraw. The Cheraw citizens' group paid $5,160 for 705.55 acres of land just south of U.S. Highway 1 and immediately donated the land to the State Forestry Commission for the creation of a recreation and forest demonstration area.[8] Wannamaker sent the state forester the deed dated March 22, 1934, for the land, with a list of all the donors for the purchase. Wannamaker recognized the historic nature of this donation and asked Smith to "file this list in your records so that it may be available as a matter of private or historical interest at any future time."[9] Later that week Smith and a forestry commissioner visited Cheraw and walked the land. Smith was quoted in the *State* newspaper as saying that the land "lends itself to a small park very nicely."[10]

An application for a CCC camp at Cheraw was submitted to the NPS Richmond office on February 9, 1934. ECW director Robert Fechner approved the state park project for CCC work in mid-March, with initial authorization for South Carolina Camp SP-1 for six months.[11] That May the local newspaper trumpeted that the park on "US 1, probably the most widely traveled roadway in the state, will bring thousands of visitors from all sections of the country . . . and will establish Cheraw as the 'Gateway City' of South Carolina."[12]

State Forester Smith began correspondence with the commanding officer at Fort Moultrie, Colonel F. F. Jewett, regarding the moving of CCC enrollees to the Cheraw area for development of South Carolina's first state park. After revisiting the Cheraw site, Smith expressed his concerns over the limited acreage and the evidently unwritten policy of ECW to clear-cut areas where it intended to set up camps. Smith asked Jewett to refrain from sending enrollees to Cheraw until further notice from the State Forestry Commission and asked Jewett to "drop a letter" to the commanding officer reinforcing the concerns about the possible damage to the park environment through the "promiscuous cutting of trees." Smith also asked Jewett to investigate the possibilities of constructing buildings for the CCC camp that could be used for park purposes after the camp was disbanded. Jewett responded to Smith: "We will do nothing toward moving the company into that area until you further inform us as to your desires in this matter. When the Company moves in the Commanding Officer will be given explicit instructions relative to his saving all the trees near the camp site. We understood that the camp at Chesterfield was to be occupied for a period of at least a year and were planning on wooden constructions. If however, it will only be for six months, we will probably have to make a tent camp out of it, constructing only a mess hall."[13]

CCC Company 445 moved to Cheraw in July 1934 to begin work on a CCC campsite (which they named Camp Cherokee) and on a state park. Authorized for a six-month period, the enrollees found themselves residents of a tent camp, which apparently did not satisfy some of their hopes. Company 445, made up entirely of young, white, South Carolina residents, had been organized in May 1933 at Fort Moultrie, near Charleston, and had served most of the first year at Fort Moultrie, with three months near Conway. Evidently the enrollees had liked their proximity to the Atlantic coast and did not like what they saw on their first impressions of the Cheraw site, for the 1936 yearbook states that "when the members of the Company arrived at the present Camp site, they like all other new enrollees, were a little downhearted. The life was naturally new to them. But they have found out in the meantime that life is swell at Camp. It has given them rugged bodies and has stimulated and developed beneficial interests."[14] The camp newspaper, the *Cherokean*, reminisced about the first days at camp in the May 20, 1935, edition, giving an idea of the initial condition of the early camps, as well as the activities in which enrollees participated. When Company 445 arrived on July 5, 1934, there were four barracks, a recreation building, a mess hall, and a "practically waterless shower house." Roads were many and confusing, and there was only occasional electrical power. According to the *Cherokean*, "half the time, the pump didn't give forth water, and the other half it wouldn't give anything." The camp newspaper proudly reported that only four months later, roads had been cleared, additional structures built (including officers' quarters and an infirmary), recreational areas constructed (including a tennis court, baseball diamond, horseshoe court, volleyball court, and basketball court), and the camp had won recognition for both Best Mess and Best Camp in District I. Commanding Officer Captain D. W. Traxler complimented the men on their cooperation and achievements during the first few months in camp.[15]

At first the camp was authorized for only a six-month stay, which was then extended for another six months. In 1935 the federal government decided to purchase an additional 6,800 acres of land adjacent to the state park for development as an RDA. With this added land and a much larger project, the CCC camp was given a longer authorization, and the enrollees erected more permanent camp buildings, including four barracks, a dining hall, a recreation hall, and officers' and NPS supervisors' quarters. According to Jack Wilson, a Cheraw teenager in the 1930s, the CCC camp had a "very military appearance, with typical barracks, white-washed rocks outlining paths and roads, everything extremely neat and orderly."[16] The camp and park project at Cheraw set the standard for other similar projects throughout the state.

The CCC camp at Cheraw ran much like other CCC camps. In addition to the daily work projects, educational and recreational opportunities were available to the enrollees. Frank Damon, an enrollee who quickly rose to the rank of leader and served as the company clerk, remembers playing tennis, going swimming, and serving as the editor of the camp newspaper. According to Damon, the education adviser "taught the enrollees to read and write as quite a few of them could do neither." Enrollees organized a baseball team and held dances in the recreation hall. The enrollees also maintained cordial relationships with the Cheraw citizens. Damon remembers that "we were invited to the homes of the local people for dinner quite often and to parties at their houses."[17] The *Cherokean* bears out this relationship. An editorial in the June 10, 1935, issue (written by editor Frank Damon) states: "To my way of thinking, there has always existed a very close relationship between the people of Cheraw and Camp Cherokee. . . . We appreciate this much more than we are able to say or even show. . . . We are all glad that there exists between the people of Cheraw and Camp Cherokee such a close relationship. We all hope that it will grow stronger and closer as time goes by."[18] Evidently the enthusiasm with which the Cheraw citizens had pursued a CCC camp and state park was extended to the enrollees building the park, and the relations between the CCC enrollees and the local people were quite good. The local citizens were delighted that their efforts in obtaining a park had been successful, and most of these CCC enrollees were white native South Carolinians or from elsewhere in the Southeast and were for the most part considered locals.

After the CCC enrollees set up their campsite, they began construction on the state park facilities. In his 1933–34 annual report, the state forester was able to report that a small lake for bathing and boating, picnic shelters, and an administration building were under construction, as well as various roads, trails, and landscaping projects around the CCC camp and the park. Smith also had received a letter from Wannamaker, who continued his interest in the park project, giving the State Forestry Commission "permission to make any plantings desired by you on our lands opposite Cheraw State Park for highway

Cheraw State Park picnic shelter covered with snow and ice, winter 1936–37.
Photograph courtesy of South Carolina Department of Archives and History

beautification purposes" and promising that these areas would be maintained by the property owners.[19]

In September 1934 the Richmond office approved drawings and estimates for a picnic grouping at Cheraw consisting of one shelter with benches, nine tables, and five outdoor fireplaces. The Dogwood Picnic Shelter at Cheraw State Park is the oldest CCC-constructed building in the South Carolina state park system, and remains one of the premier examples of CCC construction in the state parks. NPS officials viewed this picnic shelter as an early success; the District Office requested photographs, negatives, and blueprints of the shelter for its [the shelter's] inclusion in a booklet being produced on park structures in Washington (the resulting publication was Albert Good's *Park Structures and Facilities*), and the shelter was featured in the September 1935 issue of the *Kiwanis Magazine*. The Dogwood Shelter and Barbecue Pit opened formally to the public on May 18, 1935, with a barbecue supper for NPS personnel, other state park superintendents, and prominent local residents, including Wannamaker. Other Cheraw CCC projects completed in 1934–35 included the tables and outdoor fireplaces mentioned above, a public campground, two latrines, and an earthen dam to raise the level of Lake Cherokee, a seven-acre lake that had been a pond on the property. The CCC men added a diving platform and board to enhance their swimming opportunities. Locals who came to swim at Lake Cherokee also used the diving board and platform. By the spring of 1935 the CCC camp newspaper reported that churches, Sunday school classes, and groups from the local high school were using the park for cookouts and picnics, as well as for hiking, swimming, and other recreational activities.[20] Project landscape architect Harold Welden impressed upon the enrollees the significance of their building projects in an article in the *Cherokean:* "It happens to be our business to build a State Park and indirectly to provide a place where future generations can enjoy the beauties and recreational facilities of Nature at her best." The successful work at Cheraw did not go unnoticed by federal officials, as the camp newsletter reported in November 1935 that Welden was being transferred to New York State to lead similar projects there, and that he had "distinguished himself in making this park beautiful and inviting."[21]

The federal government acquired an additional 6,800 acres of land immediately adjacent to Cheraw State Park in the summer of 1935 under the submarginal land program for development as an RDA. The land was owned primarily by the Hancock Insurance Company and the Atlantic Life Insurance Company; tenant farmers occupied and farmed the land. The creation of the RDA displaced some 160 people in twenty-nine families. The Resettlement Administration (RA) relocated these families, and the Works Progress Administration (WPA) razed their houses and other farm buildings. "Several hundred" WPA workers joined the CCC enrollees in the development of the RDA. In August 1935 the local CCC company received word that the RDA projects would begin, and by November construction of a 1,300-foot-wide dam and the 300-acre Lake Juniper had started, utilizing both CCC and WPA labor at the RDA.[22] The *Cherokean* reported that the dam would be made of 2,600 cubic yards of concrete, reinforced with 104,000 pounds of steel, and that the construction would take approximately a year to complete and would be "something to be proud of in the years to come."[23] Although developed under the auspices of the federal government, unlike other federal projects viewed as a part of the NPS system, the Cheraw RDA was considered from its beginnings to be a part of Cheraw State Park, and the land was leased to the South Carolina Forestry Commission for operations until it was turned over to the state in 1944.[24]

The WPA workers were drawn from otherwise unemployed or underemployed men from around the area, including the towns of Society Hill, Chesterfield, and Pee Dee, and north to the North Carolina state line, as well as from the immediate Cheraw vicinity. Unlike the CCC enrollees who lived, worked, and played together, the WPA workers trucked into the area each day and only remained there during working hours, returning to their homes and families each night. It does not appear that the WPA and CCC enrollees fraternized together, and WPA workers left very few records of their work and life, especially when compared to those left by the CCC workers through their yearbooks, camp newspapers, and reunions. Cheraw's CCC workers did note that the WPA workers, under the direction of a Mr. Plumer, made "great headway" in the clearing of the land that became the lake. Although federal records indicate that the WPA was heavily involved with the development of the RDA, historians at the South Carolina Department of Archives and History concluded that while these records provide a clear indication of the funding sources for these projects through the Federal Emergency Relief Administration (FERA) rather than ECW, the bulk of the actual work itself was most likely conducted by the CCC rather than WPA workers.[25]

Other projects conducted throughout 1935, 1936, and 1937 at the Cheraw RDA in conjunction with Cheraw State Park included the clearing of land for two group camps, the construction of a caretaker's house, the development of a fish hatchery, and the construction of the group camps. The caretaker's house was the first major building constructed at Cheraw, and the *Cherokean* reported that it was the largest project under way in August 1935. The caretaker's house is a one-and-one-half-story building, with a side-gable roof and two dormer windows in the gable. The house has a one-story side-gable addition. Log construction over a stone basement foundation gives the house a rustic feel. CCC workers used standardized NPS designs, coupled with locally available materials to give the residence a South Carolina character. Enrollees quarried stone from local quarries for the foundation, and cypress and yellow pine, obtained from the Lake Juniper excavations, were used for the framing and siding of the building. In accordance with the ECW commitment to manual labor, the roofing shingles were hand-riven cypress shingles. The NPS, obviously pleased with the effort of the South Carolina CCC in the execution of its standardized designs, expressed to local officials that the caretaker's house "makes a very impressive showing." The State Forestry Commission reported in 1942 that the superintendents' houses at all the parks "were designed and constructed in keeping with the atmosphere of a State Park, yet the point of rusticity was not carried so far that comfort and usefulness were sacrificed," and pointed out that the homes had modern conveniences, being "equipped with running water, bathrooms, and lights."[26] In South Carolina's state parks, as throughout many of the other states, "rusticity" combined with the conveniences of the modern age, creating an unintentional but new, identifiable, uniquely American architectural style.[27]

While the houses met NPS expectations, the development and construction of the fish hatchery project created some controversy among the NPS and state forestry officials associated with Cheraw. J. E. Bost, director of fish culture for the South Carolina Department of Game and Fish, advocated the hatchery, as it would provide a means of stocking the two lakes at Cheraw as well as other lakes and streams in the area. The NPS worried that a fish hatchery would take

Cheraw State Park caretaker's house, winter 1936–37. Photograph courtesy of South Carolina Department of Archives and History

much-needed funding away from the development of recreational areas. Bost worked out a deal with the State Forestry Commission and the NPS, by which the Department of Game and Fish would provide the money for materials, but the WPA and CCC workers at Cheraw would provide the manpower for construction of a warden's house and nineteen fish-rearing pools and two supply lakes. Construction began in the spring of 1937 with labor supplied by the WPA. CCC enrollees took over the work at the fish hatchery in June, constructing twelve rearing pools, the most of any South Carolina state park. They did not complete construction of the hatchery and warden's house until the summer of 1941. Two years later the State Forestry Commission deeded the 206 acres that make up the fish hatchery to the U.S. Fish and Wildlife Service.[28]

The two group camps—Camp Forest and Camp Juniper—were designed to serve organized clubs and groups, such as the Boy Scouts, Girl Scouts, 4–H Clubs, churches, and others. Built to NPS specifications, the group areas contained unit camps of several cabins laid out in a circular fashion around a central administration building, dining hall, infirmary, and bathhouse. CCC workers also constructed furniture for use in the cabins and recreational buildings. The camps were located at some distance from the lakefront intentionally, in order that swimming and other water activities would take place only with supervision. Originally Camp Forest was designed to accommodate 120 campers, while Camp Juniper initially would serve approximately 60. By summer 1937 Camp Forest was practically completed. The CCC began construction of Camp Juniper in early 1938; however, budget restrictions dictated that the buildings at Camp

Juniper would be simpler than those at Camp Forest. The changes included the "elimination of all porches [and] a radical simplification of all framing details."[29] The extant buildings at the group camps bear out this distinction; Camp Forest's buildings are more detailed and finished in appearance, while Camp Juniper's are much more rustic and modest, without porches.

Camp Forest opened in July 1937, and the State Forestry Commission boasted that there were some 700 campers per week in August 1937. Camp Juniper opened in May 1939. The State Forest Service administered the camps' operation from the beginning. The group camps provided camping facilities for a variety of nonprofit groups, primarily made up of children. The State Forest Service employed a camp director, a dietician and cooks, a lifeguard, a first aid attendant or nurse, and other camp helpers. The sponsoring organizations provided their own leaders and programming; however, these organizations often asked State Forestry Commission personnel to provide programs both at the camps and for local groups. Shortly after the opening of Camp Juniper in May, the group camps were closed during July and August 1939 as a result of outbreaks of "infantile paralysis" (polio) in North and South Carolina. In the summers of 1942 and 1943 the recreational programs in the group camps faltered again, evidently in part because of gasoline rationing and the difficulty in obtaining transportation for the campers. However, servicemen stationed in the area during the early 1940s made good use of Cheraw's recreational facilities, including using the lake for swimming and diving.[30]

After completing the majority of the construction projects, the CCC turned to returning the land to its "natural state" in April 1938. The federal government had purchased over 6,000 acres for the construction of the RDA; most of this land was unfit for further farming production. However, South Carolinians had used this land for farming, primarily of cotton, timber, and tobacco, for decades. The RA had moved the farm families from these submarginal lands, and their houses and other farm buildings had been abandoned. During the park-building activities of the mid-1930s, the CCC and the WPA had used the empty buildings for storage facilities and the farm roads as access to worksites. The CCC razed the abandoned houses, barns, and outbuildings, and harrowed and planted old roadbeds in an attempt to "obliterate all signs of mankind," a project that was completed by the fall of 1939.[31]

While attempting to erase man-made buildings at the RDA, the CCC and the NPS increased the presence of people in the Public Use Area throughout 1939. The recreation building, an amphitheater, a picnic shelter, and a boat dock were among the largest of the construction projects completed in 1939. Cheraw State Park officially opened that July, although the polio outbreak caused the park to close almost immediately.[32]

Another construction project undertaken in 1940 caused a great deal of controversy among the locals, the State Forestry Commission, and the NPS. Local businessmen, who sought to increase the income opportunities generated by tourism to their state park and recreational area, wanted to attract more tourists through the construction of family cabins like those being built in other state parks in nearby resort areas, such as those at Myrtle Beach State Park in Horry County, South Carolina, and in North Carolina. The State Forestry Commission objected to this idea, believing that Cheraw State Park attracted primarily residents of the Pee Dee region who would use the park mainly as daytime visitors, and that there was no reason to provide overnight accommodations other than camping. In addition, the Forestry Commission argued, the majority of the users of Cheraw State Park were of lower income and could not afford the rental fees that cabins would require. L. C. Wannamaker, who had been the driving force behind the purchase and donation of the land for the state park, appealed directly to the NPS, and in turn the NPS directed the Forestry Commission and the CCC to construct eight cabins to accommodate families. The cabins are frame construction, similar to the other structures at Cheraw, and feature cross-gable roofs, paired and triple six-over-six windows, and screened porches. The CCC had completed the family cabins by the summer of 1941, signaling the end of CCC work at Cheraw State Park. The CCC camp officially closed in October of that same year.[33]

During the earliest years of its operation, Cheraw State Park and RDA were extremely successful. In 1941 the State Forestry Commission reported that Cheraw had the second highest attendance of South Carolina's sixteen state parks, hosting over 156,000 guests. The controversial family cabins were proving to be extremely popular, as were the cabins in four other parks. The Cheraw community continued to support the operation of the park, as they had its creation, as is evidenced by the fact that the local government agreed to underwrite the operating funds in order to keep the parks open after the South Carolina General Assembly appropriated no funds for the operation of the park bathhouses in 1941.[34]

Although the development of a recreational area and state park were the primary goals of the work of the CCC at Cheraw, other CCC-related activity in the area included reforestation and fire control. Due to overharvesting and fires, more than 1,600 acres in the RDA had been stripped of practically all vegetation. Timber-type surveys were undertaken to determine what types of trees and shrubbery grew in the area. These surveys revealed a large variety of trees and shrubs, including several species of pine, poplar, black locust, walnut, and oak, as well as fruit trees, flowering trees such as dogwood, and several shrubs, including holly, honeysuckle, jasmine, trumpet vine, and sand myrtle. These 1,600 acres in the RDA were reforested with a variety of pine, poplar, black locust, and walnut trees. In addition to reforestation efforts, the CCC also undertook a fire prevention program in cooperation with the Sandhill Agricultural Demonstration Project, adjacent to the park and the RDA. The CCC enrollees at Cheraw received training in fire prevention and fire protection, and were given full responsibility for fire protection in the area, as there was "no plan of organized [fire] control in this county." In addition to planning for and constructing fire towers and stringing telephone lines between the towers, the CCC constructed over nine miles of "fire motor ways" and installed fire tool boxes and fire pumps.[35] Although not directly related to the recreational work at Cheraw, these CCC efforts at fire prevention reinforced the goals of reforestation and conservation that President Roosevelt had set out for the CCC at the beginning of his administration, and provided the enrollees with valuable education in forestry and fire control.

The development of Cheraw State Park and the RDA provides a good example of the state park development undertaken by the CCC in South Carolina. Due to the interest and financial contributions of the citizens of Cheraw, Cheraw State Park has the distinction of being the first state park begun in the state. The shelters, barbecue pits, cabins, group camps, lakes, roads, and trails that the CCC built still stand as testimony to the lives and work of the CCC enrollees who made SP-1 their home for several years. Of the 118 CCC-constructed structures erected at Cheraw in the 1930s, approximately 100 still stand, and most are still in use. Through the work of CCC Company 445 and the WPA, and with the support of the NPS, the State Forestry Commission, and the local citizenry, the park developed at Cheraw provided the impetus for the development of other parks and the state park system in South Carolina.

Cheraw State Park is an example of the type of park developed under the NPS's RDA program, and its development parallels the development of the state park system in South Carolina. Though it was the first South Carolina state park to get under way, in March 1934, Cheraw State Park was one of the last to open to the public, in July 1939 (although the RDA had opened earlier, for limited use). Although Cheraw did not meet the "major population center" provision, the proactive stance taken by Cheraw locals attracted NPS officials, and when the local committee purchased and donated over 700 acres of land, setting up a CCC camp quickly followed. Shortly after starting the state park, the federal government moved to acquire the 6,800 additional acres of submarginal farming land as an extension to the state park for recreational use. Thus Cheraw State Park met two of the four priority areas as identified by Linda Flint McClelland, and became an example for the development of other parks throughout the state.

The CCC also constructed waysides along principal highways, starting in Virginia and South Carolina. Developed under the auspices of the NPS, the NPS and the states planned that the waysides, like the RDAs, would eventually become a part of the state park system. The NPS established six wayside parks on major thoroughfares in South Carolina, ranging from twenty-nine to sixty-two acres.

The NPS planned for the waysides to serve the growing population of American autocampers, providing a rest stop on major federal highways for travelers. Unlike the state parks and RDAs, waysides were designed as rest stops, not destination points, and offered only bare necessities for travelers, such as water fountains and picnic tables, and some had shelters and bathroom facilities. Some waysides also provided housing for superintendents. NPS officials gave some care in selecting the sites for waysides, choosing to locate them in areas with scenic overlooks or where short trails could provide a place for travelers to stretch their legs. However, the larger RDAs proved to be more popular, and the NPS only developed thirteen waysides, seven in Virginia and six in South Carolina. In South Carolina, and likely in Virginia, the waysides became as popular among local residents for picnicking, fishing, and other day-use family activities as they were for their intended audience, the tourist and traveler, especially in areas where other state park facilities were not readily available to locals. As the popularity of the wayside parks did not meet the anticipated demand, additional wayside programs in other states did not develop, in favor of expanding the RDA program, making the existing wayside park in South Carolina a unique example both for the state and the country.[36]

In 1935 the NPS asked the South Carolina Forestry Commission to recommend locations throughout the state for consideration by the RA, which would purchase in small acreage. The Forestry Commission responded by recommending twelve sites in the counties of Greenville, Greenwood, Aiken, Colleton, Kershaw, Cherokee, Marlboro, and Georgetown. In the fall of 1935 the RA purchased six tracts in Greenville, Greenwood, Aiken, Colleton, Kershaw, and Georgetown counties, ranging in size from twenty-nine to sixty-two acres. The RA turned the property over to the NPS in early 1936. Work began on the Greenville and Greenwood areas by the summer of 1936, with the understanding that after completion, the waysides would be turned over to the Forestry Commission's Division of State Parks. Four of the six waysides were fully developed (Greenville, Greenwood, Kershaw, and Colleton), and the commission began leasing them from the NPS on June 1, 1940.[37] The NPS turned five of the six wayside tracts over to the Forestry Commission by June 1942, including the acreage in Aiken County. No real park development had occurred at Georgetown Wayside, and it was transferred to another branch of the federal government for "military purposes."[38]

Colleton State Park. Originally constructed as the Colleton Wayside by Company 1428, Colleton State Park features this unusual enclosed picnic shelter. Photograph by the author

Colleton State Park. This picnic shelter at Colleton is a typical rectangular plan constructed by the CCC. Photograph by the author

The Colleton Wayside, near Walterboro, was one such South Carolina wayside. The approximately thirty-five acres in Colleton County lie near the intersection of U.S. Highway 15 and State Highway 65 (and within a mile of Interstate 95) along the banks of the Edisto River. Colleton Wayside provides a good example of the layout of the other waysides in the state, and includes parking areas, water fountains, grills, picnic tables, two picnic shelters, one enclosed shelter, and bathroom facilities. The picnic shelters are very simplistic in style when compared to some of the shelters at other South Carolina state parks of the era, with wood posts supporting a gable roof with exposed rafter tails. Original roofing material was hand-riven wooden shingles, but these have been replaced by composition shingles. Colleton Wayside also features a scenic walking trail leading to the banks of the Edisto River. These facilities were all constructed by the CCC, likely Company 1428 or 5468, both of which were stationed in Colleton County during the period of development.

Of the six waysides planned for in South Carolina, Colleton is the only extant wayside, and is now known as Colleton State Park. Other wayside areas were incorporated into nearby existing state parks, including the Wildcat Wayside in Greenville County, now a part of the Mountain Bridge Wilderness Area, or turned over to other state departments, including as right-of-way for projects of the South Carolina Department of Transportation.[39] Colleton State Park is the only remaining evidence of the NPS wayside development in the state, and is acknowledged as the seventeenth state park developed by the CCC in South Carolina, although it did not gain state park status until much later.

Kings Mountain National Military Park

Kings Mountain Recreational Development Area

Kings Mountain State Park

The final type of RDA was developed adjacent to existing national parks, for the recreational opportunities for those who were visiting those parks. In South Carolina, this option became available at Kings Mountain National Military Park in York and Cherokee counties, which had become a part of the national military parks system in 1931. In August 1933 President Roosevelt signed Executive Order 6166, transferring all historic sites, military battlefields, and monuments from control of the Department of Agriculture and the War Department to the NPS.[40]

Kings Mountain National Military Park is the site of perhaps the most important military engagement in the South during the Revolutionary War. In October 1780 a group of Patriots from the backcountry of present-day Tennessee, North Carolina, and South Carolina banded together to oppose Loyalist troops assisting the British army advancing northwest from Charleston after that city fell to the British in May. These opposing forces met at Kings Mountain, just south of the North Carolina border. Major Patrick Ferguson commanded the Loyalist troops, while Colonels Isaac Shelby, John Sevier, Charles McDowell, William Campbell, James Williams, and William Hill commanded the Patriot backcountry militia, often called "the Over-mountain Men" for their long march across the Appalachians. While Ferguson and his men camped and fortified the top of the ridge of Kings Mountain on October 7, 1780, the Patriots surrounded them on all sides and then attacked at about three o'clock that afternoon. Ferguson refused to surrender even when his second-in-command pleaded that further resistance was futile. After Ferguson fell mortally wounded, the Loyalists raised the white flag of surrender. Rather than taking the remaining Loyalists prisoners, however, the Patriots shouted "Tarleton's Quarter," in memory of fellow Patriots who had been killed rather than imprisoned in earlier battles with British and Loyalist troops. Although several Patriot officers tried to prevent the slaughter, over 300 Loyalists were killed or wounded before the militiamen fell back and imprisoned another 600.[41]

With the defeat of Ferguson's troops at Kings Mountain, the remainder of the British forces in the South abandoned their advance through the Carolinas and withdrew to a defensive position in South Carolina for the winter of 1780–1781. Meanwhile, Patriot forces throughout the Carolinas, revitalized by the victory of the Over-mountain Men at Kings Mountain, began the task of retaking Carolina towns that had fallen to the British, including Camden and Ninety-Six. Although the British forces in the newly united colonies did not surrender for another year following the battle of Kings Mountain, this battle was the effective turning point of the war in the South. It led to a revitalization of the Patriot movement in the South and along the East Coast and eventually to the surrender of the British forces at Yorktown, Virginia, on October 19, 1781.[42]

Although the battle of Kings Mountain was a significant military event during the American Revolution, very little commemorative action marked the site in the decades following the Revolutionary War. Commemorative efforts at Kings Mountain began in 1810, when a group of veterans gathered in Abingdon, Virginia, to remember their service as Patriots. In 1815 Dr. William McLean, of North Carolina, returned to Kings Mountain and erected a tablet to honor fallen comrades, which also memorialized Patrick Ferguson, marking the first actual commemorative monument erected at Kings Mountain. This event drew only a few participants, due in part to the difficulties in reaching Kings Mountain. These difficulties were lessened in the early 1850s with the construction of the Charlotte & South Carolina Railroad, which included a link from Yorkville to Chester. In October 1855 a celebration marking the seventy-fifth anniversary of the battle of Kings Mountain drew over 15,000 participants, including local spectators, military companies, and Masons.[43]

Although a few American veterans' organizations had formed after the Revolution, such as the Society of the Cincinnati, for the most part veterans' organizations did not organize until after the Civil War. The Grand Army of the Republic (GAR) organized in Illinois in 1866, followed by the United Confederate Veterans (UCV), women's auxiliaries, and hereditary societies such as the Sons of the Revolution (SR), Colonial Dames, the Daughters of the American Revolution (DAR), and the United Daughters of the Confederacy (UDC), all of which had formed by 1894. These veterans' organizations, women's auxiliaries, and heredity societies focused their efforts on commemorative activities to mark historic battlefields and other important historical sites, and in the South these sites were associated primarily with the Civil War. They also pressured the federal and state governments to purchase land for cemeteries and for battlefield preservation. In large part because of the efforts of these highly influential groups, Congress passed legislation to survey, preserve, and mark domestic battlefields in 1926, which included provisions to honor the battlefields associated with the American Revolution.[44]

Following the seventy-fifth anniversary of the battle of Kings Mountain, citizens of Yorkville, South Carolina, and Kings Mountain, North Carolina, organized a committee in 1879 to begin preparations for the centennial celebration. The Kings Mountain Centennial Association (KMCA) organized on July 25, 1879, with delegates from North Carolina, South Carolina, Tennessee, and Virginia attending. The KMCA resolved to "celebrate the battle's centennial and to purchase a suitable monument."[45] In addition to private donations, the states of North Carolina and South Carolina contributed $1,500 and $1,000, respectively, to the KMCA in early 1880, and the KMCA purchased thirty-nine and a half acres of battlefield land from local farmers. In October 1880 three days of celebration commenced, called Reunion Day, Military Day, and Centennial Day. Four young women, representing the states of North Carolina, South Carolina, Tennessee, and Virginia, unveiled a new granite monument, known as the "Centennial Monument," commemorating participants in the battle, accompanied by special songs, poems, and fireworks. The Centennial Monument is a twenty-eight-foot-high, gray granite shaft on an eighteen-foot-square base, surrounded by four tablets explaining the significance of the battle and dedicating the monument "to the patriotic Americans who participated in the Battle of Kings Mountain." The following year, in 1881, Lyman Draper of the State Historical Society of Wisconsin published *King's Mountain and Its Heroes: History of the Battle of King's Mountain, October 7th, 1780*. Although a great deal of attention was paid to Kings Mountain in 1880–1881, Kings Mountain received so few visitors in the ensuing years that a journalist entitled an 1893 travel piece in the *Magazine of American History*, "A Battlefield That Is Seldom Visited—Kings Mountain." The KMCA for the most part had disbanded in the years following the centennial celebration, and in 1899 transferred its ownership of the battlefield property to the Kings Mountain Chapter of the DAR, which formed the Kings Mountain Centennial Battlefield Association (KMCBA) to administer the property.[46]

The KMCBA (known by 1930 as the Kings Mountain Battleground Association [KMBA]) used its influence with state leaders in North and South Carolina to pressure Congress to agree to erect a monument on the battlefield, and for the federal government to acquire the almost forty acres owned by the KMCBA in 1906. The federal government authorized a monument in 1906 and erected it in 1909, accompanied by a celebration that attracted over 8,000 spectators, including the governors of Georgia, North Carolina, South Carolina, Tennessee, and Virginia, and the president of Wofford College. No representatives of the federal government attended, which indicated the lack of interest of the federal government in the battlefield property. Located near the spot where Patrick Ferguson surrendered to the Patriots, the U.S. Monument was designed by the architectural firm of McKim, Mead, and White, and cost approximately $25,000. This monument is much larger than the Centennial Monument, eighty-three feet high, and is white, rather than gray, granite. Bronze tablets adorn the base, detail the significance of the battle, list the commanders of both forces and those killed in the battle, and dedicate the monument to the Patriots who participated in the battle. A year after the construction of the monument, the War Department transferred the battlefield property back to the KMCBA, stating that the battlefield lacked distinctiveness and that the War Department would not commit itself to creating a national military park. Undaunted, the KMCBA resumed care of the battlefield. Its members maintained the site, erected additional markers, and continued to ask Congress to establish a national military park at Kings Mountain. The KMCBA also protected and maintained the existing markers, including the 1815 McLean marker, which had been vandalized, by enclosing them with wrought-iron fencing. In addition to its continued maintenance of the property, the KMCBA also began planning for the sesquicentennial celebration of the battle of Kings Mountain, to be held in October 1930.[47]

While the federal government previously had been uninterested in the establishment of Kings Mountain as a national military park, President Herbert Hoover attended the sesquicentennial celebration and addressed the 75,000 people who attended on October 7, 1930. Like previous commemorative celebrations, the sesquicentennial featured songs and poems written especially for

the occasion. Federal officials and even a representative of the British government joined local and state dignitaries. New commemorative markers, including a new memorial for Ferguson's grave, were erected. An allegorical pageant
highlighted the sesquicentennial celebration. The DAR erected a marker shortly
after the sesquicentennial to mark the spot where Hoover stood while giving
his speech.[48]

While plans for the sesquicentennial had been made, congressional representatives from both North and South Carolina continued their work to ensure
that Kings Mountain became a part of the national military park system under
the War Department. Hoover's participation in the celebration was a less-than-
subtle indication that the federal government would soon add the battlefield to
the War Department's responsibility. Although Secretary of War Dwight Davis
did not believe that Kings Mountain warranted federal protection, Congress
established Kings Mountain National Military Park on March 3, 1931, with
Hoover's approval. Congress appropriated $225,000 for additional land acqui-
sition and park development, although it appears that the War Department
made little use of this money, as no additional land was acquired, and no additional monuments or structures were erected.[49]

In 1933 President Franklin Roosevelt issued Executive Order 6166, which
transferred all battlefields and historic sites administered by the War Department and the Department of Agriculture to the NPS. This executive order included the approximately forty acres of Kings Mountain Battlefield Park that had
been donated by the KMBA. The NPS appointed the Kings Mountain Battlefield Commission, which optioned some 1,000 acres of land by November
1933.[50] Roosevelt's executive order transferred ownership of the Kings Mountain Battlefield land from one federal agency to another, but other Roosevelt
programs would greatly impact thousands of acres of battlefield and surrounding lands. The programs of the Public Works Administration (PWA), the Emergency Relief Agency (ERA), the RA, and the CCC would dramatically change
the Kings Mountain landscape in only a few years with the development of both
the national military park and the adjacent Kings Mountain RDA, which became
Kings Mountain State Park.

Additional appropriations for land acquisition and development originally
came through the PWA in 1934, and the NPS developed a planning document
that would eventually incorporate over 10,000 acres of surrounding land. The
NPS made arrangements to develop an additional RDA near the Kings Mountain National Military Park through CCC work. In the three years following
Executive Order 6166, the NPS concentrated its work at Kings Mountain on
land acquisition, beginning actual construction on the RDA in 1936, and new
construction at the national military park in 1937.[51] Some 10,000 acres of land

in York and Cherokee counties were acquired, much through the work of the RA, which assisted over thirty families in the project area in relocating from their farms and land in an area that had seen better days. Almost 100 farm buildings, including houses and outbuildings, were left behind from these families and others in the area that moved, structures that were eventually razed by the CCC in the years of park development.[52]

Local citizens overwhelmingly supported the arrival of the CCC in York County. In May 1935 the community learned that one Soil Conservation Service and two NPS camps would be stationed in their county. Commanding officers met with city officials and businessmen to discuss the needs of the camps and how the camps' locations would benefit the community. Colonel Walter K. Dunn, commanding officer of District I, told the community leaders that it was their duty to welcome these men and make them feel at home. It appears that the local citizens followed these instructions, and more than 2,000 people attended a welcoming reception for the first young men to set up permanent camp near Clover for work at Kings Mountain in July 1935.[53]

The RDA at Kings Mountain developed similarly to that at Cheraw, with a man-made lake, two group camps, residences, and picnic shelters. The NPS developed and administered the RDAs at Cheraw and Kings Mountain, and used WPA labor and ERA workers drawn from the local communities of Clover, York, Sharon, Blacksburg, and surrounding areas to construct park facilities from 1937 to 1942. According to South Carolina Department of Parks, Recreation, and Tourism (SCPRT) historian Al Hester, these local laborers constructed much of the group camp known as Camp York as well as the dams, bathhouse, and a picnic shelter at the RDA.[54] Additional work at the RDA and at the national military park during the 1930s was performed by the men of the CCC. While the State Forestry Commission developed a state park in conjunction with the Cheraw RDA, the state had very little connection with the park development in York and Cherokee counties until the 1940s, other than operating the group camps beginning in 1938.[55] However, state officials recognized that the federal government expected to turn the RDA over to the state after its development, and accordingly made plans for future operations of the RDA as a state park.

In 1936 the NPS drew up plans for the RDA's administration building. The original 1936 plans called for a small, one-story vernacular building, reminiscent of the early architecture of the upper Carolina region. Park officials deemed these plans too small, and additional plans were drawn up in 1937. The new plans called for a one-and-a-half-story symmetrical colonial revival building with an ell, a style chosen to reflect the historic significance of the park as well as being a popular American architectural style in the 1930s. The NPS planned to use the building to house offices, public restrooms, and a museum; the basement of the building originally housed restrooms for African American visitors to the park. The exterior of this building is symmetrical and features three dormer six-over-six windows, with the central entry flanked by two six-over-nine windows on each side. This building features a full front porch and is of stone construction with an interior stone chimney. The interior of the building also reflects the colonial revival style, complete with panel doors, chair rails, and reproduction colonial-style light fixtures.[56]

The NPS provided additional colonial revival plans for the superintendent's residence in 1940. The CCC began construction of the residence in September 1940, and completed the exterior of the building by November 1941. Following the entry of the United States into World War II and the disbanding of the CCC camps, the interior of the building was not finished until the mid-1940s. Like the administration building, the superintendent's residence is a one-and-a-half-story colonial revival building with an ell, which in this case houses a garage in the basement portion of the ell. The superintendent's residence has three bays on the first floor; the front entrance features a panel door with pilasters and a six-light transom flanked on either side with six-over-nine windows. Unlike the administration building, the superintendent's residence does

Kings Mountain National Military Battlefield, near York. The headquarters building at Kings Mountain demonstrates the CCC version of the Colonial Revival style. Photograph by the author

not have a front porch. Three six-over-six dormer windows in the gable roof and a gable-end chimney are the other main features of this frame structure.[57] Both the administration building and the superintendent's residence are listed as contributing properties in the Kings Mountain National Military Park National Register Historic District (listed 1995), and remain part of the national park.

In addition to the construction work at Kings Mountain, CCC enrollees found themselves doing a variety of work, as did most enrollees. The young men worked as foresters, truck drivers, cooks, mechanics, medical aids, masons, and landscapers, among a plethora of other occupations. One position at Kings Mountain was fairly unique, however. After building the "Visitor's House," a log structure designed to look like a pioneer cabin, two CCC boys were housed there on weekends, and served as interpretative guides for the battlefield.[58]

Other New Deal–era buildings still exist in the part of the RDA that was turned over to the state in 1942, including an elaborate stone bathhouse, picnic shelters, cabins, and numerous other structures such as water fountains, walls, roads, and trails. Although most of the shelters and other buildings that the CCC built at Kings Mountain are very similar to the picnic shelters and other structures at other South Carolina state parks, one picnic shelter at the RDA is unique. Shelter 1 (now identified as KM-S1) features an enclosed gable end made of round peeled log, rather than frame as in many of the other enclosed shelters. While the CCC and NPS tried to use natural materials as much as possible, they also tried to invoke the history of the area, and the log structure at Kings Mountain State Park should remind visitors of the typical log cabins that were home to the Over-mountain Men of the Carolinas who fought for the Patriots at Kings Mountain. The log shelter also features a stone chimney in the enclosed end, with a stone fireplace and brick-lined firebox.

The CCC also constructed two dams, creating two lakes, including the 8.5-acre Lake Robert Crawford, the focal point of the day-use area at the state park, and the 62.5-acre Lake York, created for the park's two group camps. The group camps, Camp York and Camp Cherokee, were designed with similar goals as the group camps at the Cheraw RDA, so that the "underprivileged children, farm clubs, and groups from the cities will be enabled to enjoy the healthful outdoor life during the summer months, at a low cost, under proper supervision," as stated by the State Forestry Commission.[59] Both camps feature a mess hall, staff quarters, and administration building, with cabin groups and latrines. Camp York has thirty sleeping cabins of four distinct types, all generally rectangular in shape with gable roofs, and primarily board-and-batten siding, with porches on the front of three of the four cabin types. Camp Cherokee features similar buildings, but as at Cheraw State Camp, this group camp is simpler architecturally. There are two cabin types at Camp Cherokee; as at Camp

Kings Mountain State Park. Shelter 1 is reminiscent of log construction used by the "Overmountain Men" and is one of the more unusual CCC-constructed shelters in the SC State Park system. Photograph by the author

York, the cabins are rectangular in plan with gable roofs, and of board-and-batten siding, with weatherboard siding in the gable ends. One group of the cabin types (six cabins) features projecting front porches with a gable roof, while the other type (sixteen cabins) do not have porches. Although many of the camp buildings, including the mess halls and sleeping cabins at both Camp York and Camp Cherokee, have been weatherized and updated, they maintain integrity and are all listed as contributing resources in the National Register nomination for Kings Mountain State Park.[60]

The period of CCC construction at Kings Mountain coincided with the NPS's work at the National Military Park, and the State Forestry Commission had very little input in the development of the RDA, other than the awareness that it would eventually fall under its jurisdiction once the federal government deeded the land to the state. However, as the CCC completed the recreational facilities at the RDA, the Forestry Commission administered these facilities as at other state parks, and Kings Mountain hosted the first Park Training Institute for state park employees as well as a week-long School for the Conservation of Natural Resources for South Carolina clubwomen, both in 1940.[61]

The federal presence in South Carolina's parks was essential in laying the foundation for a state park system in the state. The NPS, the RA, the WPA, and the CCC worked together to create the RDA at Cheraw, which became the first park developed in South Carolina. In turn, the State Forestry Commission worked with and learned from these federal agencies to plan for and develop a larger park system, utilizing labor provided by the young men of the CCC. These federal agencies worked together to obtain and improve several thousands of acres of land in South Carolina for the purposes of recreation of residents and tourists alike. The waysides at Colleton and elsewhere, and the new recreational facilities at Kings Mountain, attracted tourists, while putting to use lands that were not usable for farming, and put to work hundreds of young men through the work of the CCC. The State Forestry Commission watched, commented, and learned from the NPS, and, utilizing many of the same resources, developed South Carolina's state park system.

CHAPTER 6

Forestry Work and State Park Development

The South Carolina Forestry Commission and the Civilian Conservation Corps

After President Roosevelt proposed Emergency Conservation Work (ECW) in March 1933, the state foresters met in Washington, D.C., to learn the terms of the program and how it might benefit the forestry programs in the individual states. Members of the South Carolina Forestry Commission, which had been established in 1927, and the state forester returned to Washington to garner federal support in the acquisition of state forests within South Carolina. Organizations throughout the state, including chambers of commerce, women's clubs, and other civic organizations, lobbied for a release of the stringent requirements for appropriate land upon which to base conservation and forestry projects. The federal government agreed that it was in the best interest of the nation to provide fire control assistance to private landowners, and extended ECW to land where other associations existed to protect the land.[1] Although other federal agencies, such as the Department of Agriculture and the Soil Conservation Service, utilized Civilian Conservation Corps (CCC) workers and funding from ECW, the majority of CCC work in South Carolina, including state park development, was performed through the State Forestry Commission.

The first work conducted by the CCC in South Carolina related to fire prevention and fire protection through the construction of fire towers and their telephone connections throughout the coastal areas of South Carolina. The State Forestry Commission adopted a policy of constructing fire towers upon donated ten-acre tracts, along with small houses for the watchman and his family, who would live on-site. According to the Forestry Commission, this work would be undertaken without any expense to the state, while costing ECW over $150,000. This proposal for ECW in South Carolina was approved in Washington, and initially only one camp was approved, near Walhalla in Oconee County. By early June sixteen CCC camps were established in South Carolina, primarily for work related to fire prevention and protection under the auspices of the South Carolina Forest Service. Eleven of the counties hosting the new CCC camps would be locating the camps on privately owned forestland under protection through a cooperative program with the Forestry Commission; the other four counties were members of the Coastal Forest and Game Protection Association. The *State* newspaper in Columbia reported the types of work that the CCC enrollees would conduct, including "soil erosion, forest improvement, fire protection, trail construction, building of lookout towers, and all types of reforestation," and quoted State Forester H. A. Smith, who stated that this was "needed work that could not have been carried out" without the benefit of ECW. Smith also echoed Roosevelt when he stated that "thirty-five hundred boys cannot be taken from their homes into the counties of South Carolina without returning to their homes with a somewhat different conception of what forestry really means."[2] At the end of fiscal year 1932–33, the Forestry Commission lauded the work of the commissioners and the state forester in securing these initial camps in the Forestry Commission's first report dealing with ECW in South Carolina. The annual report lamented that "it is to be regretted, however, that she does not have the State Forest areas upon which real forestry can be practiced through the use of these camps."[3] The lack of funding at the state level would become a familiar refrain in the Forestry Commission's annual reports during the New Deal decade.

The Unemployment Relief Councils throughout the state selected the young men for CCC work, and over 8,000 applications were on file by mid-April 1933. South Carolina had filled the state's quota of 3,500 junior enrollees by the first week of June. Following their two-week conditioning period, for the most part, the South Carolina men selected stayed in the state for their work projects, even though the *State* pessimistically predicted that "it is doubtful whether there will be any projects in this state," in part as a result of the lack of state forests or state park land.[4] By the end of the first three months of ECW some 3,500 young men were working in South Carolina, with supervisory personnel numbering 160. The State Forestry Commission's annual report also listed 144 Chevrolet trucks that had been supplied for the transportation and work of the CCC men, along with orders in excess of $100,000 for small tools and equipment, which "in every case orders were placed with local stores," thus contributing to the local economies within the state.[5] By the end of June 1933 ECW in South Carolina had been judged a success, as is evidenced by the applications for fifty-six additional camps throughout the state. The Forestry Commission enthusiastically concluded its annual report with high praise for the work and the young men of the CCC:

> No report on the Emergency Conservation Project would be complete without a word as to the humanitarian side of the project. Thirty-five hundred boys are in the forests of South Carolina working for the preservation

of one of our greatest natural resources. They are performing all of the things that are necessary directly or indirectly for the protection of woods. They have come from town and country, from factory, office and school. They came unused to manual labor—ignorant of forest values—many even with contempt for contact with the soil. Some were undernourished and many were unversed in the ordinary regarding rules of health. Those boys today have a different attitude in regard to forest land. They have learned the joys of actual labor, of construction, of accomplishment. They are no longer afraid of manual labor, and where contact with the soil is necessary to achieve results, that contact is made. Almost without exception the boys have broadened out physically and mentally and they will return to their homes with a different viewpoint toward our greatest natural resource.[6]

Statements like these demonstrate that during the course of CCC work, officials realized the impact that the work was having not only changing the landscape and providing recreational opportunities for the state's residents but changing the lives of the young enrollees as well.

Although the State Forestry Commission obviously understood the importance of what the CCC and ECW offered the state of South Carolina as well as the young men of the state, this high praise for the program failed to influence the state legislature, which did not appropriate funding for the development of state forests or state parks, although the legislature added the development and operation of state parks to the responsibilities of the Forestry Commission, basically giving the commission additional responsibilities without providing any additional funding. During the first year of ECW projects in South Carolina, the federal government allowed for work to be conducted on private lands within forest protective associations, with an initial investment of over $5 million in the state.

In its report to the South Carolina General Assembly, the State Forestry Commission pointed out that the annual appropriations for forestry had never been more than $13,000, and that the value of the fire towers and housing constructed through ECW in the previous year exceeded the entire appropriations for forestry work in the state during the life of the commission. In addition to federal expenditures in the state, private landowners in the coastal counties spent over $14,000 on state forestry projects during the fiscal year, again, more than the state's expenditure for forestry in the entire state. The commission's report drew attention to the opportunities that ECW offered for expanding the state's forestry program, observing, "The time has come for South Carolina to place its forestry organization upon a sound financial basis . . . unless additional

Oconee State Park, Walhalla. Company 3449, Camp S-75. Photograph courtesy
of South Carolina Department of Parks, Recreation, and Tourism

funds are made available by the State . . . no request can be made for new Civilian Conservation Corps camps and it is extremely doubtful if we will be able to retain the ones we have."[7]

In spite of the lack of financial support of the state for forestry projects, the CCC and the State Forest Service accomplished a great deal during the CCC's first full year. Educational programming across the state included forestry schools for "farm boys," a training program for vocational teachers, and films and lectures by James D. Graham, a nationally known forestry expert, in the state's CCC camps. Fire prevention and protection programs were extended as well, especially given the severe fire season in 1933–34, when CCC camps engaged in fire fighting across the state. ECW projects included improvements to the fire towers, houses, and farms constructed for the watchmen in the previous year. The State Forestry Commission concluded detailing the fire protection program by stating, "what could easily have been one of the most severe fire seasons in the history of South Carolina was prevented very largely due to the presence of the Civilian Conservation Corps camps and the wholehearted cooperation of the boys."[8]

Although most South Carolina CCC workers during the first year were involved in forestry projects such as fire prevention, the biggest achievement for ECW in South Carolina during its first full year was the establishment of the state park system. From July 1933 to June 1934 the State Forestry Commission began planning for state parks and state forest parks on property in Aiken, Chesterfield, Sumter, Horry, and Dorchester counties, with additional plans to acquire park property along the southern coast, in the upstate mountains, in Chester County, and in the central northern part of the state, in order to establish a state park accessible to every citizen of South Carolina within a fifty-mile drive. The commission proudly highlighted the fact that while New York State had spent in excess of $50 million acquiring and developing state park lands, "the South Carolina system has not cost South Carolina one cent."[9] Using CCC camps designated to work on Forestry Commission lands for development of forestry parks was a creative use of ECW, but assisted in the development of some of the first parks in the state. ECW's state park program provided for the establishment of South Carolina's first state parks, and created a framework in which parks could be obtained, built, and administered. Even without a strong financial commitment on the part of the state legislature, ECW and CCC work in South Carolina provided a solid foundation for the state parks program.

Aiken State Park

The early CCC work at the Cheraw Recreational Demonstration Area (RDA) inspired other communities to seek CCC camps and the development of state park lands in their areas. State Forester H. A. Smith visited Aiken County in the early summer of 1933 to locate a CCC camp there to work on forestry projects. By the end of June Camp P-55 had been established at Montmorenci, ten miles outside of Aiken. Company 1438, made up almost entirely of South Carolina natives, arrived at P-55 in June 1933, and worked on forestry projects on private lands. By the spring of 1934 ECW was beginning to concentrate more and more on publicly owned lands, and local government officials in Aiken County feared that their CCC camp would be lost.[10]

In the summer of 1934 Aiken County purchased 700 acres of land along the banks of the Edisto River from four property owners for a little over $3,000, and then donated the land to the state; additional purchases later that year brought the total to more than 800 acres. State Forester Smith announced in August that this acreage would be set aside as a "state forest park and public recreation place," to include picnic grounds, bathing facilities, fishing ponds, and a bathhouse. With state-owned land acquired for the building of a state park, the Montmorenci camp was retained, and redesignated S-55 in October 1934. CCC Company 1438 began work there building Aiken State Park, and was replaced in early 1936 by Company 4470, an African American company, which worked at Aiken from January 1936 until December 1939. Company 4470 built the bulk of Aiken State Park, which officially opened to the public in August 1936, the third South Carolina state park to open to the public. That company constructed a superintendent's residence, two picnic shelters, and three fishing cabins by 1939, along with several auxiliary structures and dams for three small lakes. It also stocked the lakes with some 20,000 bass for fishing and built roads throughout the park. The county government officials hoped that the purchase and donation of this land for state park development would spur the federal government to purchase more land for the development of an RDA, like that at Cheraw. The county identified an additional 25,000 acres of land that could be secured at reasonable prices for its creation. The federal government never purchased more land in Aiken County, although the state purchased an additional 200 acres for Aiken State Park in 1954.[11]

The work of the CCC continued in fiscal year 1934–35, with the addition of new camps in South Carolina to assist in both forestry work and state park work. While other camps in South Carolina worked under the jurisdiction of the Department of Agriculture and the Soil Conservation Service, most camps in the state fell under the jurisdiction of the State Forestry Commission both for forestry work and state park work. The growth of forestry work in South Carolina required twelve new camps being approved in 1935, in addition to the eighteen camps already working in forestry- or park-related projects in the state. The importance and extent of the work of the Forestry Commission evidently reached the members of the legislature, as they appropriated funds to hire two new assistant state foresters to better administer the fire protection and state parks programs. The educational programs from the previous year continued, with increased interest at forestry schools, and additional educational programming in forestry in the CCC camps. The Forestry Commission, through the work of CCC participants, created forestry exhibits that were exhibited throughout the fall of 1934 at thirteen county fairs and at the state fair in Columbia. By the end of the fiscal year exhibits had been scheduled for the fall of 1935 in nineteen counties and again at the state fair. Forestry Commission personnel gave over fifty talks throughout the state to civic groups, and State Forester Smith gave radio talks broadcast from WIS in Columbia and WBT in Charlotte, North Carolina, and gave a nationwide broadcast on the state's newly established state park system from Washington, D.C. The Forestry Commission also sponsored a series of essay contests and poster contests for schools in the counties with fire protection systems or forest associations, as well as distributing 38,000 pieces of forestry educational literature in schools across the state. The commission carried its educational mission through to its state park work as well,

Chester State Park, Chester. The entrance to Chester State Park consists of a hand-carved stone wall on either side of the entrance drive. Photograph by the author

Chester State Park, Chester. Picnic shelter no. 1 at Chester overlooks the lake and was probably originally constructed by Company 4475 in 1935. Photograph by the author

hoping that by exposing Carolina schoolchildren to "the great outdoors," an environmental ethic would be inculcated "into the minds of our younger generation," for, in the words of the state forester, "he that loves a tree will protect a tree."[12]

Fiscal year 1934–35 was one of the most important to the fledgling state park program, as eight state parks were under construction by the end of the fiscal year. These parks included Cheraw, Edisto/Givhans Ferry, Poinsett, Myrtle Beach, Table Rock, Aiken, Edisto Beach, and Chester. In addition to these parks, the State Forestry Commission made plans for recently acquired land at Kings Mountain and on Paris Mountain, and for forestry land in Lee and Oconee counties. By 1934–35 the commission had established a written policy for state park recreational areas for which the CCC provided the funds and labor. The Forestry Commission's annual report for 1934–35 included paragraphs detailing the work completed at each park.[13]

State park land in 1935 totaled over 25,000 acres, all donated by private citizens, organizations, or county governments. The federal government provided the money and labor for park development, primarily through the work of the CCC, with assistance from the National Park Service (NPS) and the United States Forest Service. The State Forestry Commission recognized early on that the state would be responsible for the administration and operation of the parks. The commission proposed to raise money for park operation through the sale of concessions and from rental fees of camping sites and cabins; early revenue predictions were so optimistic that the commission also proposed to return 50 percent of any profits above actual expenses to the local school system in the county in which the park was located.[14] With an established methodology for the creation of state parks in South Carolina, new assistant state foresters in charge of ECW and state parks, and project funding and labor provided by the federal government through the CCC, South Carolina quickly extended its state park system. Governor Olin Johnston appointed L. C. Wannamaker of Cheraw as a commissioner on the State Forestry Commission, due in part to his dedication to the foundation of Cheraw State Park, and Wannamaker's influence pushed the momentum in state park work. The Forestry Commission obtained no additional land for new state parks during the fiscal year, but stayed busy working on lands that had already been obtained. Besides working on improvements at the already existing parks, and beginning work on the four parks planned for in the 1934–35 annual report, the new wayside park program was begun in South Carolina during the 1935–36 fiscal year. While the Forestry Commission recommended possible sites for the location of waysides and approved NPS plans for developments within the state, the NPS obtained the land and supervised the construction projects. In addition to the new waysides and the RDAs, nine CCC camps worked on state park projects throughout the state, and during the fiscal year over $258,000 had been expended on such work in South Carolina, exclusive of federal funding that paid, clothed, and housed the CCC workers. The Forestry Commission again demonstrated its pride in the work that had been done in the state parks by giving each park project a full paragraph in the annual report detailing the type of work finished or under way at each park, including the construction of fourteen cabins, ten shelters, three residences, and the completion of bathhouses at Myrtle Beach, Givhans Ferry, Paris Mountain, and Poinsett. The report stated that work at Givhans Ferry had been completed to such an extent that the CCC company (Company 2413) had been moved to another project, with a side camp from the company at Edisto Beach (Company 4480) brought in to complete the unfinished work there. Other indications of the parks' progress in the annual report are the interest demonstrated by citizens of the state as well as requests from outside the state for notices and articles to be printed in travel and outdoor magazines.[15]

In addition to the state park work undertaken in 1935–36, the CCC participated in other types of forestry work under the direction of the State Forest Service, including the development of state forests in Aiken, Oconee, Greenville, and Lee counties, and timber-type surveys in all counties in which a CCC camp was located. These state forests also saw development of what was originally termed "state forest parks," using CCC camps assigned to forestry projects, but in reality were developed and administered as additional state parks. The State Forestry Commission published a booklet, *The South Carolina Civilian Conservation Corps Forester,* for use in developing a forestry course through the CCC educational program. The commission also established a central warehouse near Camden, a concrete pipe plant in Sumter County, and a central repair shop for heavy equipment at Sumter. CCC enrollees staffed these facilities and received valuable vocational training in mechanics and pipe construction.[16]

Givhans Ferry State Park

The state park developed adjacent to the RDA at Cheraw had been designated as SP-1. SP-2, near Ridgeville in Dorchester County, began development during fiscal year 1934–35. On October 11, 1934, the state acquired from the local government land on the banks of the Edisto River for SP-2, originally called Edisto State Park. Like the land donated for other state parks, this land transaction contained conditions that the land must be used for a state park, and also that the State Forestry Commission and the state park would not pollute the river. Veteran Company 2413 moved to Dorchester County in October, and construction at SP-2 commenced rapidly. By March 1935 Project Superintendent James

Graham reported that the enrollees had not only set up their camp but had begun a major reforestation project and had completed a boathouse and a rest shelter, and had begun a picnic shelter on the park property, while also being designated the best camp in District I. Additionally the CCC was working with the state highway department to relocate a portion of State Highway 65 where it traveled through the park, and a "wading pool for kiddies" was being constructed on the banks of the Edisto. The park was renamed Givhans Ferry State Park by August 1935, to reduce confusion with the newly created Edisto Beach State Park on Edisto Island in nearby Charleston County.[17]

Poinsett State Park

In August 1934 Sumter County residents purchased a little over 1,000 acres of land, which was donated to the county for the purpose of the development of a recreational area and game refuge. The county government donated the land to the state for a state park, and in October 1934 CCC Company 421 began work at SP-3, Poinsett State Park. The park was named for South Carolina native Joel Roberts Poinsett. Poinsett was a true renaissance man—a naturalist, architect, engineer, and statesman (including secretary of war under President Martin

Poinsett State Park, unidentified CCC enrollees constructing Poinsett bathhouse, March 19, 1936. Photograph courtesy of South Carolina Department of Archives and History

Poinsett State Park trailside shelter, August 21, 1937. Photograph courtesy
of South Carolina Department of Archives and History

Van Buren). Poinsett, who has become immortalized in the flower bearing his
name, the poinsettia, is buried at the Church of the Holy Cross in Statesburg,
just down the road from the entrance to the state park.[18]

Initially Company 421 was one of the first CCC companies in South Carolina, organized in April 1933 in Kershaw County under the direction of Project
Superintendent R. A. Conard, who quickly was promoted to assistant state forester. Foreman J. S. H. Clarkson, a Camden resident, became project superintendent, and the company was moved to Sumter County. After setting up camp
facilities, the CCC began a road-building project in November 1934 and cleared
ten acres of land for a lake the next month, while also building footpaths, parking areas, and foundations for park buildings. By the summer of 1935 the CCC
had completed exterior work on the caretaker's house, the lake spillways, a picnic shelter, and various footpaths, bridges, and landscaping projects. Foundations had been laid for the bathhouse and lodge, and the CCC boys and some
members of the public were already swimming in the lake, although it had not
yet been completely filled. Unsupervised swimming led to a few near-drownings
and resulting heroics by CCC enrollees. The camp newspaper, *Poinsett Pointers*,
reported that 266 people visited the incomplete park on Sunday, May 12, and
that both a high school forestry class and a Boy Scout troop had utilized the
park. Red bud and longleaf pine nurseries had also been established on park-
land, fulfilling both forestry and state park missions.[19]

The architectural projects at Poinsett made good use of native materials, highlighting the local coquina rock in the picnic shelter and bathhouse construction.

The CCC administration gave careful consideration to the appearance of the buildings, especially the bathhouse and the caretaker's residence, as is evidenced by the correspondence between C. G. Mackintosh, the regional inspector, and H. E. Weatherwax, the regional officer in Richmond, Virginia, during the summer of 1935. Changes in plans for interior details at the bathhouse and exterior details at the caretaker's residence kept both projects from being completed that summer. The bathhouse, as originally constructed, served as a multipurpose building, containing a concession area, a kitchen and dining room, and a loggia, in addition to shower, dressing, and restroom facilities. Original plans called for the interior of the dining room to be covered with wood siding, although Clarkson suggested leaving the interior stonework exposed, highlighting the native coquina rock. This space has now been converted to office space and a nature museum for Poinsett State Park. Another architectural concern during the summer of 1935 was the exterior of the caretaker's house. Although the CCC had finished the construction of the house by the end of June 1935, several details remained unresolved, including the question of painting or whitewashing the cypress weatherboards and the brick used in construction of the foundation and chimneys. Regional Officer Weatherwax responded that in his opinion, the cypress weatherboarding should remain unpainted and allow to weather naturally, to a "delightful tone," and recommended the painting of trim work in gray to match the weatherboards, while painting the brickwork in the foundation and chimneys white, brown, or red, "mainly because the color of the brick used is not very attractive and because there is a difference in the brick used in the foundation and in the chimneys."[20] Similar correspondence throughout 1935 and 1936 regarding finish work and aesthetics for other projects at Poinsett is found in project files for picnic shelters. Weatherwax reported, for instance, that working shutters were added to a completed shelter to "add to the architectural appearance of the structure . . . and [provide] protection to persons who seek shelter in the building during windblown rainstorms."[21] These examples of aesthetic concern at Poinsett demonstrate the care and thought that went into the architectural elements in the state parks that the CCC constructed.

As noted earlier, work at Poinsett State Park was not without controversy during mid and late 1935. In July George Buell visited Sumter to inform the town leaders the CCC camp could be moved and that the work at Poinsett would either be completed by a "Negro CCC camp," or the camp itself would be abandoned and the state park work halted. County commissioners, city councilmen, and other town leaders discussed these options with Buell, State Forestry Commission officials, and even Senator Byrnes, expressing their desire to retain the white CCC camp and their opposition to its replacement with

Poinsett State Park, Sumter. This postcard from the 1940s features boating on
the CCC-constructed lake at Poinsett State Park. Author's collection

African Americans. Despite these objections, Company 421 was transferred to
Rock Hill for work in soil conservation. Superintendent Clarkson was transferred to Kings Mountain, and landscape architect Norman House received a
promotion to superintendent at Table Rock. Company 421 held a dance at Poinsett in honor of Clarkson in late July, and invited members of the community
to attend. Clarkson left Poinsett on August 3, 1935, and Company 421 left two
weeks later.[22]

F. H. Murray replaced Clarkson as project superintendent at Poinsett, and
Company 4475, made up of African Americans, arrived on September 5. Following a two-week conditioning period, during which time enrollees' work was
evaluated for skilled positions, Company 4475 began work surfacing park roads
and filling in the borrow pit, where rock for the spillway and other structures
had been obtained. They also completed the caretaker's house. In October the
African American company completed the road-surfacing and borrow pit oblit-
eration projects and, working with local experienced carpenters, finished a
shelter and the caretaker's garage, and did additional work on the bathhouse.
Although Superintendent Murray bragged that the African American enrollees
were "good workers" and that they worked efficiently, the community was dissatisfied with their presence. Company 4475 was transferred to the new state
park land at Chester on November 7, 1935, after only two months at Poinsett.

Poinsett State Park, unidentified CCC enrollees with CCC-constructed furniture for cabins, March 1, 1938. Photograph courtesy of South Carolina Department of Archives and History

Work at Poinsett ceased for about two months, until Veterans Company 2413 moved from Givhans Ferry to replace Company 4473 in February 1936, primarily working on landscaping projects, finishing structures that had been left incomplete, and building two overnight cabins. By the time of the park's official opening in summer 1937, park facilities included the dam and lake; bathhouse and beach area; caretaker's residence, barn, and garage; picnic areas and two shelters; and two one-bedroom cabins for overnight camping. Poinsett State Park officially opened in the summer of 1937, the second state park open to the public.[23] Veterans Company 2413 then moved to Greenwood County in the western part of the state to construct Greenwood State Park, becoming the only CCC company in the state to work on three state parks.

Lee State Park

Lee State Park, in Lee County in the central part of the state, was one of the parks originally classified as a "state forestry park." Most of the land set aside for the park was donated to the state by Lee County, which had acquired most of it through tax delinquency proceedings, while other adjacent lands were purchased from landowners. A small cadre of CCC enrollees arrived at the site on June 24, 1935, to begin preparations for Company 4471, which arrived on August 16, 1935, and named the camp Camp Robert E. Lee. The CCC camp was located across the road from the present-day park entrance. In addition to developing state park facilities at Lee, Camp P-88 also functioned as a more traditional forestry camp, conducting timber-type surveys, reforesting the area, and working with private landowners; a side camp from P-88 built the fire tower and watchman's house near Dovesville. Lee State Park opened to the public in June 1941, although many of the facilities were completed before then, and the public had been using the area while the rest of the park was under construction. At Lee, Company 4471 constructed the entrance gates, the Loop Road through the park, artesian wells, picnic shelters, cabins, and other structures. Miles Chalmers, an enrollee at Lee from 1937 to 1939, recalled building the Loop Road with mostly shovels and picks: "We thought it was hard then, but when you think about it, it was a lot of fun."[24]

Paris Mountain State Park

From the beginning of state park work in South Carolina, State Forestry Commission officials desired the construction of a state park in the mountainous areas of the upcountry. In December 1934 several local organizations in Greenville met regarding the watershed property at Paris Mountain, which had been preserved to provide reservoirs for the city of Greenville. At this meeting the city council, the Chamber of Commerce, the Water Commission, and the local Park Commission agreed to donate 1,100 acres to the state, with the stipulation that the land be used for the development of a state forest park. The state officially acquired the land in April 1935, and CCC Company 440 (S-90, Camp Palmetto) began work on the state park in the fall.[25]

By the end of the year the CCC had constructed a stone bathhouse, an athletic field, a picnic area, a parking area, and two miles of unpaved road. The reservoirs formerly impounded by the use of the area as a watershed were used as lakes and swimming areas within the state park, while a fourth reservoir, outside the park boundaries, continued to be used as a water source for nearby Greenville.[26] The bathhouse is located beside Lake Placid, one of the three lakes constructed from the reservoirs. A rectangular frame building, it is covered in

Lee State Park, near Bishopville. This picnic table uses locally found materials, including a mill grindstone. Although the seats have been replaced, the new ones mimic the CCC construction originally located here. Photograph by the author

rough rubble masonry with a gable roof. A shed roof extension with stone pillars covers a front porch running the full length of the lakeside elevation. A few alterations have occurred to the building, including the addition of a concession area on the west and a low stone wall on the porch. However, these additions echo the rustic style of the bathhouse, and the building retains a high degree of integrity.

While the work proceeded rapidly at Paris Mountain, it evidently did not please everyone, as demonstrated by a report from the regional inspector, C. G. Mackintosh, to the Regional Office in Richmond. This report, which was forwarded to Conrad Wirth in Washington, D.C., details an inspection that Mackintosh conducted in January 1936, "without use of official car or uniform," in which he labeled "the whole scheme [at Paris Mountain] a gigantic fiasco."[27] Mackintosh acknowledged that the land at Paris Mountain was desirable for park development, but he believed that this "forest park" should have been left in a more natural state rather than developed primarily for recreational use. Mackintosh contrasted what he called the "superb and abundant" forests and ground cover at Paris Mountain with the poor quality of land being developed for most other state parks in South Carolina. In his opinion, the masonry construction at the bathhouse "would not be pleasing to the author of *Park Structures*," and he decried the development of the beach and swimming area "using not too clean sand."[28] Mackintosh's report took four pages to sum up his opinion of the failings of the work at Paris Mountain, concluding with his recommendation that "this area be taken over yesterday for development as a Metropolitan or Municipal County Park and that the Third Regional Office technical staff be promptly dispatched there to determine a policy and program

Lee State Park. This water fountain made of stone rubble construction demonstrates the CCC's preferred use of locally available materials in a variety of construction projects. Photograph by the author

Paris Mountain State Park, bathhouse, ca. 1940. Photograph courtesy
of South Carolina Department of Parks, Recreation, and Tourism

for halting the gross misuse of Federal Funds."[29] In spite of Mackintosh's misgivings regarding the early proceedings at Paris Mountain State Park, the CCC and State Forest Service continued to develop the area as a state park, complete with recreational facilities.

Similar to the desire to promote cooperative recreation at the RDAs at Cheraw and Kings Mountain, park development at Paris Mountain included facilities for larger groups. CCC construction continued through 1940, including four additional picnic shelters, the superintendent's house, an amphitheater (1940), and a group camp known as Camp Buckhorn (1936–37). Camp Buckhorn, situated northwest of Lake Buckhorn, consists of a lodge, staff cabin, nine camper cabins, a latrine, a fire ring / council circle, and a parking area. The lodge is a T-shaped building with a cross-gable roof and three porches, covered in board-and-batten siding, over a partial basement foundation of rubble stone construction. The south elevation, facing the lake, has a shed-roof porch supported by rubble piers. The staff cabin, located near the lodge, is a one-story square frame building on rubble piers. The camper cabins are physically separated from the lodge and staff cabin by a small creek, and all nine are square frame buildings on stone foundations. Two of the camper cabins have exterior stone chimneys. Detailing at the lodge, staff cabin, and camper cabins has similar decorative elements, such as craftsman-style exposed rafters and heavy porch posts and rails. Originally roofed with hand-riven wooden shingles, the roofs have all been replaced with composition shingles.[30]

By 1940 Paris Mountain State Park could boast that it was the most extensively used of all of South Carolina's state parks, with over 157,000 visitors annually, in part a result of the large population centers nearby in Greenville. Both the naturalistic setting, so prized by Mackintosh early in the park's development, and the recreational opportunities of swimming and picnicking were great draws for Greenville residents. The group camp facilities were popular almost immediately with youth groups from Greenville and the surrounding areas.[31] Forestry Commission officials sought to open a segregated park for African Americans in Greenville County by the late 1940s, goal that was partly a result of the success of Paris Mountain State Park and partly because of the growing population of African Americans in the upstate. Indeed Camp Buckhorn, the site of the former CCC enrollee camp, was initally considered as the most desirable site for an African American park. Because of the opposition of white property owners in the area, this plan was quickly dropped. Eventually the Pleasant Ridge park property was purchased near Cleveland and operated first as a segreageted park for African Americans and then as a state park until 1988. The park was turned over to Greenville County in 1988 and is now operated as a municipal park.[32]

While the CCC performed a variety of valuable work under the administration of the State Forestry Commission, the annual reports continually regard the state park work as the most important to the general public, and spend most of the space allotted in detailing the work at the state parks. The work completed at several of the state parks throughout the early years of ECW in South Carolina demonstrate a high attention to detail in recreational and park planning as well as to the architectural details in the individual structures. The state followed the federal government's lead in developing its recreational facilities at the state parks, and in doing so created a foundation for a growing state park system. In a creative use of CCC camps assigned to forestry projects, the Forestry Commission began developing "forestry parks" on publicly owned forestry land, which then added to the emerging state park program. Although the majority of the New Deal state park land was acquired in the early years of the CCC program, it was the last half of the decade that saw the greatest period of construction and public use in South Carolina's new state parks.

CHAPTER 7

South Carolina's "Breathing Spaces"

Opening and Operating the State Parks during the New Deal Decade

Franklin Roosevelt's goals of conservation, recreation, and economic benefits through the Civilian Conservation Corps (CCC) became firmly entrenched in the rhetoric of the South Carolina State Forestry Commission by mid-decade. Construction and development of several state parks and the federal recreation areas were well under way. For the most part, the latter half of the 1930s saw the Forestry Commission learning to operate the state parks, while at the same time continuing their growth and beginning acquisition and construction at others. During the last half of the 1930s, state park administration in South Carolina became institutionalized, with the formal founding of the Division of State Parks under the State Forestry Commission.

The State Forestry Commission demonstrated a strong environmental and preservation ethic, and highlighted the creation, maintenance, and use of state parks as a laudable method of reaching Roosevelt's goals. The 1936–37 annual report to the state General Assembly warned that South Carolina was "rapidly losing her beautiful scenic spots," but that through the state parks, it would be possible to "save the pieces . . . for ourselves and posterity," while at the same time doing "much work in 'human conservation.'" The report claimed that the state parks "will provide 'breathing spaces' from crowded cities; our people will learn to know and love the freedom of the great out of doors."[1] The report also highlighted the educational possibilities of state parks, including teaching children the value of "Nature" and a love for the open air that would in turn create healthy minds and bodies, and for providing a camp atmosphere for children who could not otherwise afford it. Perhaps most important, the Forestry Commission offered a definition of a state park: "A State Park may be defined as an area of land possessing unusual natural beauty, historical interest, educational value, or recreational importance, which has been acquired by the State, developed, and to be preserved forever for the use of the people in securing wholesome recreation and education."[2] This definition would assist the commission in choosing areas of land to be developed, and guide their development for several years to come. The early state parks focused primarily on land reclamation, recreation, and preservation of natural landscapes, and, to a lesser extent, education. The mention of preservation of historical sites paved the way for the development of later state historical parks.

While state park work was the main focus of the work of the State Forestry Commission in the mid-1930s, other CCC camps worked with the commission in fire prevention and development of the state forests and on approved privately owned land. In fire prevention work, CCC forestry camps constructed truck trails, fire towers, and houses for the watchmen, and connected tower stations with telephone lines, as well as fighting fires as needed. By December 1938 some sixty-five fire towers had been constructed or were under construction by the CCC in South Carolina. These camps also performed more conventional forestry work such as seed collection, nursery operation, tree planting, and timber-type surveys. Camps working on forestry projects also participated in recreational construction in state forests, similar to those in state parks, in that they built dams, bathhouses, boathouses, picnic shelters, and cabins in the state forests in Greenville, Oconee, Aiken, Lee, Barnwell, and Richland counties, which became the Paris Mountain, Oconee, Aiken, Lee, Barnwell, and Sesquicentennial state parks. In spring 1937 the central warehouse was moved from Camden to Sumter, near the site of the central repair shop and the concrete pipe plant, consolidating much of the support work for all of the state's CCC camps.[3] Although the Forestry Commission acknowledged the important contributions of the CCC to its work in general forestry projects, including timber-type surveys and fire prevention, it devoted only nine pages of its thirty-plus-page annual report to these activities, choosing to focus most of the report on the exciting developments in the state parks.

By June 30, 1937, the State Forestry Commission, in cooperation with the CCC, the National Park Service (NPS), and the United States Forest Service (USFS), had developed approximately 13,000 acres in the state parks, along with 17,000 additional acres under federal ownership in the wayside parks and the Recreational Demonstration Areas (RDAs) at Cheraw and Kings Mountain. Seven CCC camps worked on eight of the state parks, with other camps assigned to the RDAs at Cheraw and Kings Mountain. The parks at Aiken and Givhans Ferry were almost completed, with side camps providing additional support, and the forestry camps at Lee, Oconee, and Paris Mountain worked on recreational development at the state parks there.[4]

Although the State Forestry Commission lauded the work of the CCC and the assistance of the federal government in the development and creation of the state park system, the commission expressed concern about its ability to properly maintain, equip, and staff the parks once the CCC finished the building projects. While the federal government provided the funding for park facilities, the state would have to commit funding for maintenance, staff, and supplies. The financial statement showed that while the state had expended over $20,000 (in addition to federal funding) during the fiscal year, only about $4,000 had been received from cabin rentals, concessions, dressing room fees, bathing suit rentals, and other revenue-generating activities. However, the commission justified this expense by explaining that a great deal of the cost was initial set-up fees, such as the purchase of towels and bathing suits for the bathhouses, and equipping the vacation cabins with appliances, furniture, and cooking utensils. The commission reminded the General Assembly that the CCC would not always be available to provide maintenance for the state parks, nor would the CCC provide permanent caretakers: "These things are the responsibility of the State, and to secure the greatest gain from the parks, the maintenance and operation must be of a high standard."[5]

By mid-decade the fledgling state park program had blossomed into a popular recreational program around the state. The State Forestry Commission boasted that a state park was within seventy-five miles of any South Carolina resident (although the commission had made no meaningful provisions for the 40 percent of the state's residents who were African American), and that the recreational activities offered were free for the most part, providing wholesome outdoor activities for rich and poor alike. During the twelve-week period in the summer of 1936 that Myrtle Beach, Poinsett, and Aiken were officially opened, park staffs recorded attendance of almost 50,000 people, with over 42,000 guests visiting Myrtle Beach alone. The Forestry Commission hoped to use these numbers to highlight the importance of the new state park system both to the General Assembly and South Carolina citizens alike, and to convince the state's legislators to increase funding for the maintenance and further development of the state parks when CCC funding and labor would no longer be available.[6]

Among the CCC's many accomplishments in South Carolina's state parks during fiscal year 1936–37 was the completion of two bathhouses, thirty-nine cabins, nine shelters, seven water fountains, twenty-one camp fireplaces, 29 acres of landscaping (not including more than 600 acres of "vista cutting for effect"), and 8 acres of camp or picnic ground development, not to mention the more mundane (and more difficult to quantify) work of fire prevention, seed collection, weed eradication, and general emergency work. While a great amount of work was completed at the twelve parks in 1936–37, the most significant event of the year came on July 1, 1936, when Myrtle Beach State Park opened to the public, marking the first official opening of any of South Carolina's state parks. By June 1, 1937, six state parks had opened: Myrtle Beach, Poinsett, Aiken, Givhans Ferry, Oconee, and Paris Mountain. Governor Olin D. Johnston and U.S. Senator Ben T. Leppard, along with official representatives of the NPS, the

USFS, and the State Forestry Commission, spoke at formal dedication ceremonies for the state park system at Myrtle Beach on June 17, 1937, and at Paris Mountain on July 15, 1937.[7]

Myrtle Beach State Park

Established in 1912 as a partnership between Conway natives and brothers Franklin and Donald Burroughs and New York–based investor Simeon Brooks Chapin, the Myrtle Beach Farms Company was founded to enhance the coastal strand at Myrtle Beach, managing some 65,000 acres for residential and tourist development. By the mid-1920s Myrtle Beach had developed as a tourist destination, with the opening of hotels, guesthouses, a pavilion, and a bathhouse. But lack of transportation infrastructure worried many of the investors and board members of the Myrtle Beach Farms Corporation, who sold the majority of their holdings to Greenville textile magnate John T. Woodside in 1926, retaining some 1,300 acres of beachfront and commercial property in downtown Myrtle Beach. Woodside intended to develop a master-planned community, including homes, churches, schools, and all necessarily infrastructure, as well as tourist accommodations including hotels, a boardwalk, and a game preserve. As Myrtle Beach historian Barbara Stokes has observed, Woodside's "energy and vision were infectious. Unfortunately his timing was not good."[8] Woodside's textile investments received a direct hit from the stock market crash even as his Ocean Forest Hotel in Myrtle Beach opened with a grand celebration, and by 1933 Myrtle Beach Farms Corporation, which held the mortgage for the property, regained its property at a tax sale, with significant improvements.[9]

The Myrtle Beach Farms Corporation donated 320 acres, including beachfront, for a state park in August 1934, and CCC Company 1408 moved to the site for Camp SP-4 in November 1934. During the spring of 1935 Company 1408 began work on the state park, and its first permanent building, the administration building, was all but complete by May. Enrollees bragged in their camp newspaper that the building was the first park structure "throughout the parks in the United States" to receive a coat of white paint, where other buildings were left to weather naturally or were stained. The construction methods and architectural style received a great deal of attention in the camp newsletter, which commented on the administration building's relationship to the existing buildings in the Conway area, and described it as a "glorified negro shack . . . with wide clapboards indicative of Southern Colonial architecture."[10]

By its opening in July 1936 the South Carolina's first state park boasted a swimming beach, picnic area, playgrounds, large bathhouse, boardwalk, and pavilion. Although members of the State Forestry Commission did not think that the park was finished, they believed enough facilities were in place to allow

Myrtle Beach State Park, Myrtle Beach. Front elevation of bathhouse near completion, March 19, 1936. Photograph courtesy of South Carolina Department of Archives and History

Myrtle Beach State Park. This postcard from the 1940s features the impressive bathhouse at Myrtle Beach, designed to serve two hundred guests per day. Author's collection

the public to officially use the park. The public already had been "unofficially" using Myrtle Beach's recreational facilities, as was the case in the other state parks under development. The Forestry Commission hoped that by opening the parks at Myrtle Beach, Poinsett (on August 5), and Aiken (on August 19) in the summer of 1936, that it would provide valuable experience in the actual operation of state parks and their facilities. At Myrtle Beach the Forestry Commission employed a recreational director, five lifeguards, a concessions operator,

Myrtle Beach State Park. Following the demolition of the Myrtle Beach bathhouse in 1967, a camp store/cabin unit was constructed at the state park using the remaining portions of the bathhouse. Photograph by the author

Myrtle Beach State Park, Myrtle Beach. Shelter 1 at Myrtle Beach is a large version of the rectangular plan favored in many of South Carolina's state parks. This shelter is enclosed at each end, and features a large impressive fireplace and chimney. Photograph by the author

Myrtle Beach State Park, Myrtle Beach. Chimney detail, shelter 1.
Photograph by the author

a bathhouse manager, a policeman, and two "colored attendants" to serve the white park visitors.[11]

South Carolina's first state park vacation cabins were also under construction at Myrtle Beach. This experiment was both controversial and popular. Myrtle Beach locals and NPS officials feared that vacation cabins would be competition to the local hotels and guesthouses, but State Forester H. A. Smith assured them that only a few cabins would be built, and would not compete with local tourist accommodations, reminding everyone that "the real purpose behind State Parks is to give to those of the lower income bracket an opportunity to enjoy the pleasures of a resort place without running up against commercial prices."[12] Enrollees at SP-4 predicted the popularity of the vacation cabins in May 1937 when they pointed out in their newsletter that "after all, there are only five cabins and five won't go very far with a million and a quarter people in your own state wanting them." Also popular was the first state park trailer camp, which provided water and electrical hook-ups for autocampers. The innovative trailer camp was quickly copied at other popular state parks such as Poinsett, the second state park officially opened to the public.[13]

Oconee State Park

State forestry park development continued along with state park work. Oconee State Park, near Walhalla in Oconee County in the northwestern corner of the state, opened to the public in June 1937. Two years earlier Oconee County had donated 1,165 acres to the State Forestry Commission for state park development, with the stipulation that if the use of the land changed, its title would revert back to the county. Almost immediately CCC Company 3449 moved in, establishing Camp S-75 on July 16, 1935, operating as a forestry project under the direction of foreman J. R. McClees. Among their first projects, other than camp construction, was the creation of a dam and lake for swimming, and a bathhouse. By the time of the park's opening in June 1937, Oconee boasted two man-made lakes, a bathhouse, three parking areas, two picnic shelters, and roads and hiking trails.[14]

One of the first buildings constructed at Oconee, the bathhouse was constructed of rough-cut ashlar stone, quarried from nearby Stumphouse Mountain. A piazza faces the lake, with a hipped roof supported by paired square timbers (replaced in kind in the late 1940s). A gable roof on the east side of the building covers a flagstone surface, which originally served as a covered boat dock and leads to the dam spillway. Two picnic shelters sit on the northwest shore of the lake. Shelter 1 is a large structure, sited on a slope above the lake, and featuring a large stone centrally located fireplace. The gable roof is supported by chestnut log posts; its original wood shake shingles were replaced with composition shingles ca. 1950. In contrast to Shelter 1, Shelter 2 is a

Oconee State Park, bathhouse under construction, ca. 1934. Photograph courtesy of South Carolina Department of Parks, Recreation, and Tourism

smaller structure, covering only one picnic table, and features a gable roof with rough-cut ashlar stonework support pillars over a poured concrete foundation. Three sides of the shelter have a low stone wall.[15]

Oconee State Park has twenty cabins, best described as variations on the theme of rustic park architecture, and a relatively large number of family camping cabins as compared with many of the other state parks. CCC Company 3449 began construction of the first six cabins in 1935, and they were completed by the park's opening in June 1937. Located north of the lake, each of these cabins has two bedrooms and one bath, but they vary slightly from one story to one-and-one-half stories, and two of the six (Cabins 4 and 6) feature a T-shaped plan rather than the rectangular plan common to the other four. All six cabins are situated on stone rubblework foundations, but siding varies from board-and-batten siding (Cabins 1, 3, and 4) to log chinked with concrete (Cabins 2, 5, and 6).

Two additional groups of cabins were constructed in 1938. Cabins 8–13 were all constructed as one-bedroom cabins, and are more uniform than the first group. Cabin 8 was enlarged in the 1960s for staff housing at the park, and the other five cabins in this group have been altered with the enclosure of a portion of their full porches to provide an extra bedroom. However, for the most part these cabins retain their integrity and are consistent with CCC design and construction. CCC enrollees also built the final group of cabins, in 1939–40. These cabins are also located southeast of the lake in a wooded area, with porches overlooking the lake. Cabin 14 is an L-shaped, one-story cabin, with board-and-batten siding on a stone rubble foundation. Cabins 15, 17, and 19 are built to the same design and are rectangular, one-and-a-half-story buildings, with board-and-batten siding on stone rubble foundations, with full front porches facing the lake. Cabins 16, 18, and 20 are L-shaped, one-story cabins, with board-and-batten siding on stone rubble foundation piers, filled with concrete block. Half-porches are inset in the ell and face the lake. These cabins feature exterior rubble stone chimneys and stone rubblework steps leading from the porch. Including the cabins, Oconee State Park retains over sixty original CCC buildings and structures that contribute to its listing on the National Register of Historic Places.[16]

By July 1938 the CCC enrollees at Walhalla working on Oconee State Park could report in their camp newspaper, the *Oconee Mountaineer,* that they had built a "mountain playground, a vacationists' paradise" in the lake and dam, the scenic roadway, cabins, picnic shelters, bathhouse, and caretaker's residence. They credited this "paradise" to their foreman, J. R. McClees, and congratulated him on a job well done, one well rewarded with a promotion to the position of field inspector for the State Forestry Commission. At the same time, the park had grown quite popular, and automobile traffic required the construction

Oconee State Park, Walhalla. The bathhouse and people enjoying the recreational opportunities at the park are the highlights of this postcard from the 1940s. Author's collection

of additional parking areas and the widening of the road leading to the park from State Highway 24. The South Carolina Highway Department offered the enrollees a chance to use their paving equipment to widen and pave the dirt road, but gave them only five days, requiring shift work twenty-four hours a day. The enrollees stepped up to the challenge and completed the roadwork in the allotted time.[17]

The members of Company 3449 celebrated the fifth anniversary of the CCC with special articles in their camp newsletter, including one highlighting the work of the CCC in Oconee County. In addition to the state park work conducted by Company 3449, the newsletter showcased the work of Companies 439 and 462, initially assigned to F-1 and F-2 elsewhere in the county in 1933. According to the *Oconee Mountaineer*, these projects had constructed fifty miles of surfaced roads, seventeen miles of trails, fifty-five miles of telephone line, and a picnic area, as well as the Walhalla Fish Hatchery and the forty fish-rearing pools there. As part of the fifth anniversary celebration, approximately 600 guests attended an "open house" held in April 1938 at the camp, featuring tours of the state park, lectures, a camp glee club performance, and various demonstrations of CCC skills and activities such as first aid and life-saving. Since the state park work had been completed, most members of the company prepared to vacate the camp in the spring of 1938 and relocate for similar state park work at Mt. Mitchell, North Carolina, although at least ten enrollees transferred to another CCC company bound for Oregon.[18]

Fiscal year 1937–38 marked the first full year of state park operation in South Carolina, and six state parks were in full operation by that year, including Myrtle Beach, Poinsett, Aiken, Givhans Ferry, Paris Mountain, and Oconee. Some facilities were available to the public at Edisto Beach and Table Rock state parks. The group camps at the RDA at Cheraw opened briefly in August 1937, and reopened along with the group camp at Kings Mountain in June 1938. In addition to the successful operation of these state parks, the State Forestry Commission's annual report stated that four new park areas had been added to the system, including Barnwell State Park in Barnwell County, Sesquicentennial State Park in Richland County, Greenwood State Park in Greenwood County, and Hunting Island State Park in Beaufort County. By the end of the fiscal year the Forestry Commission could report that CCC camps were already at work at Barnwell and Sesquicentennial, and camps were scheduled to arrive at Hunting Island and Greenwood in the late summer of 1938, being transferred from Edisto Beach and Poinsett state parks, respectively.[19]

The CCC accomplished a great deal during fiscal year 1937–38, including the building of a dam and spillway, a road, and fish-rearing ponds at Table Rock State Park; a dam and spillway and group camp at Cheraw; a trailer camp at Myrtle Beach; completion of the bathhouse and construction of three vacation cabins at Edisto Beach; and completion of a trailer camp and three vacation cabins at Poinsett. These major construction projects were in addition to the other types of CCC construction projects and other work undertaken in the state parks. For example, the State Forestry Commission recorded that the CCC constructed seventy picnic table–and–bench combinations, thirteen fireplaces, and three lodges in the parks, in addition to constructing over 12,000 square yards of parking spaces and moving and planting over 90,000 trees and shrubs.[20]

State parks saw a dramatic increase in visitors during the year, recording over 478,000 visitors in 1937–38, a significant increase over the previous year when only a few of the parks were open, and those for only a brief time. This large number of park users provided the State Forestry Commission with a baseline by which to measure future park attendance. Visitors were not charged an entrance fee to the state parks, so funds were only generated by concessions and rental fees, and associated fees for the group camps. During the fiscal year, the parks generated slightly over $13,200 in income, including almost $4,000 in cabin rentals and almost $3,000 in group camp rentals. The vacation cabins proved to be a success during the first full year of park operation, housing over 1,600 people during the weeks the cabins were available for rental. The Forestry Commission made sure to note that of the thirty-eight vacation cabins that had been constructed, only thirty-one were available for public rental. Four of the other cabins were used to house park employees, and the remaining three were not being used because of "lack of funds to equip them."[21]

Funding remained a priority theme of the State Forestry Commission's annual report, especially related to the fledgling state park system, as it would throughout the years of CCC involvement with the parks and the commission. The first pages of the annual report lamented the fact that a lack of state funds could cost the state CCC camps, and that much available labor was not being put to use because the state's appropriations were insufficient in funding more than one construction project per park per year. The commission reported that for all activities (including forestry and fire prevention, as well as state parks), total expenditures during the fiscal year reached slightly over $205,000, and that the General Assembly had appropriated only $62,500 for the entire year. The rest of the expenses came from federal dollars and county money. In addition to the existing shortfall in state appropriations, which seems to have occurred each year, the unprecedented use of the state parks created a larger maintenance bill than previously had been anticipated.[22] The financial woes of the State Forestry Commission, especially in the area of state park operation, would plague the park system throughout the years of CCC operation.

Sesquicentennial State Park

One of the new parks added to the state park system in 1937–38 was Sesquicentennial State Park in northeast Richland County. The state capital of Columbia celebrated its sesquicentennial anniversary in March 1936, complete with pageants, balls, parades, football games, concerts, and a commemorative legislative session where the members of the General Assembly appeared in period costume, including frock coats, knee breeches, and wigs. The Columbia Sesquicentennial Commission, led by State Senator James H. Hammond, financed the various festivities through the sale of commemorative coins marking the city's momentous anniversary.[23]

At the end of the celebration year, an audit of the Sesquicentennial Commission's financial records revealed that a little over $26,000 remained from the sale of the commemorative coins, and Senator Hammond discussed the disbursement of these funds with Columbia mayor Lawrence B. Owens through the spring of 1937. The Columbia Chamber of Commerce passed a resolution at the end of 1936 recommending that the Sesquicentennial Commission spend any leftover funds for "permanent and commemorative purposes," and Hammond and Owens discussed the possibilities of erecting historical markers throughout Columbia, the establishment of a botanical garden at the University of South Carolina, and the creation of a state or municipal park to mark the sesquicentennial celebration. Hammond, Owens, the commission, the chamber of

Sesquicentennial State Park, Columbia. Shelter 1 at Sesquicentennial, although a variety of the standard rectangular plan, features the use of concrete construction, a highly unusual construction material and technique found in the state parks. Photograph by the author

Sesquicentennial State Park, Columbia. Shelter 1, interior detail. Photograph by the author

commerce, and the city council agreed to the erection of fifty-two historical markers, primarily in downtown Columbia, explaining the significance of street names and sites of historical importance, expending some $3,200 for this purpose. The commission also made a $6,000 donation to the University of South Carolina for the purpose of creating a botanical garden or arboretum, and began investigating the possibility of purchasing property for the development of a park.[24]

With the examples of Myrtle Beach, Poinsett, and Table Rock already in place, the city of Columbia asked the State Forestry Commission to investigate appropriate sites in Richland County upon which a state park could be suitably developed according to state and federal guidelines. The Forestry Commission identified two tracts upon which a state park could be developed in Richland County, the Messers Mill tract on Old Camden Road and the Dent property northeast of Columbia. After fully investigating both of these possibilities, the city of Columbia purchased 1,415.5 acres from the Dent family in August 1937 and donated the land to the state for the development of Sesquicentennial State Park.[25]

CCC Company 4469 had been established in June 1935 near the Richland/Kershaw County line along U.S. Highway 1, near the Dent property chosen for Sesquicentennial State Park. Camp P-71 had been working on forestry projects

Sesquicentennial State Park, Columbia. The large bathhouse and concessionaire at Sesquicentennial went over budget, but the Forestry Commission argued that it was really three buildings instead of one. Photograph by the author

on private lands in the Pontiac area, such as the fire tower located near the entrance of the state park. Following approval of the state park project, the enrollees immediately began work on the park, constructing a lake, bathhouse, picnic shelters, and a caretaker's residence. Work at Sesquicentennial State Park proceeded rapidly, and the park officially opened to the public in June 1940.[26]

Construction at Sesquicentennial State Park, as at the other state parks, made use of locally available materials, but in the central portion of the state, one of the most plentiful construction materials was sand, leading to park buildings unique both in the state and across the country. Although there was some hesitation and reluctance on the part of the regional forester and the landscape architects, the use of concrete construction for the park was approved as an experimental construction technique. The large bathhouse at Sesquicentennial received a great deal of attention from the regional office, and when an inspector inquired as to the projected cost of the building, he was shocked at the projected $4,000 figure. The inspector told State Forestry Commission Assistant Director R. A. Conard that Washington had imposed a $2,500 limit per building, and that he feared trouble for the park. Conard, not to be deterred, explained that the bathhouse was really three structures in one, providing not only bathhouses for both males and females but also a concession stand, so in fact he was saving money. The inspector laughed, and said, "Go ahead. We'll see if we can get away with it." By the 1950s the Forestry Commission could report that the experimental concrete construction was a success, in that not only were the buildings pleasing in appearance, but they also needed less maintenance than some of the other buildings in the state parks.[27]

Although seven state parks all over the state had opened in 1936 and 1937 (Myrtle Beach, Poinsett, Aiken, Givhans Ferry, Oconee, Paris Mountain, and Edisto Beach), and the RDAs at Cheraw and Kings Mountain were both operational, the State Forestry Commission had undertaken very little in the way of publicity to lure additional visitors to the state parks. The commission spent the first two years of parks operations learning how to establish and operate a system of parks, not on creating recreational or educational plans for visitors to the park. However, throughout the spring and summer of 1939 state park directors encouraged their employees to more fully engage the parks' visitors, by leading nature hikes, organizing recreational events and competitions, and providing instruction in swimming and diving, among other types of organized activities. The Recreational Division of the Works Progress Administration (WPA) assisted state parks employees in this effort. The more proactive activity program was well received, and the Forestry Commission reported that "this program is considered as the greatest forward step for State Parks during the past fiscal year."[28]

Sesquicentennial State Park, Columbia. The State Commission of Forestry erected this monument "dedicated to the recreation of the people" at Sesquicentennial State Park in 1941, shortly after the park opened. Photograph by the author

Hunting Island State Park, postcard ca. 1940. This park features the natural beauty of the island. Author's collection

The State Forestry Commission did not begin any new parks during 1938 and 1939, but work progressed on all parks that had already been started. The commission considered that the initial park system was complete with the twelve established parks, with only a few planned additions: a park located near the lakes created by the Santee-Cooper Power Development in the midstate; a smaller system of parks within the existing state parks for African Americans; and a system of state historical monuments "to preserve places of state-wide historical interest throughout the State."[29] Of these three additional goals, the commission had moved to provide some day-use park access for African Americans in segregated areas at planned parks, to include Hunting Island State Park and Greenwood State Park, as well as providing group camp facilities for blacks at the Sand Hills State Forest near Cheraw, and at Poinsett State Park, with plans to open at least one of these areas by the summer of 1940.[30]

The State Forestry Commission and the NPS employed CCC camps in seven state parks during 1938 and 1939—at Cheraw (adjacent to the Cheraw RDA), Poinsett, Table Rock, Kings Mountain, Edisto Beach, Hunting Island, and Greenwood. The camp employed at Edisto Beach moved to Hunting Island State Park in July 1938, leaving a small side camp at Edisto Beach through September, and the CCC camp stationed at Kings Mountain also provided labor at Chester State Park. The Forestry Commission employed eight additional forestry camps in a variety of forestry projects throughout the state, including timber-type surveys, truck trail construction, and nursery work. Also in May 1938, but unmentioned in the official annual report, was a damaging fire at Hunting Island, which destroyed the lighthouse keeper's house, where some CCC enrollees were housed; local residents recalled that enrollees were playing cards in the house when a kerosene lantern was overturned, starting the fire in the frame building, which quickly spread—not only destroying the house but a great deal of vegetation as well. A short exchange of terse correspondence between State Forester Smith and Acting Adjutant Robert W. May of District I is the only record of this incident in the Forestry Commission files.[31]

Table Rock State Park

Table Rock State Park first opened on April 4, 1938, when 500 visitors attended the official opening. Table Rock Mountain, for which the park was named, had long been a destination point in South Carolina. Located in the mountainous upstate, in Pickens County, Table Rock Mountain received its name from a Cherokee legend in which the flat-topped mountain served as a table from which the "Great Spirit" ate his meals, and was considered to be sacred to Native Americans. One of the first known written records of the area, an 1809 report on the boundary between North and South Carolina, refers to the mountain as "the Rock known by the name of Table Mountain."[32]

By 1816 adventurous tourists began climbing Table Rock to study the flora and fauna and to appreciate the grand vista afforded at the summit. William Sutherland opened the twenty-room Table Rock Hotel in 1845 to accommodate visitors to the area. The hotel provided access to several of the routes up the mountain, including routes that could be taken by horseback, at least partway, but the majority of the access was by foot. Sutherland contracted with John Masters and Daniel Carrol to construct wooden steps mounted to iron pins to further ease the journey up the mountain, and one visitor reported that there were approximately 130 of these steps.[33]

Sutherland died in 1859, and the advent of the Civil War curtailed much of the tourist industry in upstate South Carolina. Stephen Keith reopened the Table Rock Hotel in the 1870s as a summer resort, and the family continued to operate the hotel, constructing another hotel at a new location on the mountain in about 1900. Although the area enjoyed a spurt of prosperity around the turn of the century, the Keith family abandoned the hotel operation in 1912.[34]

In the early 1930s, with the state seeking to acquire land for CCC development of state parks, Table Rock Mountain received a great deal of attention. A survey by the NPS highlighted the former summer retreat as a desirable location for a state park, and in the spring of 1935 the city of Greenville donated a little over 1,000 acres, including Table Rock Mountain and the slightly larger Pinnacle Mountain, to the state for the purposes of establishing a state park. Pickens County purchased additional acreage from private owners, and donated another 1,500 acres to the state that same year. The CCC quickly moved into the area to begin development of the state park, with two veterans' companies (2434 and 2435) established in August 1935 as Camps SP-5 and SP-6.[35]

These World War I veterans enrolled in the CCC were not used to working in the mountainous terrain, and the winter of 1935 was apparently a particularly hard one. The intensive labor involved in dam building and the creation of Table Rock State Park was evidently too difficult for the men. Two junior CCC camps (Companies 5465 and 5466) replaced the veteran camps in July 1936 in order to hasten the park's development. Company 5465 (SP-5) was charged with actual park construction, including trails, roads, and all park structures, while Company 5466 (SP-6) constructed a concrete dam and spillway to create a twenty-three-acre lake, known as Pinnacle Lake. The granite dam was designed to be scenic as well as functional, and may be viewed from an overlook or from below. A path and stone steps connect the two viewing places. The dam and lake project was completed in 1937, and the camp was disbanded in June of that

Table Rock State Park, Pickens. Company 5465, Camp SP-5, June 1937. Photograph courtesy of South Carolina Department of Parks, Recreation, and Tourism

year. Pinnacle Lake was stocked with over 245,000 rainbow trout in 1938, and opened for fishing in 1940.[36]

Company 5465 constructed a number of buildings and other structures, including a bathhouse, concessions building, eight cabins, picnic shelters, a trail shelter, fish-rearing pools, houses for the park superintendent and warden, roads, numerous trails, and overlooks. Four of the cabins are of hewn-log construction, and three feature board-and-batten siding, but all are one-story, rectangular plan, with a gable roof and stone foundation. Local architects John W. Linley and Fred Ledbetter designed many of the buildings at Table Rock, with the approval of the NPS, and twenty Clemson architecture students participated in an architectural design contest for the park's built environment.[37]

The premier building for Table Rock State Park is that of the lodge, an L-shaped building with a great hall on the main level, and a dining hall, sun porch, and kitchen in the basement level. Constructed of hewn logs, the lodge is situated in a hillside so as to give the facade a one-story appearance from the front. Built over a granite foundation comprising a full basement with its own entrance, it appears as a two-story structure from the rear elevation. The lodge

Table Rock State Park, Pickens. The Hemlock Shelter at Table Rock State Park is a rock-constructed version of the rectangular shelter plan favored by the CCC in the South Carolina State Parks. Photograph courtesy of South Carolina Department of Archives and History

Table Rock State Park, Pickens. This small shelter is found trailside at Table Rock State Park. Photograph courtesy of South Carolina Department of Archives and History

has a full front porch with timber rails and a shed roof, and the interior great hall features exposed log walls, a large stone fireplace, and exposed timber rafters. The lodge affords wonderful views of Table Rock Mountain and Pinnacle Mountain, and the State Forestry Commission ensured that the design of the rest of the state park's facilities did not detract from these vistas when viewed from the lodge. The CCC completed the lodge in 1939, and the restaurant / dining hall opened in 1940.[38]

Although the CCC finished construction of the lodge in 1939, other projects did not see completion prior to the disbandment of Company 5465 in October

1941. The CCC finished work on buildings that had been started, such as the additions of doors or windows, but planned projects had to be abandoned, including a group camp, additional cabins, and riding stables.[39] Although Table Rock State Park was not developed to the fullest potential envisioned by the State Forestry Commission and the NPS, approximately forty of the CCC constructed buildings, trails, walls, and structures remain, and are listed as contributing elements in the National Register–listed Table Rock State Park Historic District.

Greenwood State Park

Following completion of most of the work at Poinsett State Park, Company 2413 transferred from SP-3 (Poinsett) to the new SP-11 to construct Greenwood State Park in Greenwood County. Although the project had been approved as early as May 1938, by this time the numbers of CCC camps were flattening out, and Greenwood simply had to wait until Poinsett could be finished, and Company 2413 did not arrive until October 1938. The county had purchased approximately 1,000 acres of land, with a two-mile stretch fronting the newly created Lake Greenwood, a portion of the impound being created by the Buzzard Roost project and the Public Works Administration (PWA). The city of Greenwood had no state park within a fifty-mile radius, and although the park land could boast "no particular interesting features from a scenic, historical, or biological standpoint" (according to the master plan for the park), the PWA-created lake provided instant recreational possibilities for the 15,000 residents of Greenwood, Clinton, Laurens, and Newberry, of which approximately one-third were African Americans. Star Fort, "the most well preserved Revolutionary British fort in this section of the country," is located seven miles from the park, near Ninety-Six, and is now a part of Ninety-Six National Historic Site.[40]

From the outset the development plans for Greenwood State Park called for two recreational areas, one for whites and one for African Americans. Both areas would provide day-use facilities, including separate swimming pools, play fields, outdoor theaters, hiking trails, a community building, and picnic areas, while the day-use area for whites would also include lake frontage, boat storage, horse stables, and a group camp. The planned "Negro Area" had no lake frontage. Throughout October 1938 the CCC enrollees surveyed the land, approximately half of which was wooded, culling undesirable trees and making truck trails to get to work sites, and beginning a tree nursery. Camp construction continued, and park construction began by January 1939 and continued throughout the year, with picnic areas being developed in both the "white" and "colored" areas. Progress at Greenwood was hampered by the dwindling enthusiasm for the CCC program at the federal level, and monthly progress reports throughout

1939 and 1940 indicate that both labor and materials were often more difficult to come by than they had been in previous years. The optimistic master plan was revised and re-revised, and by May 1941 the park boasted a landing dock and pier, picnic area development in both areas, road construction to both "white" and "Negro" entrances, custodian/caretaker dwellings in both areas, and a marine railway to assist with boat launchings at variable lake levels.[41]

By June 1939 the State Forestry Commission had acquired almost 22,000 acres of land under CCC development in fifteen state parks. In addition to the fifteen state parks, the CCC had been involved in the development of the RDAs; although under the jurisdiction of the NPS, the Forestry Commission operated these areas as state parks, and had an agreement with the NPS that they would become a part of the state park system, along with six wayside parks that the NPS had been developing since 1935. Seven of the twelve state parks under construction had opened by the beginning of the summer 1939, with two additional parks (Chester and Barnwell) scheduled to open in late summer 1939.[42]

The final years of CCC work in South Carolina were difficult ones for state park development in the state. However, the foundation for a system of state parks had been laid over the previous years. Throughout 1939–40 eight CCC forestry camps continued work on the state parks at Barnwell, Oconee, Sesqui-centennial, Lee, and Paris Mountain, while conducting additional forestry work,

Barnwell State Park, Barnwell. This t-plan picnic shelter, probably constructed by Company 4468, features a brick fireplace in the t-end. Photograph by the author

such as timber-type surveys, road construction, construction of fire towers and telephone lines, and nursery work. Company 4468, stationed at Camp P-70 in Barnwell County, not only worked on Barnwell State Park but also provided forestry work for the counties of Barnwell, Aiken, and Orangeburg, and even built a municipal swimming pool in Springfield. Five other CCC camps, working under the administration of the NPS, continued working on the parks at Cheraw, Greenwood, Hunting Island, Kings Mountain, and Table Rock. The Forestry Commission also worked with the Writers' Program of the Works Progress Administration (WPA) in preparing a smaller version of the WPA's popular American Guide series, dealing with the CCC-developed state parks, with R. A. Walker writing to Louise DuBose, assistant state director of the Federal Writers' Project, in December 1938 to correct a passage in the manuscript: "The Washington Office has listed Aiken, Oconee, Lee, and Paris Mountain as State Forest Parks. It is true that we, at one time, called these areas State Forest Parks, but they are at present designated State Parks, except that we were aided in development by CCC camps from the U.S. Forest Service instead of the National Park Service."[43]

Although the CCC and the State Forestry Commission accomplished a great deal of work at the state parks, the Forestry Commission again felt compelled to warn the General Assembly that the state needed to appropriate additional funding for the continuation of the state park program. Although the CCC continued to provide labor for the development of the parks, very little funding had been provided for staff or maintenance, and the continuation of federal funding and cooperation for the work of the CCC was dependent upon the additional contributions of the state. State Forester H. A. Smith warned in his annual report that "unless funds are provided in the future, South Carolina will find her camps moving to other States who have signified their intention of supplying these necessary funds."[44] In addition, Smith complained that his state park staff was woefully inadequate, totaling thirteen full-time employees devoted to state park work, including the nine park superintendents. Apparently the state forester envisioned a day in the near future when the CCC could no longer be relied upon to provide the labor necessary for the development of the state parks. His foresight would prove accurate.

State Forester Smith was not the only official concerned about the state's failure to adequately fund the developing state park program. CCC director Robert Fechner wrote to Governor Burnet Maybank in January 1939, echoing many of the concerns of Smith and the State Forestry Commission. Fechner reminded Maybank of the great amount of work that had been conducted in South Carolina in five years, estimating the cost to the federal government at almost $5 million. Fechner stated: "I am advised that South Carolina has only recently established a state park system, which is at the present time inadequately financed."[45] Although the financial concerns regarding the state park program had reached the highest level of the CCC, it made little difference in state funding for the park program.

Several noteworthy events affected the state parks during fiscal year 1939–40. Organized activity programs, begun in the previous fiscal year, were continued at several of the state parks, and Paris Mountain State Park hosted both a state casting tournament and a state swimming meet, while the state archery meet was held at Sesquicentennial State Park near Columbia, in addition to a variety of local tournaments being held at the various parks. Parks conducted field days and water pageants along with other community events, such as sings or folk dancing. Over 584,000 people visited the state parks during fiscal year 1939–40, more than any other year, and over twice as many visitors who had visited the parks in 1936–37, despite the fact that a polio outbreak forced the closing of the group camps at Cheraw during July and August 1939.[46]

Other than these public events, two educational events were held for the first time, including the State Park Employees Training Institute. The Park Training Institute at Kings Mountain brought together the nine park superintendents, the park personnel stationed in Columbia, and as many of the almost 100 part-time summer personnel as could attend to introduce them to one another and to give them a basic outline of the goals and objectives of the state park system. The institute was so successful that the State Forestry Commission reported that it would become an annual event. Kings Mountain also hosted the first annual School for the Conservation of Natural Resources, sponsored by the State Forest Service, the State Garden Clubs, and the State Federated (Women's) Clubs. Thirty-one clubwomen from around the state attended the weeklong school, where they enjoyed the recreational opportunities of Kings Mountain and listened to a variety of lectures on conservation, forestry, and recreation, given by local speakers as well as lectures from the USFS, the NPS, and professors from Clemson College and the University of South Carolina.[47]

The State Park Employees Training Institute was held for a second year in May 1941, this time at Cheraw, to better educate both the permanent personnel as well as the summer employees in the state park system. Use of the fourteen open parks in 1940 and 1941 swelled to over 830,000 visitors, and included a count of over 24,000 out-of-state cars, requiring a greater number of summer employees to work in the parks as lifeguards, nurses, cooks, bathhouse attendants, and concessions operators. The vacation cabins in the mountains and on the coast proved extremely popular throughout the summer months; over 5,000 people spent at least a week in a state park cottage. In addition to the training institute for park employees, the School for the Conservation of

Natural Resources was again held for South Carolina's clubwomen, and included a lecture titled "The CCC, Its Purpose and Achievements."[48]

CCC work in the state was limited during fiscal year 1940–41. Although the State Forestry Commission operated eight camps during the fiscal year, four of these camps were abandoned by the end of the fiscal year, including the camps working on the state parks at Barnwell, Lee, and Paris Mountain, and low enrollment in some of the other camps often hampered the forestry work of those camps. Additional CCC camps worked at Cheraw, Greenwood, Hunting Island, Kings Mountain, and Table Rock. Fourteen of the sixteen state parks established in the state were open to the public in fiscal year 1940–41, and very little development work was left for the CCC at the parks. No new parks were begun during that fiscal year, although the state legislature did appropriate funding for the purchase of land for a new state park along the Santee-Cooper lake. With appropriations of $15,000 each from the state and from Orangeburg County, the Forestry Commission acquired over 2,300 acres for the new Santee State Park in 1941.[49]

The State Forestry Commission included four recommendations in its 1940–41 annual report. The first recommendation addressed the need for additional funding in five areas, including maintenance, development work to retain the CCC camps, the hiring of additional personnel both at the state office and at the parks, more and better equipment at the parks, and extending the recreational program offered to schoolchildren. The other recommendations addressed the recurring need for a "system of recreational areas for colored people," the acquisition of areas of historical importance, and an increase in advertising the state parks both within South Carolina and in neighboring states.[50]

Although the early history of the South Carolina state parks is an overall positive story, detailed throughout the State Forestry Commissions annual reports, the parks certainly met with challenges, financial and otherwise. The southern coastal state parks at Edisto Beach and Hunting Island were both damaged in August 1940 when a hurricane struck the southern coast of the state. While Hunting Island sustained only limited damage, due primarily to the limited development of the site, the established park at Edisto was badly damaged. Three of the five vacation cabins were destroyed, while the other two sustained heavy damage, and several picnic shelters were destroyed or damaged. The Forestry Commission estimated the damage at Edisto Beach to be in excess of $25,000. In 1941 the General Assembly appropriated $6,000 for repairs at Edisto Beach State Park, allowing for the two damaged cabins to be repaired and the picnic shelter on the beach to be rebuilt. The cabins were moved from their beach location slightly more inland, to provide a greater degree of protection from later storms. The CCC camp at Hunting Island repaired the

Edisto Beach State Park beach cabin, ca. 1940. Photograph courtesy of South Carolina Department of Parks, Recreation, and Tourism

Edisto Beach State Park guard house and entry gate, ca. 1940. Photograph courtesy of South Carolina Department of Parks, Recreation, and Tourism

Edisto Beach State Park picnic shelter, ca. 1940. Photograph courtesy
of South Carolina Department of Parks, Recreation, and Tourism

damage at that park as one of their final projects, while further plans for development at Hunting Island were put on hold "until after the war," according to the Forestry Commission's annual report.[51]

During fiscal year 1941–42 the State Forestry Commission saw many changes, in great part because of the entry of the United States into war with Germany and Japan. Prior to the nation's entry into the war, H. A. Smith, the state forester, resigned his post to accept a position with the Tennessee Valley Authority in Alabama. Six foresters left South Carolina for better-paying positions in other states, while five others enlisted in the armed forces following Pearl Harbor. The CCC camps in South Carolina, as in the rest of the country, were disbanded, leaving behind unfinished projects at several of the state parks, including Cheraw, Table Rock, Hunting Island, Greenwood, Barnwell, and Kings Mountain. The Forestry Commission's continual lament for additional funding from the General Assembly, especially during the final years of CCC work, sounded more urgent as the federally funded labor pool disappeared: "Now that the only source for development work thus far provided has been cut off it is imperative that some plan for developing the parks be provided. The most serious situation in connection with the development work is the lack of funds to make the necessary surveys and planning."[52]

Funding became an even greater issue during fiscal year 1941–42 when it became apparent that operating expenses of the parks would exceed estimates, due in part to the disbanding of the CCC camps and the additional maintenance on park buildings the state would be required to take on. In order to keep the bathhouses open through summer 1942, local governments agreed to underwrite the operating costs at Barnwell, Cheraw, Poinsett, Sesquicentennial, and Table Rock. Finally, the General Assembly authorized a special appropriation of an additional $14,000 in order to keep the parks open through the year.[53]

While the United States' entry into the war affected staffing of the state parks, it also affected their use. Park usage again saw an increase, climbing to over one million visitors during fiscal year 1941–42, but by the summer of 1942 it had become necessary to curtail park operation to day use only in six of the parks. The state parks also provided for new visitors, serving as bivouacs for enlisted men. The State Forestry Commission estimated that 80 percent of visitors to Sesquicentennial State Park were soldiers, many from nearby Fort Jackson, and British soldiers used the group camps at Cheraw State Park while their ship was being repaired at Charleston. Selected state parks hosted military maneuvers, and the three coastal parks, Myrtle Beach, Edisto Beach, and Hunting Island, were garrisoned for military lookout stations.[54]

Of the goals and recommendations that had been set out in the previous year's annual report, in 1941–42 the State Forestry Commission reported some progress on at least two recommendations. "Colored Areas" had been established in four areas of the state, including areas adjacent to Hunting Island State Park and Greenwood State Park (neither of which had officially opened), in the Sand Hills State Forest near Cheraw, and in the Poinsett State Forest near Poinsett State Park, but the activities allowed at these areas were limited primarily to picnicking and swimming, as there were no funds to allow for further developments of these areas. Plans had been made for two state historical monuments, including the General Sumter Burial Grounds in Poinsett County, which had been donated to the state and Eutaw Springs and which the Forestry Commission had approved for acquisition, but again a lack of funding was cited as preventing the acquisition of this site. The Forestry Commission tried to convince the state legislature of the importance of preservation of the state's historic sites: "Each succeeding year brings to light other areas of historical significance in South Carolina. The existence of many areas of such nature are brought to our attention each succeeding year. Much of the historical material is being allowed to rot and decay because of improper care and maintenance. Funds are not available to carry on this very important work which deals with the record of the past history of South Carolina."[55]

While the annual reports of the State Forestry Commission continually reported increased park visitation, and more recreational usage beyond swimming, picnicking, and camping, the tone of the reports could best be characterized as doubtfully optimistic. The commission continued to report the growing numbers of park visitors and the variety of recreational opportunities available at the parks in hopes of convincing the state legislators that the new state parks were vital projects to provide to the citizens of South Carolina, and that provisions needed to be made for the African American citizens of the state, who were, for the most part, excluded from the parks because of mandated segregation. The commission also expressed interest in historic preservation through the identification and acquisition of the state's most historic sites. However, the tone of the annual reports in the late 1930s and early 1940s reveals a great deal of frustration that funding was not available for these important programs, and that the state park program under way was endangered for the same reason.

The contributions of the CCC from 1936 until the end of the CCC program are invaluable. Although administered by the state through the State Forestry Commission and its Division of State Parks, the CCC carried out the bulk of construction and maintenance work at the new and continually growing state parks. Throughout the period of CCC work in the South Carolina state parks, the Forestry Commission continually reminded the General Assembly of the estimated dollar value of the CCC labor, and that this work, paid for by the federal government, needed to be matched by the state government, to demonstrate that the state was interested in continuing this program. The looming war left much of the future of expanding the existing state park system in doubt, but a strong foundation had been laid through the CCC construction of sixteen state parks and six wayside areas in South Carolina.

The story of the work of the CCC in South Carolina is the story of the beginning of the state park system in South Carolina developed by a relatively new state government department, the State Forestry Commission, which had been created by legislative action in 1927. Because of the creation of ECW as a result of the New Deal, the Forestry Commission used the new but existing governmental framework to administer the new state parks program. Learning from the NPS's work in the state in the RDAs first at Cheraw and later at Kings Mountain, the Forestry Commission emulated this example in developing smaller recreational areas on land acquired by the state both for park and forestry purposes. In what may have been a unique use of camps designated for "forestry" projects under the USFS, the Forestry Commission used some of those CCC camps to develop recreational facilities on state forestry lands, which then became state parks, and were administered as such. By 1937 the administration of the state parks was such a part of the Forestry Commission that a new Division of State Parks was set up under the commission.

Although World War II ended the heavy federal involvement in the development of South Carolina's state parks, it did not end the development and

Table Rock State Park, square dance in lodge, July 1958. Photograph courtesy of South Carolina Department of Archives and History

Table Rock State Park, lodge at night, summer 1958. Photograph courtesy of South Carolina Department of Archives and History

administration of those parks. In fact, one additional state park was added to the state park system almost immediately, when Santee State Park opened in 1942. Park usage increased throughout the decade of the 1940s, and park-goers demanded more recreational opportunities as well as additional creature comforts, such as the electrification of group cabins, and the addition of refrigerators at the family cabins, a luxury that many private residences did not have in the 1940s. As the economy not only recovered but prospered, American recreational desires changed, and South Carolina was no exception. Additional parks were added to the state park system, but park facilities grew more and more utilitarian as administrative, personnel, and maintenance costs system-wide grew. As roads improved and vehicles became more prevalent, more and more people were able to travel to spend a few hours or a few days at a state park, and the coastal parks grew exponentially in popularity for their cheap accommodations, in cabins, for autocampers, and new in 1955, at family campgrounds. For example, Myrtle Beach hosted over 50,000 campers in that year. The Forestry Commission hoped to add additional cabins to increase revenue, but cabins cost money up front, have additional maintenance costs, and require additional personnel for reservations, cleaning, and maintenance. The 1960s saw a new movement in the development of new state parks, as historic sites, mentioned early in the state park administration from the 1930s, were finally added to the park system, without the more typical recreational development that had become associated with South Carolina's state parks. Also during the 1960s African Americans, who had long been dissatisfied with the less than equitable treatment they found in the state park system, sued the state in 1961 in order to have equal access to all the state parks. Rather than integrate, the state attorney general ordered the parks closed in 1963. However, due in part to the desire of South Carolinians to have their parks opened, and due largely to the leadership of Governor Robert McNair, the parks had reopened, integrated, by 1966. All of these state park activities were taking place under the jurisdiction of the Division of State Parks within the State Forestry Commission; meanwhile the Forestry Commission was still trying to do regular forestry work as well. State parks were somewhat of a distraction from the commission's other important work. At the same time, the state began realizing the importance of tourism to the Palmetto State's economy, and that state parks were part of that burgeoning industry in South Carolina. Legislative action in 1967 created yet another new state department, that of Parks, Recreation, and Tourism. Thus the work of the CCC in South Carolina not only led to entrenchment of the newly created Forestry Commission by augmenting its work in forestry and fire prevention throughout the state, but indirectly created yet another new state department some twenty-five years after the CCC program ceased to exist.

CHAPTER 8

Learning from the Parks

Resources and Interpretation in South Carolina

Like many of the other New Deal programs, the record of the Civilian Conservation Corp (CCC) is mixed. The New Deal and the CCC provided opportunities for hundreds of thousands of Americans in a myriad of ways, from the most basic provisions of food and shelter, to providing jobs and technical educations for the unemployed and destitute, to providing career opportunities for unemployed professionals. Conversely, New Deal programs have been castigated for their shortcomings, especially in their failure to make equal provisions for African Americans. The CCC, in spite of its successes, has been soundly criticized in several areas, including its military overtones, the perceived shortcomings of its educational program, and the racial discrimination that echoed throughout the larger society in the 1930s. However, in spite of some of the program's most glaring oversights, the achievements of the CCC deserve to be celebrated and studied, as do the individual participants in the program throughout the 1930s. The CCC met President Roosevelt's dual goals of conservation of land and of men, and the results of the program and the larger successes of the New Deal can best be seen when studied at a more localized level than when viewing the program as a whole.

The legacy of the New Deal in South Carolina also includes shortcomings as well as accomplishments. The rural poor and textile workers saw only limited improvement through New Deal programs such as those offered by the Agricultural Adjustment Administration and the National Recovery Administration, but any improvement was better than none at all. Many other New Deal programs in the state were burdened with bigotry, incompetence, or corruption at all levels. But the tangible evidence of the New Deal in South Carolina points to numerous successful programs that changed the landscape of the state while at the same time improving the lives of the thousands of South Carolinians who received assistance through the Works Progress Administration, the Public Works Administration, and the CCC.

Participants and historians alike have lauded the CCC as one of the most successful programs of the New Deal, both in terms of what the program provided for its enrollees and the long-term products they created. In addition to the short-term financial support and room and board provided at a time when many young men had few other options, and the vocational and educational opportunities that the enrollees received while serving, CCC participants often made use of their on-the-job training, either professionally or avocationally. Architectural historian Phoebe Cutler cites one CCC alumnus who patterned his residence in New Jersey after the state parks he helped create, complete with a lake and beach. Other participants at various levels of the program used the knowledge gained during their service to move into professional jobs as foresters, park rangers, or contractors, as well as using the militarily styled organizational structure of the CCC to ease the transition into military life in the army or navy, especially important during the war years of the 1940s.[1]

CCC architecture, especially in state and national parks, also points to the success of the program. Many CCC-constructed buildings remain in state parks across the country, and many state historic preservation offices have documented these structures through surveys and by nominating and listing them on the National Register of Historic Places. Texas architectural historians documented over 400 extant CCC structures in Texas state parks during that state's 1983 celebration of the fiftieth anniversary of the New Deal. One Texas state park, Bastrop State Park in Bastrop County, became a National Historic Landmark in 1997 as a result of the extent of the park's original development through the CCC program.[2] Other states, including Arkansas, Florida, Massachusetts, Minnesota, North Carolina, Tennessee, and Virginia, among others, have also listed state parks on the National Register for their association with the CCC.

The South Carolina Department of Archives and History (SCDAH) has recognized the value of the contributions of the CCC to the state, especially in the area of park development. The SCDAH has also recognized the value of the program to the men of the state, and several programs have attempted to further document the work of the CCC boys in South Carolina and to use their work to teach South Carolinians of all ages about the Depression and New Deal in South Carolina. These innovative programs have included documenting several parks in the statewide Survey of Historic Properties; the listing of four state parks on the National Register of Historic Places; an educational packet of documents and photographs detailing the work of the CCC in the state for middle and high school students; a National History Day exhibit entry where middle school students researched the lives and work of CCC enrollees, including interviews with some of the participants; and an exhibit and public program celebrating the work of the CCC and including reminiscences of former enrollees.

The Historical Services Division of the SCDAH, working with the South Carolina Department of Parks, Recreation, and Tourism (SCPRT), has identified at least 377 buildings and structures related to the work of the CCC in the statewide survey program, including state park buildings as well as other CCC constructions such as fire towers. In addition to these buildings are several man-made lakes, smaller structures such as water fountains and grills, and miles of park roads originally laid by the CCC. Of course, not all of the buildings have retained enough integrity to be considered eligible for listing on the National Register of Historic Places, but a great many have. These surveys have resulted in four South Carolina state parks (Paris Mountain, Table Rock, Oconee, and Kings Mountain) being listed on the National Register of Historic Places for their association with the work of the CCC. Kings Mountain National Military Battlefield is also listed on the National Register, and Poinsett State Park is eligible for listing, while other parks have individually eligible buildings or smaller districts within the state park boundary (such as the group camps at Cheraw State Park). Although listing on the National Register provides only a nominal degree of protection (from federal projects through the Section 106 process), researching and nominating these buildings and districts to the National Register has often resulted in a great deal of local publicity, and CCC alumni in the area are often consulted both for the nominations themselves and for newspaper stories, giving local residents access to New Deal history in their own backyards. In addition, these nominations more fully document the historical resources found within the parks.

The document packet prepared by the Education Service Area of the SCDAH contains a brief explanation of the role of the CCC during the New Deal for both teachers and students, and provides exercises and assignments using photographs and documents, including maps, correspondence, memorandums, and various governmental forms to aid students in their use of primary documents for historical research. The documents were drawn from files in the state archives and from the National Archives, and many of the exercises were based on educational activities at the National Archives. The project does more than teach students about the role of the CCC in their state; it also introduces them to primary document research and historical interpretation, engaging them in a study of the New Deal work program that was designed to reach young men who were close to their own age. More than eighty photographs of CCC work in state parks throughout South Carolina are included for the students to examine, along with a "photograph analysis worksheet," allowing the students to delve further into the historical events pictured. Although the document packet has been out of print for several years, it is available on a CD-ROM, along with other document packets on other South Carolina subjects.[3]

The SCDAH also sponsors the state level of the National History Day competition, and the state competition is held at the SCDAH building in Columbia. In 2000 two students from the Cheraw area entered the exhibit competition highlighting the work of the CCC in building the state park at Cheraw, and they interviewed CCC alumni in Columbia and Charleston. Although the exhibit did not go on to the national competition, it did receive high marks from the competition's judges for the students' use of personal interviews and their research into how the New Deal and the CCC had impacted their local community.

The SCDAH moved into its new building on the outskirts of Columbia in 1998, and one feature of the new building was a small exhibit hall, which has hosted rotating exhibits, complemented by online exhibits. In the spring of 2000, the exhibit topic was the CCC and South Carolina state parks. Tara Mitchell Mielnik, then outreach coordinator at the SCDAH, served as curator of the exhibit, and Tim Belshaw served as exhibit designer. In addition to researching the archival files in the state archives, and the various state parks files at the SCPRT, the outreach coordinator spoke with eighty alumni of the CCC living in South Carolina, and numerous relatives and friends who retained letters, books, and other memorabilia that were included in the exhibit, along with documents, maps, blueprints, and photographs from the SCDAH and the SCPRT office.

The exhibit featured panels discussing the program in general, the daily life of CCC enrollees, the architecture and buildings of the state parks, and the experiences of African Americans in South Carolina's CCC, while exhibiting documents that included a membership card, certificates, and various correspondence between local, state, and federal officials, as well as photographs of camps and projects, along with a variety of other memorabilia. An online exhibit on the SCDAH accompanied the exhibit, featuring several of the photographs on display. The exhibit featured an opening reception with more than fifty CCC alumni and their families present. Albert Hester, historian with the SCPRT, gave a brief slide show on the importance of the CCC in the development of the park program in the state, and many enrollees gave vignettes of their life in the CCC and how it impacted their later lives. A common theme throughout the evening was that "the CCC was the best thing that could have happened to me." The exhibit and program are a groundbreaking example of combining archival materials, oral history, material culture, and the built environment to provide public programming that examines the impact of the CCC on a state, local, and individual level.

The SCPRT has long acknowledged its strong connection to the work of the CCC in the development of the first state parks as the genesis of that department. Many of the extant buildings in the CCC state parks have small metal markers to designate them as constructed by the CCC. Sesquicentennial State Park erected a special monument in 1984 to honor the work of the CCC there, while Oconee State Park is home to the CCC Workers Statue, also known as

"Iron Mike," one of the fifty six-foot statues of a CCC enrollee erected throughout the country by the National Association of Civilian Conservation Corps Alumni. Greenwood State Park, now called Lake Greenwood State Recreational Area, maintains an interactive exhibit at its CCC museum within the conference center. The SCPRT also mentions the CCC involvement at each of the state parks on its Web site, and SCPRT staff, especially historian Al Hester, worked closely with the SCDAH in developing the National Register nominations for each of the listed parks.

While historians may continue to debate the true successes of the New Deal and the CCC, the men who served in South Carolina proudly point to the buildings, dams, roads, and trails in seventeen of the state parks, allowing their work to stand as testimony of their experiences seventy years ago. South Carolina's state park system has grown from those initial state parks, begun under the direction of the NPS and the South Carolina Forestry Commission, to a system of forty-seven parks, natural areas, recreational areas, and historic sites, administered under the South Carolina State Park System in the SCPRT. The State Park Service and the SCPRT are a direct outgrowth of the State Forestry Commission's work with the CCC in the establishment of a state park system, and SCPRT's work in historic preservation, environmentalism, recreation, and tourism development is directly linked to the foundation of a state park system begun by the CCC in the 1930s.

The CCC was one of the most successful New Deal programs in South Carolina, providing hundreds of young men with employment, education, and basic needs such as food, clothing, and shelter, all opportunities that were otherwise difficult to find in the depression years of the 1930s. While most of them only spent a few years in the CCC, even seventy years later these men still recall their CCC experience as one of the most valuable of their lives. Many of them speak fondly of the projects they helped with, and they point proudly to the tangible products of those projects, which still stand today. In South Carolina, the most significant of these projects are the seventeen state parks that the CCC built during the 1930s and that formed the nucleus of the state park system in South Carolina.

The seventeen CCC-constructed state parks all over the state provide a unique learning laboratory for a variety of subjects. Early in the life of the state park system, state forestry officials touted the parks as a place for adults and children alike to learn to appreciate nature, to study plants and animals, and to learn about the state's historical treasures, while at the same time improving their physical health through outdoor recreational activities. Seventy years later the parks still provide those opportunities, while also providing a place to study the remnants of one of the most successful programs of the New Deal in the work of the CCC.

A List of Civilian Conservation Corps Camps in South Carolina

Co. No.	Camp/ Project	RR Location	Post Office	Date Occupied	Camp Name/ Comm. Location	Organized at	Project Notes	FN
408	AF-2	Pontiac	Columbia	2/1/1941		Moultrie		1, 2
416	NP-19	Whittier	Ravensford	11/30/34			?	1
419	P-53	Effingham	Florence	6/22/33	Camp Lawrence	Mc		1, 2
420	P-57	Nichols	Nichols	6/28/33				1
421	P-52	Camden	Blaney	6/23/33	Kershaw	Mc		1, 2
421	SP-3	Wedgefield	Sumter	10/20/34	Sumter		Poinsett SP	1, 2, 5
421	SCS-10	Rock Hill	Rock Hill	8/17/35	Tom Johnston			1
425	P-8 (F-11)	Edgefield	Modoc	11/2/34		Benning		1, 2
438	F-5	Whitmire	Union	11/23/34	Andrew Jackson (?)			1
439	F-1	Walhalla	Mountain Rest	5/18/33	Ellison Smith (12 mi. NW)	Moultrie		1, 2, 4, 5
440	P-51	Greenville	Cleveland	5/30/1933	Palaette (25 mi. NW)	Moultrie		1, 2
440	S-90	Greenville	Greenville	2/1/37	Camp Palmetto (7 mi. N)	Moultrie	Paris Mtn SP	1, 2
440	P-94 (S-94)	Orangeburg	Elloree	9/17/40		Moultrie		1, 2
441	P-66	Alston	Parr Shoals	6/13/33		Moultrie		1, 2

441	SCS-2	Greer	Greer	7/3/34	Highlands (2 mi. NW)	Moultrie		1, 2
441	P-62	Kingstree	Kingstree	6/22/33				1
441	SCS-16	Fountain Inn	Fountain Inn	9/29/33 (9/29/39)	Quillen (1 mi. NW)	Moultrie		1, 2, 3
442	NP-3 (RDA)	Cheraw	Cheraw					2
442	P-56	Moncks Corner	Moncks Corner	6/19/33	Pinopolis (4 mi. NW)	Moultrie		1, 2, 5
442 (462?)	F-2	Walhalla	Seneca	6/15/33	Wade Hampton (27 mi. NW)			1
443	P-60	Summerville	Summerville	6/16/33				1, 2
443	SCS-3	Greer	Greer	10/9/34	Camp Buie (12 mi. N)	Moultrie		1, 2
445	P-58	Charleston	Ft. Moultrie	6/29/33	Edgar Allan Poe	Moultrie		1, 2
445	P-65	Conway	Conway	4/—/34	Peter Horry	Moultrie		2
445	SP-1	Cheraw	Cheraw	7/4/34	Jefferson Davis (3 mil. S)		Cheraw SP	1, 4, 5
446	AF-1	Fort Jackson	Columbia	1/27/41	On Reservation	Moultrie		1, 2
449	P-7	Greenwood	Bradley	11/2/34	Camp Wrailey (12 mi. SE)			1
452 (458?)	F-5	Whitmire	Union	11/23/34	(10 mi. S)	Mc		1, 3

Co. No.	Camp/ Project	RR Location	Post Office	Date Occupied	Camp Name/ Comm. Location	Organized at	Project Notes	FN
461	P-57	Nichols	Nichols	6/25/35 6/20/33	Victor Blue (city limits)	composite		1, 2
462	F-2	Walhalla		6/15/33		Mc		2, 3
1204	F-3	Charleston	Witherbee	10/19/33	William Moultrie (1 mi. E)	Dix		1
1207 (1201?)	F-4 (F-2?)	Charleston	Awendaw	10/19/33	Francis Marion (27 mi NE)	Dix		1, 2, 5
1221	P-67	Astill	Luray	10/19/33		Dix		1, 2
1407	F-6	Newberry	Whitmire	10/24/34	(6 mi. S)	Benning		1, 2
1408	P-61	Georgetown	Georgetown	6/17/33		Benning		1, 2, 3
1408	SP-4	Myrtle Beach	Myrtle Beach	11/9/1934	Peter Horry 5 mi. SW	Benning	Myrtle Beach SP	1, 2, 4
1409	P-65	Conway	Conway	6/26/33				1, 2
1409	SCS-1	Spartanburg	Switzer	6/9/34	Camp Sparta 5 mi E Spburg	Benning		1, 2, 3
1417	P-60	St. George	Summerville	6/14/33	Dorchester 12 mi SE	Benning		1, 2
1417	SCS-11	Chester	Rodman	8/17/33	Richard Lacy, 9 mi N (or Edward Lacy?)	Benning		1, 2

1417	SCS-15 (SCS-18?)	Lancaster	Lancaster	9/8/39	Andrew Jackson 1 mi SE	Benning		1, 2
1428	P-54	Walterboro	Jacksonboro	6/25/33		Benning	Colleton County	1, 3
1428	P-68	Stokes	Stokes	7/14/33	William Loundes 5 mi NW	Benning See side camp for 4468	Colleton SP?	1, 2
1429	S-74	Aiken	Montmorenci	6/24/35	Joseph Wheeler 5 mi SW	Benning	Aiken SP?	1, 2
1429	MP-1	York	York	8/18/35	Camp Hawthorne 12 mi N	Benning	Kings Mtn NMP	1, 2
1437	P-59	Ridgeland	Ridgeland	6/27/33				1
1438	P-55 S-74	Aiken	Montmorenci	6/24/33		Benning	Aiken SP? (see co. 1429)	1, 2
1448	AF-3	Fort Jackson	Columbia	1/31/41		Moultrie	Army	1, 2
1449	F-7	Greenwood	Bradley	11/2/34	Camp Bradley 13 mi SW	Benning		1, 2
2413-V	P-64	Hardeeville	Hardeeville	8/11/33		Moultrie		1, 2
2413-V	SP-2	Ridgeville	St. George	10/5/34	(10 mi S)	Moultrie	Givhans Ferry	1, 2, 3
2413-V	SP-11	Chappell	Ninety Six	9/23/38	Camp Greenwood (5 mi S)	Moultrie	Greenwood SP	1, 2
2413-V	SP-3	Wedgefield	Wedgefield	2/5/36	Poinsett (6 mi S)	Moultrie	Poinsett SP	1, 2, 3

Co. No.	Camp/ Project	RR Location	Post Office	Date Occupied	Camp Name/ Comm. Location	Organized at	Project Notes	FN
2414-V	P-63	Sumter	Sumter	7/13/33	W.D. (W. S.?) Miller 6 mi SW	Moultrie		1, 2, 3
2414-V	F-91	Sumter	Sumter	7/15/38		Moultrie		1
2434		Pickens		Aug 1935				3
2435		Pickens		Aug 1935				3
3437	AF-4	Columbia	Columbia	1/13/42	Camp Pontiac 13 mi NE		Stationed at Sesqui?	1
3449	S-75	Walhalla	Walhalla	7/16/35	10 mi N	Mc	Oconee SP	1, 4
3450	SCS-4	Abbeville	Abbeville	8/3/35	Camp Selleck 2 mi W	Mc		1, 2
3451	SCS-5	Laurens	Laurens	8/18/35	1 mi E	Mc		1, 2, 3
3451	SCS-29 (SCS-20)	Goldville	Goldville	6/15/40	2 mi E	Mc		1, 2
3452	SCS-6	Greenwood	Greenwood	8/1/35	Star Fort 2 mi E	Mc		1, 2, 3
3452	SCS-23	Edgefield	Edgefield	8/20/40		Mc		2
4432-C	BF-1	Hardeville	Hardeville	8/21/35	2 mi S	Screven		1
4464 (C or no?)	F-9	Georgetown	McClellanville	7/10/35	Camp Elmwood 20 mi S	Moultrie		1, 2
4465-C	F-10	Whitmire	Clinton	9/2/35	8 mi E			1, 2

4465-C	F-6	Whitmire	Newberry	10/9/37	12 mi N		See Co1407	1, 2
4465-C	F-94	Orangeburg	Elloree	11/13/41				1
4466	MP-1	York					CRL newspaper, Buell files	
4467	P-61	Georgetown	Georgetown	6/17/33	Lafayette 3 mi N	Moultrie		1, 2, 3
4468	P-70	Barnwell	Barnwell	7/3/35	Johnson Hagood 3 mi W		Barnwell SP	1, 2, 3, 4
4469	P-71	Columbia	Columbia	7/5/35	Pontiac 13 mi NE	Moultrie	Sesqui SP	1, 2, 3, 4
4470-C	S-74	Aiken	Montmorenci	6/24/33	Joseph Wheeler 10 mi SE	Moultrie	Aiken SP	1, 4
4470-C	S-75	Camden	Camden	1/15/36				2
4471	P-88	Alcott	Bishopville	8/16/35	Robert E. Lee 3 mi. SW		Lee SP	1, 2, 4
4472	SCS-7	Newberry	Newberry	3/23/35	Bernard O'Neal (O'Neil) 1 mi S	Moultrie		1, 2, 4
4473	SCS-8	Union (Beaufort?)	Kelton	8/22/35	Pinckney 8 mi. N	Moultrie		1 2
4474	SCS-9	Gaffney	Gaffney	8/25/35	Daniel Morgan 1 mi SW	Moultrie	Initially began as a side camp to Co445 at Cheraw	1, 2, 3

Co. No.	Camp/ Project	RR Location	Post Office	Date Occupied	Camp Name/ Comm. Location	Organized at	Project Notes	FN
4474	SCS-21	Spartanburg	Spartanburg	6/3/40	John McSwain 4 mi NW	Moultrie		1, 2
4475 (is this 4476?)	SP-9	Chester	Chester	7/27/35	Lakeview 2 mi W		Chester SP	1, 2
4475-C				9/5/35			Poinsett SP	
4475-C				11/7/35			Chester SP	
4475-C	F-11	Meriweather	Modoc	6/12/37 4/12/37	9 mi N	Moultrie		1, 2, 3
4476-C	SP-9	Chester	Chester	7/27/35		Moultrie		2
4477	SCS-12	Winnsboro	Winnsboro	8/24/35	Camp Gaillard 1 mi SW	Moultrie	District Cook & Baker School located at this camp	1, 2
4477	SCS-24	Alcott	Bishopville	5/1/41	3 mi. SW	Moultrie		1, 2
4479	SP-7	Kings Mtn.	Kings Mtn.	7/25/35	Patrick Ferguson 10 mi SE	Moultrie	Kings Mtn SP	1, 2, 4
4480	SP-8	Moggette (?)	Edisto Island	8/21/35	John Laurens 22 mi SE	Moultrie	Edisto Beach SP	1, 2
4480	SP-10	Beaufort	Frogmore	7/9/38	19 mi SE	Moultrie	Hunting Island SP	1, 2

4486	SCS-14	Liberty	Liberty	8/26/35	Camp Bryson 3 mi W	Mc		1, 2, 3
4486	SCS-17	Calhoun	Clemson	11/2/39	2 mi E	Mc		1, 2, 3
4487-C	SCS-15	Anderson	Anderson	8/25/35	Cochrane 3 mi NE	Mc		1, 2
4487-C	SCS-22	Due West	Due West	6/18/40	Monroe Young 1 mi NE	Mc		1, 2, 4, 5
4487-C	SCS-23	Crafton	Edgefield	11/1/41				1
4488	SCS-13	Carlisle	Union			Mc		2
5412-C	F-3	Not readable		8/5/35				1
5418-C	F-3	Charleston	Withersbee	10/19/33	William Moultrie 1 mi E	Moultrie		1, 2, 4
5419-C	F-4	Charleston	Awendaw	8/5/35	Francis Marion 27 mi NE	Moultrie		1, 2
5419-C	MP-2 (BF-2)	Charleston	Awendaw	10/14/37		Moultrie		1 2
5419-C	SCS-19	Ward	Saluda	10/4/39	3 mi W	Moultrie		1, 2, 3
5423	Army	Pacolet	Pacolet	3/16/41	15 mi. E			1
5423-C	SCS-?	Spartanburg						3
5465	SP-5	Pickens	Pickens	7/8/36	20 mi NW	Mc	Table Rock SP	1, 2

Co. No.	Camp/ Project	RR Location	Post Office	Date Occupied	Camp Name/ Comm. Location	Organized at	Project Notes	FN
5466	SP-6	Pickens	Pickens	7/8/36	20 mi NW	Mc	Table Rock SP	1, 2
5468	P-68	Walterboro	Walterboro	4/2/38	5 mi NW	Screven		1, 2
5468	P-93	Green Pond	Walterboro	6/1/40	8 mi E	Screven		1, 2
6466	SCS-20	Goldville	Goldville	7/10/41	2 mi E			1
6466	SP-10	Beaufort	Frogmore	11/1/41			Hunting Island SP	1

Notes

1. Letter from M. P. Vermette, southeast region director, NACCCA to Rowena Nylund, South Carolina PRT, 18 November 1991, with attached "Day Report" for South Carolina from NACCCA files. In files at SC PRT. Same information available on-line at www.ccclegacy.org/south__carolina.htm. Most spelling inaccuracies have been corrected.

2. "Civilian Conservation Corps Camps in the State of South Carolina." Files, Historical Services, South Carolina Department of Archives and History. List compiled from the federal records. Notation on list: "Many companies were moved or disbanded before their assigned projects were completed and then later a different company would be assigned to the same site with the original project number, and in a few cases with the original occupation date. Some Companies only stayed in place for a few months and missed being on the Semi-Annual reports to the Adjutant General's Office, therefore there is no written record. The Federal Records are faded and in some cases numbers and dates are illegible."

There are differences for companies 4475/4476 in these two records. This list indicates the 4475/4476 were "Colored" companies, but list compiled from NACCCA does not. Also, NACCCA lists 4475 twice but does not list 4476.

Also see companies 5412-C, 5418-C, 5419-C. NACCCA lists as "Colored Companies" but SCDAH list does not indicate "C".

3. See Waller article from the *Historian* and camp newspapers published by these camps.

4. CCC camp newsletters, Center for Research Libraries, Chicago, Illinois.

5. Calvin Monroe Young was born a slave at Due West, S.C., in 1859. He went to Biddle University at age twenty-three, graduating with an A.B. in 1891 and an S.T.B. in 1894. He served as a pastor in Rock Hill until 1906, when he was called to the presidency of Williams Institute, later renamed Harbison Institute. He served in that capacity until his death. He married Clarkie Hannah Hughes of Greenville, S.C., and later Sarah Naomi Russell of Blackstock, S.C. He was president of Harbison Institute in Abbeville, S.C., during the fire of 1910 and helped to relocate the school to Irmo, S.C., the following year. He died in 1929.

Preface

1. See Edgar A. Nixon, ed., *Franklin D. Roosevelt and Conservation, 1911–1945*, vol. 1 (New York: Arno Press, 1972).

2. "Roosevelt's Forest Army" is just one of the many nicknames the CCC received during its nine-year existence and is the title of Perry H. Merrill's book about the CCC, *Roosevelt's Forest Army: A History of the Civilian Conservation Corps, 1933–1942* (Montpelier, Vt.: by the author, 1981). For a more complete administrative history of the CCC, see John A. Salmond, *The Civilian Conservation Corps, 1933–1942: A New Deal Case Study* (Durham, N.C.: Duke University Press, 1967).

3. Although the CCC built sixteen state parks during its work period in South Carolina, the program also developed six waysides along national highways. One of these waysides later became Colleton State Park, bringing the total of CCC-built parks to seventeen.

4. This introductory material is taken from "A Lasting Legacy: The Civilian Conservation Corps and South Carolina's State Parks," a brochure for an exhibit by the same title, written by the author. The exhibit was on display at the South Carolina Department of Archives and History from December 1999 through June 2000. The author was exhibit curator, and Tim Belshaw was exhibit designer.

Chapter 1. Depression and the New Deal in South Carolina

1. Don Barton, *The Clemson-Carolina Game, 1896–1966* (Columbia, S.C.: State Printing Company, 1966), 120–125.

2. Jack Irby Hayes Jr., *South Carolina and the New Deal* (Columbia: University of South Carolina Press, 2001), 7–8. Hayes's book is the best history of South Carolina's experience during the New Deal and should be consulted by anyone interested in learning more about the impact of the various New Deal programs in the state.

3. Ibid., 8. The impact of the cotton textile industry on many aspects of life in South Carolina in the decades prior to the Depression is fully discussed in David L. Carlton, *Mill and Town in South Carolina, 1880–1920* (Baton Rouge: Louisiana State University Press, 1982). The lives of cotton mill workers in Georgia and the Carolinas during these same decades have been examined in Jacquelyn Dowd Hall et al., *Like a Family: The Making of a Southern Cotton Mill World* (Chapel Hill: University of North

Carolina Press, 1987). For a closer look at the lives and political feelings of South Carolina mill workers through the first half of the twentieth century, see Bryant Simon, *A Fabric of Defeat: The Politics of South Carolina Millhands, 1910–1948* (Chapel Hill: University of North Carolina Press, 1998).

4. Hayes, *South Carolina and the New Deal,* 7–9; Walter Edgar, *South Carolina: A History* (Columbia: University of South Carolina Press, 1998), 499. See also Gilbert C. Fite, *Cotton Fields No More: Southern Agriculture, 1865–1980* (Lexington: University Press of Kentucky, 1984), 91–138, for the impact of the cotton industry upon the South during the Depression.

5. Hayes, *South Carolina and the New Deal,* 9, 56–57; Edgar, *South Carolina,* 499–500; John Hammond Moore, *Columbia and Richland County: A South Carolina Community, 1740–1990* (Columbia: University of South Carolina Press, 1993), 339–40; Walter J. Fraser Jr., *Charleston! Charleston! The History of a Southern City* (Columbia: University of South Carolina Press, 1989), 379.

6. Hayes, *South Carolina and the New Deal,* 9–12; Moore, *Columbia and Richland County,* 338–39.

7. Quoted in Hayes, *South Carolina and the New Deal,* 11.

8. Hayes, *South Carolina and the New Deal,* 10–12; D. Clayton Brown, "Modernizing Rural Life: South Carolina's Push for Public Rural Electrification," *South Carolina Historical Magazine* 99 (January 1998): 66; "Chapter Celebrates CCC Anniversary," *Charleston (S.C.) Post and Courier,* April 2, 1998.

9. David M. Kennedy, *Freedom from Fear: The American People in Depression and War, 1929–1945* (New York: Oxford University Press, 1999), 192.

10. Richard Lowitt and Maurine Beasley, eds., *One Third of a Nation: Lorena Hickok Reports on the Great Depression* (Chicago: University of Illinois Press, 1981), 158–159.

11. Paul Lofton, "The Columbia Black Community in the 1930s," *Proceedings of the South Carolina Historical Association* (1984): 89; I. A. Newby, *Black Carolinians: A History of Blacks in South Carolina from 1895–1968* (Columbia: University of South Carolina Press, 1973), 245–50; Edwin D. Hoffman, "The Genesis of the Modern Movement for Equal Rights in South Carolina, 1930–1939," *Journal of Negro History* 44 (October 1959): 348, 360–62.

12. *Charleston (S.C.) News and Courier,* May 19, September 28, 1932.

13. Hayes, *South Carolina and the New Deal,* 8–13.

14. Moore, *Columbia and Richland County,* 340.

15. Hayes, *South Carolina and the New Deal,* 16–18; Edgar, *South Carolina,* 500–501.

16. Edgar, *South Carolina,* 501.

17. Anthony J. Badger, *The New Deal: The Depression Years, 1933–1940* (New York: Noonday Press, 1989), 194.

18. Hayes, *South Carolina and the New Deal,* 39–40, 45; William E. Leuchtenburg, *Franklin D. Roosevelt and the New Deal, 1932–1940* (New York: Harper Torchbooks, 1963), 120; T. H. Watkins, *The Hungry Years: A Narrative History of the Great Depression in America* (New York: Henry Holt, 1999), 169–171; Badger, *New Deal,* 190–200; Robert S. McElvaine, *The Great Depression: America 1929–1941* (New York: Times Books, 1984), 151; Kennedy, *Freedom from Fear,* 170–189.

19. Hayes, *South Carolina and the New Deal,* 44–45.

20. Ibid., 122–15, 136; McElvaine, *Great Depression,* 149–150; Badger, *New Deal,* 152–169; Kennedy, *Freedom from Fear,* 200–213. For a larger survey of the general impact of the Agricultural Adjustment Act, see Theodore Saluoutos, "New Deal Agricultural Policy: An Evaluation," *Journal of American History* 61 (September 1974): 394–416; and Van L. Perkins, *Crisis in Agriculture: The Agricultural Adjustment Administration and the New Deal, 1933* (Berkeley: University of California Press, 1969). Pete Daniel's *Breaking the Land: The Transformation of the Cotton, Tobacco, and Rice Cultures since 1880* (Chicago: University of Illinois Press, 1985) provides a study of the way in which the AAA and other New Deal agricultural programs sought to balance the availability of technology with the needs of southern agriculturalists.

21. Kennedy, *Freedom from Fear,* 212–13.

22. Hayes, *South Carolina and the New Deal,* 126–127; Senator E. D. Smith quoted in Kennedy, *Freedom from Fear,* 213.

23. Brown, "Modernizing Rural Life," 75–78. For an example of the student projects at the University of South Carolina that contributed to the passage of the South Carolina Rural Electrification Act, see W. S. Smith, "Rural Electrification in South Carolina" (M.S. thesis, University of South Carolina, 1932).

24. Brown, "Modernizing Rural Life," 76–85; Hayes, *South Carolina and the New Deal,* 134–135; Badger, *New Deal,* 177–118.

25. Hayes, *South Carolina and the New Deal,* 129–130.

26. Ibid., 132–133; William David Hiott, "New Deal Resettlement in South Carolina" (M.A. thesis, University of South Carolina, 1986), 6–8, 100–101. Paul K. Conkin's *Tomorrow a New World: The New Deal Community Program* (Ithaca, N.Y.: Cornell University Press, 1959) is widely acknowledged as the definitive (if early) study of the resettlement programs of the New Deal.

27. Quoted in Hall et al., *Like a Family,* 297.

28. Lofton, "Columbia Black Community," 91.

29. The failure to unionize textile workers in the state left a lingering legacy; by 1980 less than 7 percent of the state's labor force was unionized. The difficulties of unions organizing in the South is discussed in J. Wayne Flynt, "The New Deal and Southern Labor," in *The New Deal and the South,* ed. James C. Cobb and Michael V. Namaroto, 63–95 (Jackson: University Press of Mississippi, 1984). The general textile strike of 1934 has received much recent attention. See Simon, *Fabric of Defeat,* for example, as well as Janet Christine Irons, *Testing the New Deal: The General Textile Strike of 1934 in the American South* (Chicago: University of Illinois Press, 2000); and John A. Salmond, *The General Textile Strike of 1934: From Maine to Alabama* (Columbia: University of Missouri Press, 2002).

30. Hayes, *South Carolina and the New Deal,* 100, 118–119; Kennedy, *Freedom from Fear,* 177–189; McElvaine, *Great Depression,* 158–162. See also Flynt, "New Deal and Southern Labor"; and Simon, *Fabric of Defeat.* For a detailed account of NRA's effect on the textile industry in the South, see James Hodges's aptly titled *New Deal Labor Policy and the Southern Cotton Textile Industry, 1933–1941* (Knoxville: University of Tennessee Press, 1986).

31. Hayes, *South Carolina and the New Deal*, 56–57; Badger, *New Deal*, 227–35. Until the 1937 constitutional amendment, the state constitution provided state pensions to be given only to Confederate veterans and their widows. The early effects of Social Security throughout the South are discussed in James T. Patterson, *The New Deal and the States: Federalism in Transition* (Princeton, N.J.: Princeton University Press, 1969), 85–101; and George Brown Tindall, *The Emergence of the New South: 1913–1945* (Baton Rouge: Louisiana State University Press, 1967), 487–91. The development of Social Security at the national level is placed into larger historical context in William Graebner, *A History of Retirement: The Meaning and Function of an American Institution, 1885–1978* (New Haven, Conn.: Yale University Press, 1980).

32. Hayes, *South Carolina and the New Deal*, 58–60; Badger, *New Deal*, 200–227. Despite the massive variety of projects conducted under the auspices of the WPA, until recently the only comprehensive study of the WPA was Donald Howard, *The WPA and Federal Relief Policy* (New York: Russell Sage, 1942). A recent survey of the work and impact of the WPA is Nick Taylor, *American Made, The Enduring Legacy of the WPA: When FDR Put the Nation to Work* (New York: Bantam Books, 2008). A plethora of works have discussed various aspects of the WPA's legacy. For the national context on the New Deal's youth programs, including the NYA, see Richard A. Reiman, *The New Deal and American Youth: Ideas and Ideals in a Depression Decade* (Athens: University of Georgia Press, 1992). For the NYA project in South Carolina, see *Report of the State Commission of Forestry, July 1, 1937, to June 30, 1938* (Columbia: General Assembly of South Carolina, 1938), 38–39. Later chapters of this study discuss the impact of the CCC on the lives of South Carolina's young men.

33. Lofton, "Columbia Black Community," 91; Hoffman, "Genesis of Equal Rights," 361. After teaching at Columbia's Booker T. Washington High School, Modjeska Monteith Simkins became South Carolina's only full-time, statewide, African American public health worker when she was appointed as director of Negro Work for the South Carolina Anti-Tuberculosis Association. See Jill K. Hanson, "'A Room of One's Own': Preserving Twentieth-Century Women's History in Columbia, South Carolina" (M.A. thesis, University of South Carolina, 1994).

34. Ellen Woodward, "Hot Lunches for a Million School Children," [1937?], Record Group 69, National Archives, http://newdeal.feri.org/texts/500.htm, accessed December 12, 2002.

35. Hayes, *South Carolina and the New Deal*, 61–62; Badger, *New Deal*, 205–7. While the WPA's women's programs provided relief for women, these programs were often the most expendable; officials in several states complained that the women's projects were always the first to be closed down. Susan Ware highlights the WPA's women's projects as well as the larger experience of women in the New Deal in *Beyond Suffrage: Women in the New Deal* (Cambridge, Mass.: Harvard University Press, 1981).

36. South Carolina Federal Writers' Project, *South Carolina: A Guide to the Palmetto State*, American Guide Series, Works Projects Administration (repr., New York: Oxford University Press, 1963); South Carolina Federal Writers' Project, *South Carolina State Parks*, American Guide Series, Works Projects Administration (Columbia: South Carolina State Forest Service, 1940); South Carolina Federal Writers' Project, *Palmetto Pioneers: Six Stories of Early South Carolinians* (Columbia: South Carolina Federal Writers'

Project, 1938); Works Progress Administration of South Carolina, *Research and Records Work in South Carolina* (Columbia: n.p., 1940); Roberta V. Copp, "South Carolina's Historic Records Survey, 1935–1942" (M.A. thesis, University of South Carolina, 1988), 25–52. For African American slave narratives collected by the WPA, see Belinda Hurmence, ed., *Before Freedom, When I Just Can Remember* (Winston-Salem, N.C.: John F. Blair, 1989), a collection of twenty-seven WPA slave narratives from South Carolina.

37. Hayes, *South Carolina and the New Deal,* 41–43, 63–64; Taylor, *American Made,* 289; Lise C. Swensson and Nancy M. Higgins, eds., *New Deal Art in South Carolina* (Columbia: South Carolina State Museum, 1990), 30–32.

38. Sidney R. Bland, *Preserving Charleston's Past, Shaping Its Future: The Life and Times of Susan Pringle Frost* (Columbia: University of South Carolina Press, 1999), 89–94; Fraser, *Charleston! Charleston!* 383–84. See also Susan G. Hiott, "New Deal Art in South Carolina," http://people.clemson.edu/hiotts/pwap.html, accessed December 14, 2001. Charleston benefited from an inordinately large amount of New Deal money, especially from the WPA and the PWA, in part as a result of Mayor Burnet Maybank's political alliance with Senator James Byrnes and his personal friendship with Harry Hopkins. See Marvin L. Cann, "Burnet Maybank and Charleston Politics in the New Deal Era," *Proceedings of the South Carolina Historical Association* (1979): 39–48.

39. Hayes, *South Carolina and the New Deal,* 41–43, 63–64; Swensson and Higgins, *New Deal Art,* 20–32.

40. Hayes, *South Carolina and the New Deal,* 71–73.

41. Ibid.; Fraser, *Charleston! Charleston!* 386–88; Cann, "Burnet Maybank," 44. For the impact of the Charleston Navy Yard during the decade immediately following the New Deal, see Fritz P. Hamer, "A Southern City Enters the Twentieth Century: Charleston, Its Navy Yard, and World War II, 1940–1948" (Ph.D. diss., University of South Carolina, 1998).

42. Hayes, *South Carolina and the New Deal,* 75–84; Fraser, *Charleston! Charleston!* 386–88. For a complete discussion of the history of Santee-Cooper and its impact in the state, see Walter Edgar, *History of Santee Cooper: 1934–1984* (Columbia, S.C.: R. L. Bryan, 1984). See also "History of Santee Cooper," http://www.santeecooper.com, accessed December 17, 2002, and December 2, 2009.

Chapter 2. Emergency Conservation Work and the Civilian Conservation Corps

1. William E. Leuchtenburg, *The FDR Years: On Roosevelt and His Legacy* (New York: Columbia University Press, 1995), 49–53; Cole Blease Graham Jr., "James Francis Byrnes," in *The South Carolina Encyclopedia,* ed. Walter Edgar, 114–115 (Columbia: University of South Carolina Press for the Humanities Council, 2006).

2. Leuchtenburg, *Franklin D. Roosevelt and the New Deal,* 41–52; Salmond, *Civilian Conservation Corps,* 10–11; Nixon, *Franklin D. Roosevelt and Conservation,* 138–149.

3. Nixon, *Franklin D. Roosevelt and Conservation,* 138–149; Salmond, *Civilian Conservation Corps,* 12–23. Congressman Byrns of Tennessee begrudgingly sponsored the bill at Roosevelt's request; he regarded the "scheme as idealistic and unfeasible" but realized the need to provide some sort of employment for young men. See Ann B. Irish, *Joseph W. Byrns of Tennessee: A Political Biography* (Knoxville: University of Tennessee Press, 2001), 169–170.

4. Nixon, *Franklin D. Roosevelt and Conservation,* 151; Salmond, *Civilian Conservation Corps,* 27–29; Charles W. Johnson, "The Army and the Civilian Conservation Corps, 1933–1942," *Prologue* (Fall 1972): 141.

5. Salmond, *Civilian Conservation Corps,* 30.

6. Ibid., 31; William G. Robbins, *American Forestry: A History of National, State, and Private Cooperation* (Lincoln: University of Nebraska Press, 1985), 140; James Wright Steely, *Parks for Texas: Enduring Landscapes of the New Deal* (Austin: University of Texas Press, 1999), 37.

7. Salmond, *Civilian Conservation Corps,* 26–31. An excellent introduction to the early organization and its first year of work is Joseph Speakman, "Into the Woods: The First Year of the Civilian Conservation Corps," *Prologue* 38 (Fall 2006), http://www .archives.gov/publications/ prologue/2006/fall/ccc.html, accessed November 13, 2006.

8. The *State,* April 21, 1933, and April 23, 1933.

9. Salmond, *Civilian Conservation Corps,* 34–35; Steely, *Parks for Texas,* 38.

10. Quoted in Johnson, "The Army and the Civilian Conservation Corps," 139.

11. Raymond Gram Swing, "Take the Army Out of the CCC," *Nation* 141 (October 25, 1935): 459–60.

12. James's 1906 Stanford address was published in 1910. For a recent reprint of this essay, see Joyce Carol Oates and Robert Atwan, eds., *The Best American Essays of the Century* (New York: Houghton Mifflin, 2001). See also Terry A. Cooney, *Balancing Acts: American Thought and Culture in the 1930s* (New York: Twayne, 1995), 157–165.

13. Neil Maher, *Nature's New Deal: The Civilian Conservation Corps and the Roots of the American Environmental Movement* (New York: Oxford University Press, 2008), 18–19, 34–37.

14. James F. Byrnes, *All in One Lifetime* (New York: Harper & Brothers, 1958), 109.

15. Kenneth Holland and Frank Ernest Hill, *Youth in the CCC* (Washington, D.C.: American Council on Education, 1942; repr., New York: Arno Press, 1974), 24.

16. Johnson, "The Army and the Civilian Conservation Corps," 139–144; Salmond, *Civilian Conservation Corps,* 31–32.

17. Johnson, "The Army and the Civilian Conservation Corps," 145–146.

18. Charles W. Johnson, "The Army, the Negro, and the Civilian Conservation Corps," *Military Affairs* 36 (October 1972): 87.

19. Steely, *Parks for Texas,* 38; Alison T. Otis et al., *The Forest Service and the Civilian Conservation Corps: 1933–1942* (Washington, D.C.: U. S. Forest Service, 1986), 9.

20. *Bugle* (Company 4468, P-70), July 8, 1936, Barnwell, S.C. Microfiche from Center for Research Libraries, Chicago (hereafter cited as CRL).

21. "Civilian Conservation Corps Camps in the State of South Carolina, 1933–1942," photocopied report, Research Files, State Historic Preservation Office, South Carolina Department of Archives and History, Columbia (hereafter cited as SHPO, SCDAH).

22. Nadine Cohodas, *Strom Thurmond and the Politics of Southern Change* (New York: Simon and Schuster, 1993), 73.

23. Salmond, *Civilian Conservation Corps,* 48–50; Merrill, *Roosevelt's Forest Army,* 19. See also the general description of the CCC program in the *State* (Columbia, S.C.), May 28, 1933.

24. Salmond, *Civilian Conservation Corps,* 49–53.

25. *State* (Columbia, S.C.), May 21, 1934.

26. *Hilltop* (Company 4470), November 15, 1935, Cassatt, S.C.; *Bugle* (Company 4468), July 8, 1936, Barnwell, S.C., both in CRL.

27. Salmond, *Civilian Conservation Corps,* 105–16, 158. For the Cheraw camp, see the *Cherokean,* June 10, 1935, CCC camp newsletters, CRL.

28. Robert Fechner, "My Hopes for the CCC," *American Forests: The Magazine of the American Forestry Association* (January 1939), http://www.newdeal.feri.org/forests/af139 .htm, accessed May 2, 2000.

29. Salmond, *Civilian Conservation Corps,* 168.

30. *Pinopolian,* January 24, 1935, CCC camp newsletters, South Carolina Historical Society, Charleston (hereafter cited as SCHS).

31. Salmond, *Civilian Conservation Corps,* 168; Ned H. Dearborn, *Once in a Lifetime: A Guide to the CCC Camp* (New York: Charles E. Merrill, 1936), 45–47. Dearborn's book, published early during the life of the CCC, was intended to provide an overview of CCC camp life for new and prospective enrollees, to give them a taste of the educational and vocational opportunities they would have, and to encourage them to make the most of these opportunities. As Dearborn says on page 3, "One of the big reasons for preparing this Guide was to help you find out just what sort of work you are best fitted for or what kind of job you think you would best fit in. It will guide you through this great experience upon which you are beginning and which will leave its wholesome mark on you for the rest of your life."

32. Salmond, *Civilian Conservation Corps,* 168.

33. Ibid., 53, 167–168.

34. Steely, *Parks for Texas,* 39; Salmond, *Civilian Conservation Corps,* 121.

35. John Paige, "The CCC: It Gave a New Face to the NPS," *CRM Bulletin* 6 (September 1983): 2.

36. Phoebe Cutler, *The Public Landscape of the New Deal* (New Haven, Conn.: Yale University Press, 1985), 84.

37. Ibid., 85.

38. Ibid., 86–87.

39. Paige, "CCC," 2–3; Allen R. Coggins "The Early History of Tennessee's State Parks, 1919–1956," *Tennessee Historical Quarterly* 63 (Fall 1984): 314; Carroll Van West, *Tennessee's New Deal Landscape* (Knoxville: University of Tennessee Press, 2001), 199–201. Shelby Bluffs State Park had been acquired by the state in July 1939 for development as a state park for the large African American population in the Memphis area. It was later renamed to honor Dr. Thomas O. Fuller. In January 1962, 187 acres of the original 616-acre park were transferred to Memphis State University (now the University of Memphis) in order to protect the archaeological remains. The Chucalissa site was listed in the National Register of Historic Places in 1973 and as a National Historic Landmark in 1994. See also Carroll Van West, "Chucalissa Village," and Ruth D. Nichols, "T. O. Fuller State Park," both in *Tennessee Encyclopedia of History and Culture,* ed. Carroll Van West, 157–18, 904 (Nashville, Tenn.: Rutledge Hill Press, 1998).

40. Quoted in Arthur Schlesinger, *The Coming of the New Deal* (Boston: Houghton Mifflin, 1988), 338.

41. Salmond, *Civilian Conservation Corps*, 180, 193–16, 200–201; Johnson, "The Army and the Civilian Conservation Corps," 154–155.

42. Salmond, *Civilian Conservation Corps*, 196–17; Johnson, "The Army and the Civilian Conservation Corps," 155.

43. Salmond, *Civilian Conservation Corps*, 211–17.

44. Thomas P. Rutledge to J. D. Duford, January 22, 1941; Enrollee reports from September and October 1941, both in Hunting Island State Park files, box 12, South Carolina Forestry Commission (hereafter cited as SCFS), CCC files, SCDAH.

45. Thomas J. Allen to R. A. Walker, March 7, 1942, Hunting Island State Park files, box 12, SCFS, CCC files, SCDAH.

Chapter 3. "A good set of boys here and I like it fine"

1. Holland and Hill, *Youth in the CCC*, 13. Neil M. Maher's recently published *Nature's New Deal* explores these themes of environmentalism and the promotion of outdoor recreation, and their influence on both the resulting physical and political landscapes following the New Deal decade.

2. The Center for Research Libraries in Chicago contains what may be the most complete collection of camp newsletters on microfilm, including over sixty titles in South Carolina.

3. Holland and Hill, *Youth in the CCC*, 141.

4. Johnson, "The Army, the Negro, and the Civilian Conservation Corps," 82.

5. Holland and Hill, *Youth in the CCC*, 58–61. As time passed the average age of a CCC enrollee decreased, as the older, more experienced enrollees found other employment or left the CCC to be married or for other reasons. The experiences of African American and other minority enrollees will be examined in greater detail in a following chapter.

6. Ibid., 47.

7. Wilbert Bernshouse, "Autobiography," [1996], handwritten manuscript, photocopy in author's possession.

8. James P. Dawkins in National Association of Civilian Conservation Corps Alumni, Chapter 36, "Fort Moultrie Chapter of the NACCCA," typewritten booklet, [1984], photocopy in author's possession (hereafter cited as NACCCA).

9. *State* (Columbia, S.C.), May 17, 18, 19, 22, 29, 30, June 1, 5, 1933.

10. Wilbert Bernshouse, Fort Benning, Ga., to his mother, Sumter, S.C., May 19, 1933, photocopy in author's possession. Spelling in the original.

11. Ibid.

12. NACCCA.

13. *State* (Columbia, S.C.), June 4, 1933.

14. Ibid., June 4, 10, 14, 1933.

15. Ibid., July 27, 1934.

16. NACCCA; *State* (Columbia, S.C.), July 27, 1934; *Ditch Diggers Digest*, May 8, 1935, CCC camp newsletters, SCHS. Cmar recalled that their "big disappointment" stemmed from the hope that these New York City recruits would be sent to California.

17. Patrick Clancy, "Conserving the Youth: The Civilian Conservation Corps

Experience in the Shenandoah National Park," *Virginia Magazine of History and Biography* 105 (Autumn 1997): 463–67.

18. NACCCA.

19. *State* (Columbia, S.C.), June 4, 1933.

20. Jeffrey Ryan Suzik, "'Building Better Men': Education, Training, and Socialization of Working-Class Male Youth in the Civilian Conservation Corps, 1933–1942" (Ph.D. diss., Carnegie Mellon University, 2005), 107–18.

21. NACCCA.

22. Holland and Hill, *Youth in the CCC,* 191.

23. For the scholarly treatment of the way the Great Depression threatened masculinity and how the CCC contributed to redefining masculinity in the mid-twentieth century, see Bryant Simon, "'New Men in Body and Soul': The Civilian Conservation Corps and the Transformation of Male Bodies and the Body Politic," in *Gender and the Southern Body Politic,* ed. Nancy Bercaw, 131–160 (Jackson: University Press of Mississippi, 2000). For a comparison of the way that the work of the CCC transformed both the natural landscape and the bodies of the CCC boys while at the same time providing nationalistic political symbolism, see Neil M. Maher, "A New Deal Body Politic: Landscape, Labor, and the Civilian Conservation Corps," *Environmental History* 7 (Summer 2002): 435–61. The above-cited Suzik dissertation also examines the politicization of the CCC enrollees.

24. NACCCA; *State* (Columbia, S.C.), June 4, 1933; *Hi-Land Hi-Lights,* October 1937, CCC camp newspapers, SCHS.

25. *Pinopolian,* March 28, 1935, CCC camp newsletters, SCHS.

26. Frank A. Damon, Charleston, S.C., to the author, March 16, 2000; Dearborn, *Once in a Lifetime,* 45–47.

27. Holland and Hill, *Youth in the CCC,* 38–42; I. V. Butler, Charleston, S.C., to the author, November 23, 1999; *Hi-Land Hi-Lights,* CCC Camp newsletters, SCHS, n.d.

28. Bernshouse, "Autobiography."

29. NACCCA.

30. Ibid.; *State* (Columbia, S.C.), June 21, 1933.

31. *District I Opener,* November 23, 1935, CCC camp newsletters, SCHS.

32. *Hi-De-Hi-De-Ho,* July/August 1938, Anderson, S.C., CRL; *Hi-Land Hi-Lights,* October 1937, November 1938, CCC camp newsletters, SCHS; "Missing Persons" folder for Myrtle Beach State Park, box 16, SCFS, CCC files, SCDAH.

33. NACCCA; Damon to the author, March 16, 2000.

34. NACCCA; CCC District I Yearbooks, CCC files, South Carolina Department of Parks, Recreation, and Tourism (hereafter cited as SCPRT); *Pinopolian,* February 7, 1935, CCC camp newsletters, SCHS.

35. *Cherokean,* May 20, 1935; and *Poinsett Pointers,* April 29, 1935, CCC camp newsletters, SCHS; E. E. Jamison medal and letter in CCC files at SCPRT; *Mountaineer* (Company 4479), January 12, 1938, CRL. See also Robert Waller, "*Happy Days* and the CCC in South Carolina," *Historian* 64 (Fall 2001): 52.

36. NACCCA.

37. Ibid.

38. Ibid.

39. Bernshouse, "Autobiography."

40. *District I Opener,* November 23, 1935; and *Cherokean,* May 20, 1935, CCC camp newsletters, SCHS. For the account of listening to *War of the Worlds,* see the *Mountaineer* (Company 4479), October 30, 1938, CRL.

41. NACCCA.

42. William H. Taylor, Aiken, S.C., to the author, November 1, 1999. Taylor mistakenly attributed the songs to Dorsey, but they were originally recorded and performed by Glenn Miller's band.

43. Steely, *Parks for Texas,* 36.

44. NACCCA.

45. Ibid.

46. Weekly Report, CCC Company 445, Fort Moultrie, S.C., November 11, 1933–December 30, 1933, Frank A. Damon Personal Collection, Charleston, S.C., photocopy in author's possession; *State* (Columbia, S.C.), June 10, 1933.

47. *Pinopolian,* December 15, 1934, January 24, March 7, 1935, CCC camp newsletters, SCHS; *Oconee Mountaineer* (Company 3449), February 21, 1938, Walhalla, S.C., CRL; *Clover Clacker* (Company 4479), October 26, 1935, CRL.

48. *York (S.C.) Observer,* March 16, 1993.

49. Weekly Report, CCC Company 445, Fort Moultrie, S.C., November 1, 1933, Damon Collection, photocopy in author's possession.

50. Weekly Reports, CCC Company 445, Fort Moultrie, S.C., January 20, 27, February 3, 1934, Damon Collection, photocopies in author's possession; *Bugle* (Company 4468), November 4, 1935, Barnwell, S.C., CRL.

51. Butler to the author, November 23, 1999.

52. Damon to the author, March 16, 2000.

53. Weekly Report, CCC Company 445, Fort Moultrie, S.C., November 11, 1933, Damon Collection, photocopy in author's possession.

54. Weekly Reports, CCC Company 445, Fort Moultrie, S.C., December 23, 30, 1933, Damon Collection, photocopies in author's possession.

55. *Pinopolian,* January 24, March 7, 1935, CCC camp newsletters, SCHS.

56. For example, historian Jerrell H. Shofner recounts a situation in Sebring, Florida, where three CCC men robbed a diner and were shot while fleeing by the owner, then later arrested. See Jerrell H. Shofner, "Roosevelt's 'Tree Army': The Civilian Conservation Corps in Florida," *Florida Historical Quarterly* 65 (April 1987): 453–55, for this and other incidents. See also Clancy, "Conserving the Youth," 463–67.

57. NACCCA.

58. Holland and Hill, *Youth in the CCC,* 108, 127. See also Stephen O'Neal Rich, "The Civilian Conservation Corps: A Life-Changing Experience" (M.S.W. thesis, California State University, Long Beach, 2003).

59. Blanche Cook, *Eleanor Roosevelt,* Vol. 2, *1933–1938* (New York: Viking Press, 1992), 88–91; Kennedy, *Freedom from Fear,* 144.

60. Cook, *Eleanor Roosevelt,* 2:88–91; Badger, *New Deal,* 206; Waller, *"Happy Days,"* 44.

61. Olen Cole Jr., *The African-American Experience in the Civilian Conservation Corps* (Gainesville: University Press of Florida, 1999), 17. Cole also mentions that other

ethnic minorities in California, including Japanese, Chinese, and Filipinos, were not considered as minorities in the 1930s and that there is no separate information relating to them in California's CCC records.

62. Cooney, *Balancing Acts,* 114; Cole, *African-American Experience,* 18; Salmond, *Civilian Conservation Corps,* 23, 30–36.

63. Salmond, *Civilian Conservation Corps,* 30–36; Speakman, "Into the Woods."

64. Salmond, *Civilian Conservation Corps,* 37.

65. *State* (Columbia, S.C.), June 21, 26, 30, 1933; Waller, *"Happy Days,"* 43.

66. Mrs. Edward J. James, Simpsonville, S.C., to Governor Olin D. Johnston, Columbia, S.C., December 4, 1935, General—Dead File: Table Rock State Park, SCFS, CCC files, SCDAH.

67. General—Dead File: Table Rock State Park, SCFS, CCC files, SCDAH.

68. H. E. Weatherwax, Regional Officer, to C. G. Mackintosh, Spartanburg, S.C., January 2, 1936, General-Dead File: Table Rock State Park, SCFS, CCC files, SCDAH.

69. Ibid.

70. E. Thomas Sims and Julie Turner, "Table Rock State Park Historic District," National Register of Historic Places Registration Form, SCDAH, 1989, 8/6. See also Table Rock State Park, SCFS, CCC files, SCDAH; Table Rock Project Files, SCPRT; and *Pickens (S.C.) Sentinel,* May 7, 1936.

71. *Cherokean,* June 10, 1935, CCC camp newsletters, SCHS.

72. Quoted in Nixon, *Franklin D. Roosevelt and Conservation,* 147.

73. Johnson, "The Army, the Negro, and the Civilian Conservation Corps," 82; Cole, *African-American Experience,* 14. Olen Cole's *The African-American Experience in the Civilian Conservation Corps* is to date the only book-length study of African American enrollees in the CCC, and his book is primarily a case study of the experience in California. The classic study of African Americans nationally during the New Deal decade remains Harvard Sitkoff, *A New Deal for Blacks: The Emergence of Civil Rights as a National Issue, The Depression Decade* (New York: Oxford University Press, 1978). For the experience of African Americans in another New Deal program in the South, see Nancy L. Grant, *TVA and Black Americans: Planning for the Status Quo* (Philadelphia: Temple University Press, 1990).

74. Charles Johnson, "The Army, the Negro, and the Civilian Conservation Corps," 82; Salmond, *Civilian Conservation Corps,* 91; Cole, *African-American Experience,* 14; Hayes, *South Carolina and the New Deal,* 165; Edna Kennerly, "The Civilian Conservation Corps as a Social Resource in South Carolina" (M.S.W. thesis, University of South Carolina, 1940), 46. For more on the New Deal experience of South Carolina's African American population, see JoAnn Deakin Carpenter, "Olin D. Johnston, the New Deal, and the Politics of Class in South Carolina, 1934–1938" (Ph.D. diss., Emory University, 1987), 335–41; Newby, *Black Carolinians,* 248–49.

75. Quoted in Cole, *African-American Experience,* 26.

76. Robert Fechner to Dayton Jones, California CCC selection director, July 16, 1935, as quoted in ibid.

77. Robert Fechner to Thomas L. Griffith, September 21, 1935, "CCC Negro Selection" file, box 700, General Correspondence of the Director, Record Group 35, National Archives, College Park, Md.; Cole, *African-American Experience,* 21, 26; Salmond, *Civilian*

Conservation Corps, 91. President Roosevelt's assessment of Fechner's position as "political dynamite" is quoted in Steely, *Parks for Texas,* 97.

78. Luther C. Wandall, "A Negro in the CCC," *Crisis* 42 (August 1935): 254.

79. Charles Johnson, "The Army, the Negro, and the Civilian Conservation Corps," 84–85; Watkins, *Hungry Years,* 168.

80. Sitkoff, *New Deal for Blacks,* 64–65, 74–75.

81. Kennerly, "CCC as a Social Resource," 47–48. Although Kennerly comments that the proportion of African American CCC enrollees in South Carolina was not equal to that of the general population, she devoted only a page and a half of her 100–plus-page master's thesis in social work to the situation of the "Colored" CCC camps.

82. Waller, *"Happy Days,"* 49.

83. Marian Thompson Wright, "Negro Youth and the Federal Emergency Programs: CCC and NYA," *Journal of Negro Education* 9 (July 1940): 398–99; Kennerly, "CCC as a Social Resource," 47; *Hi-De-Hi-De-Ho Newsletter* and *District I, Fourth Corps Area Annual, 1938* (Baton Rouge, La.: Army and Navy Publishing, 1938), CCC files, SCPRT.

84. *Hill Top* (Company 4470), November 1935; *Hi-De-Hi-De-Ho* (Company 4487) January–April, August, November 1937, January–April 1938, Awendaw, S.C., CRL.

85. Quoted in Salmond, *Civilian Conservation Corps,* 91–92. See also Ren Davis, "Our Mark on This Land," *Georgia Journal* (March/April 1998): 23.

86. Leslie Alexander Lacy, *The Soil Soldiers: The Civilian Conservation Corps in the Great Depression* (Radnor, Pa.: Chilton Book, 1976), 74–79; Salmond, *Civilian Conservation Corps,* 91–93; Steely, *Parks for Texas,* 94–95; *District I Yearbook 1938,* SCPRT.

87. *Sumter (S.C.) Daily Item,* July 26, 31, October 25, 26, 31, November 12, 1935.

88. "Narrative Report for Poinsett State Park SP-3, October 1st to Nov. 6, 1935," Record Group 79, Entry 41, box 123, National Archives, photocopy in Poinsett State Park Files; and Chester State Park Files, SCPRT.

89. Stephen W. Skelton, "Poinsett State Park: National Register Nomination Preliminary Research," 1989, unpublished paper in Research Files, SHPO, SCDAH, 15–16; *Sumter (S.C.) Daily Item,* July 26, 31, November 12, 1935; *District I, Fourth Corps Area Annual 1938,* 36–39; Poinsett State Park, SCFS, CCC files, SCDAH. This notation was also found on an application for camps at Table Rock State Park.

90. "Narrative Report for Poinsett State Park SP-3, March 31, 1936," Record Group 79, Entry 41, box 123, National Archives; CCC files, Poinsett State Park, SCDAH.

91. *Columbia (S.C.) Record,* April 21, 1941; *State* (Columbia, S.C.), April 21, 1941; *Pittsburgh Courier,* June 14, 1941. A concise but complete account of this incident is given by Andrew H. Myers in *Black, White, and Olive Drab: Racial Integration at Fort Jackson, South Carolina, and the Civil Rights Movement* (Charlottesville: University of Virginia Press, 2006), 24–26. I appreciate Tracy Power at the SCDAH for pointing out this source.

92. "Civilian Conservation Corps Camps in the State of South Carolina, 1933–1942," Research files, SHPO, SCDAH; National Park Service, *A Study of the Park and Recreation Problem of the United States* (Washington, D.C.: GPO, 1941), 67–68; South Carolina State Planning Board, *Parks and Recreational Areas of South Carolina,* Bulletin No. 7 (Columbia: South Carolina State Planning Board, 1941), 86. A study of the segregated

state park system and the fight for integration of the state parks is Stephen Lewis Cox, "The History of Negro State Parks in South Carolina, 1940–1963" (M.A. thesis, University of South Carolina, 1992).

93. Cox, "History of Negro State Parks," 80–109; *State* (Columbia, S.C.), July 15, 2001.

94. Hoffman, "Genesis of the Equal Rights," 346, 353.

95. Newby, *Black Carolinians,* 246.

96. Hayes, *South Carolina and the New Deal,* 158, 183.

Chapter 4. Building Opportunity

1. South Carolina Forestry Commission, *Report of the State Commission of Forestry for the Year July 1, 1930, to June 30, 1931,* 83, SCDAH (hereafter cited as SCFC, *Report 1930–1931*).

2. Quoted in Freeman Tilden, *State Parks: Their Meaning in American Life* (New York: Alfred A. Knopf, 1962), 3–5. See also John Henneberger, "State Park Beginnings," *George Wright Forum* 17 (2000): 18–19.

3. Cutler, *Public Landscape,* 8–28; Henneberger, "State Park Beginnings," 18–19.

4. Tilden, *State Parks,* 11–16; Cutler, *Public Landscape,* 8–28, 64–66. See also Dwight F. Rettie, *Our National Park System: Caring for America's Greatest Natural and Historic Treasures* (Urbana: University of Illinois Press, 1995), 6.

5. Warren James Belasco, *Americans on the Road: From Autocamp to Motel, 1910–1945* (Cambridge, Mass.: MIT Press, 1981), 3–8, 72, 106.

6. Ibid., 3–8, 76–79; John A. Jakle, *The Tourist: Travel in Twentieth Century North America* (Lincoln: University of Nebraska Press, 1985), 158–19.

7. Belasco, *Americans on the Road,* 4, 76; Jakle, *Tourist,* 158–10.

8. Cutler, *Public Landscape,* 65.

9. Edgar, *South Carolina,* 491–93; Fraser, *Charleston! Charleston!* 354–86, passim; Barbara F. Stokes, *Myrtle Beach: A History, 1900–1980* (Columbia: University of South Carolina Press, 2007), 23–26. A detailed description of the climb up Table Rock during the early nineteenth century can be found in "Description of the Table Rock of South Carolina," printed in the *New England Galaxy,* July 6, 1827.

10. Quoted in Belasco, *Americans on the Road,* 144.

11. Clarence Buxton to William Lykes, Columbia [S.C.] Chamber of Commerce, n.d. [1934], Columbia Chamber of Commerce Papers, Caroliniana Library, University of South Carolina, Columbia; Stokes, *Myrtle Beach,* 37–38.

12. SCFC, *Report 1931–1932,* 26, SCDAH; SCFC, *Report 1933–1934,* 8–9, SCDAH.

13. *South Carolina Acts and Resolutions 1933,* Act 350; Robin Copp, "The Civilian Conservation Corps and South Carolina," (unpublished paper in CCC Research Files, SHPO, SCDAH, 1985), 8–9.

14. South Carolina Federal Writers' Project, *South Carolina State Parks,* 6, 42. The CCC developed six wayside parks in South Carolina under the RDA program; one of these is now Colleton State Park.

15. Edgar, *South Carolina,* 449.

16. Albert H. Good, *Park and Recreation Structures,* 3 vols. (Washington, D.C.: National Park Service, 1938; repr., Boulder, Colo.: Graybooks, 1990); Linda Flint

McClelland, *Building the National Parks: Historic Landscape Design and Construction* (Baltimore: Johns Hopkins University Press, 1998), 429–30.

17. Albert Good, *Park Structures and Facilities* (Washington, D.C.: National Park Service, 1935), 3–4.

18. Cutler, *Public Landscape,* 77–78.

19. McClelland, *Building the National Parks,* 434; Cutler, *Public Landscape,* 90–91. Phoebe Cutler also draws on the parallels between "Government Rustic" architectural sensibilities if not architectural style in the state parks of the 1930s and architectural designs of Frank Lloyd Wright during the same period: "The Chicago renegade and the Government Rustic designers shared a ground-hugging regard for nature." See Cutler, *Public Landscape,* 78–79.

20. Otis et al., *Forest Service and the Civilian Conservation Corps,* 10.

21. Ibid., 51–52; James Bates, "Long Cane/Enoree History," http://www.fs.fed.us/r8/fms/welcome/piedmont.htm, accessed July 31, 2001. See also Peggy J. Paxton, *The National Forests and Purchase Units of Region Eight* (Atlanta: USDA Forest Service, 1950).

22. Otis et al., *Forest Service and the Civilian Conservation Corps,* 53.

23. D. Y. Lenhart, *The South Carolina Civilian Conservation Corps Forester* (Columbia, S.C.: State Commission of Forestry, 1936), 1–36.

24. McClelland, *Building the National Parks,* 417.

25. Quoted in Harlan D. Unrau and G. Frank Williss, *Administrative History: Expansion of the National Park Service in the 1930s* (Denver: NPS Denver Service Center, 1983), n.p., http://www.cr.nps.gov/ history/on-line__books/unrau-williss/adhi.htm, accessed August 8, 2001.

26. Rettie, *Our National Park System,* 6, 54; Cutler, *Public Landscape,* 70–71, 157; McClelland, *Building the National Parks,* 328, 415–17. The development of the RDAs at Cheraw, Kings Mountain, and Colleton Wayside will be discussed in following chapters.

27. Unrau and Williss, *Administrative History,* n.p. See also Seth C. Bruggeman, *Here, George Washington Was Born* (Athens: University of Georgia Press, 2008), for the expansion of NPS's work in historic sites at George Washington Birthplace National Monument for a case study of the challenges faced during the New Deal decade at NPS historic sites.

Chapter 5. Conservation and Commemoration

1. Cutler, *Public Landscape,* 70–75. See also Tilden, *State Parks,* 3–16.

2. McClelland, *Building the National Parks,* 414–15.

3. For general discussion of the RDA program, see McClelland, *Building the National Parks,* 414–20. An introduction to the South Carolina RDAs is found in Robert Waller, "The Civilian Conservation Corps and the Emergence of South Carolina's State Park System, 1933–1942," *South Carolina Historical Magazine* 104 (April 2003): 113–16. Waller refers to these areas as Recreational Development Areas, and McClelland uses the term interchangeably. NPS materials use the term "Recreational Demonstration Area." For an excellent introduction of the federal recreation areas in South Carolina at the end of the New Deal period of development, see South Carolina State Planning Board, *Parks and Recreational Areas,* 75–86.

4. SCDAH, Historical Services Division, Research files, "Cheraw State Park Survey Report," 1991, 5. As the first state park begun in South Carolina, Cheraw is the best documented of the CCC state park projects in South Carolina.

5. Robert Fechner to Burnet R. Maybank, January 14, 1939. Burnet R. Maybank papers, SCDAH.

6. "Cheraw State Park Survey Report," 5.

7. H. L. Tilghman to H. A. Smith, February 19, 1934; L. C. Wannamaker to H. L. Tilghman, February 20, 1934; H. A. Smith to H. L. Tilghman, February 20, 1934; and H. L. Tilghman to H. A. Smith 22 February 22, 1934, all in SCFS, Administration, CCC files, box 3, SCDAH.

8. Census data from http://www.census.gov/population/cencounts/sc190090.txt, accessed November 9, 2001. Affidavit concerning finances and land purchases, February 12, 1934, signed by L .C. Wannamaker and notarized by H. A. McLeod, SCFS, Administration, CCC files, box 3, SCDAH.

9. L. C. Wannamaker to H. A. Smith, March 23, 1934, SCFS, Administration, CCC files, box 3, SCDAH. A copy of the deed and the list of donors is not included with this letter in the archival records, although a partial list is on file at SCPRT.

10. *State* (Columbia, S.C.), March 28, 1934.

11. Application for Camp Cherokee, SP-1 at Cheraw, February 9, 1934; and H. E. Weatherwax (ECW District Officer) to H. A. Smith (State Forester), March 15, 1934, both in SCFS, Administration, CCC files, box 4, SCDAH.

12. *Cheraw (S.C.) Chronicle*, May 31, 1934.

13. H. A. Smith to F. F. Jewett, March 21, 1934; and Jewett to Smith, March 23, 1934, both in SCFS, Administration, CCC files, box 4, SCDAH.

14. *CCC Annual District I, 1936* (Baton Rouge, La.: Army and Navy Publishing, 1936), 31, SCPRT.

15. *Cherokean*, May 20, 1935, CCC Camp newsletters, SCHS.

16. Jack Wilson, quoted in Copp, "Civilian Conservation Corps and South Carolina," 10.

17. Damon to the author, March 16, 2000.

18. *Cherokean*, June 10, 1935, CCC camp newsletters, SCHS.

19. SCFC, *Report 1933–1934*; L. C. Wannamaker and Ethel Pegues to H. A. Smith, August 23, 1934, SCFS, Administration, CCC files, box 4, SCDAH.

20. *Cherokean*, May 20, 1935, CCC camp newsletters, SCHS; E. H. Hutchinson (Superintendent, Cheraw State Forest Park) to H. A. Smith, September 20, 1934; Smith to H. E. Weatherwax (ECW District Officer, Richmond, Va.), September 22, 1934; Weatherwax to Smith, September 27, 1934; and Weatherwax to Smith, February 13, 1935, all in SCFS, Administration, CCC files, box 4, SCDAH. See also "Cheraw State Park Survey Report," 6; and *State* (Columbia, S.C.), July 8, 1934.

21. *Cherokean*, July 31, November 12, 1935, CCC camp newsletters, SCHS and CRL.

22. *Cherokean*, August 30, November 12, 1935, April 7, 1936, CCC camp newsletters, SCHS; "Cheraw State Park Survey Report," 7–13; SCFS, Photography file, CCC files, box 3, SCDAH; SCFC, *Report 1934–1935*, 34, SCDAH; SCFC, *Report 1935–1936*, 72, SCDAH; SCFC, *Report 1943–1944*, 63–64, SCDAH; "Master Plan Report: Cheraw State Park and Cheraw Recreational Area," SCFS, Administration, CCC files, box 3, SCDAH.

23. *Cherokean,* August 30, 1935, CCC camp newsletters, SCHS.

24. SCFC, *Report 1934–1935,* 34; SCFC, *Report 1935–1936,* 72; SCFC, *Report 1943–1944,* 63–64.

25. *Cherokean,* April 7, 1936, CCC camp newsletters, SCHS; Frank Brown, Dan Elswick, and Tommy Sims, "The Establishment and Development of South Carolina State Parks," unpublished report in research files, Historical Services Division, SCDAH.

26. *Cherokean,* August 30, 1935, CCC camp newsletters, CRL; R. A. Walker (Assistant State Forester) to E. H. Hutchinson, July 31, 1935, SCFS, Administration, CCC files, box 4, SCDAH; SCFC, *Report 1942–1943,* 72, SCDAH.

27. For a discussion of how "Government Rustic" architecture combined both a longing for the nation's past with an appreciation with the conveniences of modernity, see Weber, "Vision and Reality."

28. "Cheraw State Park Survey Report," 9; SCFC, *Report 1941–1942,* 119, SCDAH; SCFC, *Report 1943–1944,* 63. The state parks at Aiken, Table Rock, Lee, and Poinsett also had fish-rearing pools.

29. "Cheraw State Park Survey Report," 8–9; E. M. Lisle (NPS Regional Officer) to P. R. Plummer (Project Manager), August 8, 1937, SCFS, Administration, CCC files, box 3, SCDAH.

30. South Carolina Federal Writers' Project, *South Carolina State Parks,* 29; SCFC, *Report 1937–1938,* 7, SCDAH; SCFC, *Report 1941–1942,* 91; SCFC, *Report 1942–1943,* 73–74; and SCFC, *Report 1943–1944,* 68.

31. "Cheraw State Park Survey Report," 9–10; SCFS, Administration, CCC files, box 4, SCDAH.

32. SCFC, *Report 1939–1940,* 98, SCDAH; "Cheraw State Park Survey Report," 10; SCFS, CCC files, box 4, SCDAH.

33. "Cheraw State Park Survey Report," 10–11; SCFC, *Report 1941–1942,* 87–88; SCFS, Administration, CCC files, box 4, SCDAH.

34. SCFC, *Report 1941–1942,* 87–94.

35. "Cheraw Recreational Demonstration Area Supplement Master Plan Report for 1940," SCFS, Administration, CCC files, box 3, SCDAH.

36. McClelland, *Building the National Parks,* 376–79, 415–416. See also South Carolina State Planning Board, *Parks and Recreational Areas,* 50–52.

37. SCFC, *Report 1935–1936,* 72; South Carolina State Planning Board, *Parks and Recreational Areas,* 76–77.

38. SCFC, *Report 1941–1942,* 86. See also South Carolina State Planning Board, *Parks and Recreational Areas,* 65, 76.

39. SCFC, *Report 1939–1940,* 99; Albert Hester, Historian, South Carolina Department of Parks, Recreation, and Tourism, to the author, June 8, 2002, in author's possession.

40. Robert W. Blythe, Maureen A. Carroll, and Steven H. Moffson, *Kings Mountain National Military Park: Historic Resource Study* (Atlanta: Southeast Regional Office, National Park Service, 1995), 95. Other national monuments and national parks in South Carolina transferred to the NPS include Castle Pinckney National Monument in Charleston, declared a national monument in 1924, and Cowpens National

Battlefield Site near Spartanburg, established as a National Battlefield in 1929. See South Carolina State Planning Board, *Parks and Recreational Areas*, 77–79.

41. Robert W. Blythe, Maureen A. Carroll, and Steven H. Moffson, "Kings Mountain National Military Park," National Register of Historic Places Registration Form, SCDAH, 1994, 8/31–8/34. For an early, complete account of the battle of Kings Mountain, see Lyman Draper, *King's Mountain and Its Heroes: History of the Battle of King's Mountain, October 7th, 1780* (Cincinnati: Peter G. Thomson, 1881; repr., Nashville, Tenn.: Blue and Gray Press, 1971), especially pages 236–309.

42. Blythe, Carroll, and Moffson, "Kings Mountain National Military Park," 8/40–8/41.

43. Ibid., 8/49–8/51.

44. Ibid., 8/42–8/48; Ronald F. Lee, *The Origin and Evolution of the National Military Park Idea* (Washington, D.C.: National Park Service, Office of Park Historic Preservation, 1973), 11, 17–19. Lee's book provides a great deal of interesting context surrounding the development of the national military parks, including the Civil War battlefields of Antietam, Chickamauga/Chattanooga, Shiloh, Gettysburg, and Vicksburg, all of which had obtained national battlefield status by 1900. Additionally, Lee served as a foreman in a CCC camp at Shiloh in 1933, before becoming assistant chief historian, chief historian, and later assistant director of the National Park Service.

45. Quoted in Blythe, Carroll, and Moffson, "Kings Mountain National Military Park," 8/51.

46. Ibid., 8/52–8/53, 8/61; Draper, *King's Mountain and Its Heroes;* Robert Shackleton, "A Battlefield That Is Seldom Visited—Kings Mountain," *Magazine of American History* 30 (July–August 1893): 38–46.

47. Blythe, Carroll, and Moffson, "Kings Mountain National Military Park," 8/53–8/55, 8/64–8/65.

48. Ibid., 8/55.

49. Ibid., 8/56, 8/83. Conversely, the Revolutionary War battlefield at Lexington and Concord, Massachusetts, received a great deal of commemorative attention at the local level, including the erection of a monument as early as 1799. However, Lexington and Concord did not become a National Historical Park until 1959, when Congress established Minute Man National Historical Park. The North Bridge at Concord is still owned locally but is managed by the National Park Service. See Edward Tabor Linenthal, *Sacred Ground: Americans and Their Battlefields* (Urbana: University of Illinois Press, 1993), 11–51.

50. Blythe, Carroll, and Moffson, "Kings Mountain National Military Park," 8–83; Blythe, Carroll, and Moffson, *Kings Mountain National Military Park*, 95.

51. Blythe, Carroll, and Moffson, *Kings Mountain National Military Park*, 96–97.

52. Kristina Dunn and Al Hester, "Kings Mountain State Park," National Register of Historic Places Registration Form, SCDAH, 2008.

53. *Rock Hill (S.C.) Evening Herald*, May 21, 22, 29, July 26, 1935.

54. Dunn and Hester, "Kings Mountain State Park."

55. SCFC, *Report 1936–1937*, 49, SCDAH; South Carolina State Planning Board, *Parks and Recreational Areas*, 79.

56. Blythe, Carroll, and Moffson, *Kings Mountain National Military Park*, 101–12.

57. Ibid., 103–15.

58. Scott Withrow, "The CCC Remembered in Upstate South Carolina: Bethany and Mountain Rest," unpublished paper in Kings Mountain State Park files, SCPRT. The Visitor's House has been moved from its original location and is now located at the Kings Mountain State Park History Farm.

59. South Carolina Federal Writers' Project, *South Carolina State Parks*, 31.

60. Dunn and Hester, "Kings Mountain State Park."

61. SCFC, *Report 1939–1940*, 88–90, 105–16.

Chapter 6. Forestry Work and State Park Development

1. SCFC, *Report 1932–1933*, 28, SCDAH; Shofner, "Roosevelt's 'Tree Army,'" 440.

2. *State* (Columbia, S.C.), June 2, 1933.

3. SCFC, *Report 1932–1933*, 29.

4. *State* (Columbia, S.C.), April 23, May 17, 18, 21, 1933.

5. SCFC, *Report 1932–1933*, 29.

6. Ibid., 31.

7. SCFC, *Report 1933–1934*, 7–8, 10.

8. Ibid., 16–17, 20.

9. Ibid., 25–26.

10. Aiken State Park history files, SCPRT.

11. *Aiken (S.C.) Standard and South Carolina Gazette,* August 13, 1934; *State* (Columbia, S.C.), August 4, 1934; Aiken State Park history files, SCPRT. Two of the cabins and some of the smaller structures burned in April 1967, when the "Windsor Fire" burned some 4,000 acres in Aiken County.

12. SCFC, *Report 1934–1935*, 13–15, 33.

13. Ibid., 31–39.

14. Ibid. See also South Carolina State Planning Board, *Parks and Recreational Areas,* 31.

15. SCFC, *Report 1935–1936*, 70–76.

16. Ibid., 62–63; *Sumter (S.C.) Daily Item,* April 20, 1935; Lenhart, *South Carolina Civilian Conservation Corps Forester,* iii.

17. "Narrative Report for Edisto State Park, SP-2, March 1st, 1935; March 31, 1935; May 1, 1935; June 1, 1935; August 3, 1935; October 1, 1935," Record Group 79, Entry 41, box 122, National Archives; Givhans Ferry State Park history file, SCPRT.

18. Stephen W. Skelton, "Poinsett State Park: National Register Nomination Preliminary Research," unpublished paper in research files, Historical Services Division, SCDAH. An interesting description of Poinsett State Park is found in Tilden, *State Parks,* 242–45; however, Tilden spends less time in describing the park's facilities or natural resources than in highlighting the career of Joel Poinsett.

19. "Narrative Reports for Poinsett State Park, December 1, 1934–June 1, 1935," Record Group 79, Entry 41, box 123, National Archives; Skelton, "Poinsett State Park," 11–14; Poinsett State Park history files, SCPRT; *Poinsett Pointers,* April 29, May 20, June 10, 1935, CCC camp newsletters, SCHS; *1936 District I Annual,* 69, SCPRT.

20. C. G. Mackintosh, Regional Inspector, to H. E. Weatherwax, Regional Officer, Richmond, Va., June 29, 1935; Weatherwax to Mackintosh, July 2, 1935, SCFS,

Administration, both in CCC files, Poinsett State Park, SCDAH; Skelton, "Poinsett State Park," 14–15.

21. H. E. Weatherwax to State Park ECW, Washington, D.C., June 18, 1935, SCFS, CCC files, Poinsett State Park, SCDAH.

22. *Sumter (S.C.) Daily Item,* July 22, 23, 26, 1935; "Narrative Report for Poinsett State Park No. 3, August 1st–October 1st, 1935," Record Group 79, Entry 41, box 123, National Archives; Poinsett State Park history files, SCPRT.

23. "Narrative Report for Poinsett State Park SP-3, October 1st to Nov. 6, 1935"; "Narrative Report for Poinsett State Park, March 31, 1936," both in Record Group 79, Entry 41, box 123, National Archives. See also Poinsett State Park history files, SCPRT.

24. Lee State Park history files, SCPRT; "Lee State Natural Area," undated brochure, SCPRT.

25. Albert Hester, "Paris Mountain State Park Historic District," National Register of Historic Places Registration Form, SCDAH, 1998, 8/11; Archie Vernon Huff Jr., *Greenville: The History of the City and County in the South Carolina Piedmont* (Columbia: University of South Carolina Press, 1995), 346–47.

26. Hester, "Paris Mountain State Park Historic District," 8/11.

27. C. G. Mackintosh to H. E. Weatherwax, January 16, 1936, and attached report; H. E. Weatherwax to Conrad Wirth, January 18, 1936, both in Record Group 79, Inspection Reports, Entry 64, box 2, National Archives.

28. Ibid.

29. Ibid.

30. South Carolina State Planning Board, *Parks and Recreational Areas,* 62–66; Hester, "Paris Mountain State Park Historic District," 7/7–/8.

31. South Carolina State Planning Board, *Parks and Recreational Areas,* 62–66.

32. For a more detailed discussion of the controversy surrounding the establishment of a seregated park for African Americans in the upststate, see Stephen Lewis Cox, "The History of Negro State Parks in South Carolina, 1940–1963" (M.A. thesis, University of South Carolina, 1992, 45–61.

Chapter 7. South Carolina's "Breathing Spaces"

1. SCFC, *Report 1936–1937,* 47. For a discussion of the evolution of the South Carolina parks management plans, see also SCPRT, "An Historic Management Perspective of the South Carolina State Parks System" (Columbia: SCPRT, [1988?]).

2. SCFC, *Report 1936–1937,* 48. Phoebe Cutler explores the linkages between outdoor recreation and the reclamation of both land and people in her *Public Landscape of the New Deal,* in a chapter titled "The New Deal and the New Play."

3. SCFC, *Report 1936–1937,* 71–73; see also South Carolina State Planning Board, *Parks and Recreational Areas,* 31.

4. SCFC, *Report 1936–1937,* 55–58, 65–69; Lee State Park history files, SCPRT.

5. SCFC, *Report 1936–1937,* 61–64.

6. Ibid., 48–49, 58–59.

7. Ibid., 55–58, 65–69.

8. Stokes, *Myrtle Beach,* 26.

9. Ibid., 18–33.

10. *SP 4 UM* (Myrtle Beach, S.C.), May 26, 1937, CRL.

11. SCFC, *Report 1936–1937*, 56–57; South Carolina Federal Writers' Project, *South Carolina State Parks*, 9; Tilden, *State Parks*, 233–36; South Carolina State Planning Board, *Parks and Recreational Areas*, 62

12. H. A. Smith to H. B. Springs, June 14, 1934, SCFS, Administration, CCC files, Myrtle Beach State Park, SCDAH; Stokes, *Myrtle Beach*, 38–41.

13. *SP 4 UM* (Myrtle Beach, S.C.), May 26, 1937, CRL. A hurricane damaged the massive bathhouse and pavilion complex in the 1960s, and it was dismantled in 1967. A portion of the complex has been reused in the state park.

14. Kevin Allen, "Oconee State Park Historic District," National Register of Historic Places Registration Form, SCDAH, 2004, 25–26; Oconee State Park history files, SCPRT.

15. Allen, "Oconee State Park," 13–14.

16. Ibid., 4–11; Oconee State Park history files, SCPRT.

17. *Oconee Mountaineer* (Company 3449), February 21, 1938, Walhalla, S.C., CRL.

18. Ibid., March 28, April 20, 1938.

19. SCFC, *Report 1937–1938*, 63, 66–71.

20. Ibid., 67–69.

21. Ibid., 71–73.

22. Ibid., 8–9.

23. James H. Hammond papers, (unprocessed), South Caroliniana Library; Moore, *Columbia and Richland County*, 366; Jane K. Simons, *A Guide to Columbia: South Carolina's Capital City* (Columbia: Columbia Sesquicentennial Commission, R. L. Bryan, 1939), 69.

24. James H. Hammond to Mayor L. B. Owens of Columbia, April 5, 1937; Owens to Hammond, April 7, 1937; Hammond to Owens, April 16, 1937; and Owens to Hammond, June 2, 1937, all in Hammond papers, South Caroliniana Library; Sesquicentennial State Park history files, SCPRT.

25. Sesquicentennial State Park history files, SCPRT; Moore, *Columbia and Richland County*, 366.

26. Sesquicentennial State Park history files, SCPRT; Waller, "*Happy Days*," 56. During the building of Sesquicentennial, one enrollee, P. Washington Porter, found time to participate in a national play-writing contest sponsored by the national CCC newsletter *Happy Days* and the Federal Writers' Project. Porter's tragedy, *Return to Death*, won national honors, and Porter traveled from Pontiac to New York City to oversee the production of his work at the WPA Federal Theater.

27. *State* (Columbia, S.C.), June 10, 1956.

28. SCFC, *Report 1938–1939*, 77–79, SCDAH.

29. Ibid., 82.

30. Ibid.; Cox, "History of Negro State Parks," 19–22.

31. Robert W. May to H. A. Smith, August 9, 1938; Smith to May, August 12, 1938, both in SCFS, CCC files, Administration, General Files. Hunting Island State Park has an interpretive exhibit related to the development of Hunting Island addressing this event as well.

32. Governor's Messages, 1809, General Assembly papers, SCDAH; Sims and

Turner, "Table Rock State Park Historic District," 8/1–/2. Freeman Tilden offers a brief sketch of Table Rock Mountain and the state park in his *State Parks*, 460.

33. Sims and Turner, "Table Rock State Park Historic District," 8/4.

34. Ibid.; "Master Plan Report for Table Rock State Park, Pickens County, South Carolina," August 18, 1939, SCFS, Administration, CCC files, Table Rock State Park, SCDAH.

35. Sims and Turner, "Table Rock State Park Historic District," 8/5–/6; see also SCFS, Administration, CCC files, Table Rock State Park, SCDAH.

36. Sims and Turner, "Table Rock State Park Historic District," 8/6–/7; *Pickens (S.C.) Sentinel,* May 7, 1936; *Greenville (S.C.) Piedmont,* May 11, 1938; "Master Plan Report for Table Rock State Park"; SCFS, CCC files, Table Rock State Park, SCDAH.

37. Sims and Turner, "Table Rock State Park Historic District," 8/7–/10. See also *State* (Columbia, S.C.), March 27, 1936, for winning drawings and results from the Clemson architectural competition.

38. Sims and Turner, "Table Rock State Park Historic District," 7/1, 8/9–/10; "Master Plan for Table Rock State Park."

39. Sims and Turner, "Table Rock State Park Historic District," 8/11; "Master Plan for Table Rock State Park."

40. "Master Plan Report for Greenwood State Park," SCFS, CCC files, Greenwood State Park, SCDAH.

41. Ibid.

42. SCFC, *Report 1938–1939*, 79–82.

43. R. A. Walker to Louise DuBose, December 16, 1938, SCFS, CCC files, General Files, SCDAH. See also South Carolina Federal Writers' Project, *South Carolina State Parks.*

44. SCFC, *Report 1939–1940*, 91–92, 102–14.

45. Robert Fechner to Burnet R. Maybank, January 14, 1939, SCFS, Administration, CCC files, General Files, SCDAH.

46. SCFC, *Report 1939–1940*, 96–98, 106–17.

47. Ibid., 88–90, 105–16.

48. SCFC, *Report 1940–1941*, 80–82, 94–98, SCDAH.

49. Ibid., 87–101, 105; SCPRT, "History of South Carolina State Parks" (Columbia: SCPRT, 1992).

50. SCFC, *Report 1940–1941*, 104–15.

51. Ibid., 88; SCFC, *Report 1941–1942*, 84, 88–89.

52. SCFC, *Report 1941–1942*, 10–11, 88.

53. Ibid., 97.

54. Ibid., 90–96; "Historic Management Perspective of the South Carolina State Parks System."

55. SCFC, *Report 1941–1942*, 98–99.

Chapter 8. Learning from the Parks

1. Chutler, *Public Landscape*, 153–54.

2. Steely, *Parks for Texas*, 194–95, 199–200.

3. [Robin Copp], *The Civilian Conservation Corps in South Carolina, 1933–1942*. Public Programs Document Packet 4, Columbia: SCDAH, 1990.

BIBLIOGRAPHY

Manuscripts and Records

Frank A. Damon personal collection, Charleston, S.C.
National Archives, Washington, D.C.
    Record Group 35
    Record Group 69
    Record Group 79
South Carolina Department of Archives and History, Columbia
    Forestry Commission, CCC files
    Forestry Commission, State Park files
    General Assembly papers
    Burnet R. Maybank papers
South Carolina Department of Parks, Recreation, and Tourism, Columbia
    George Buell Collection
    CCC files
    CCC yearbooks
    State Park history files (Aiken, Barnwell, Cheraw, Chester, Colleton, Edisto Beach, Givhans Ferry, Greenwood, Hunting Island, Kings Mountain, Lee, Myrtle Beach, Oconee, Paris Mountain, Poinsett, Sesquicentennial, Table Rock)
South Carolina Historical Society, Charleston
    Civilian Conservation Corps camp newsletters
South Caroliniana Library, University of South Carolina, Columbia
    Columbia, S.C., Chamber of Commerce records
    James H. Hammond Papers

Correspondence

Bernshouse, Wilbert, Fort Benning, Ga., to his mother, Sumter, S.C., May 19, 1933. Photocopy of letter in author's possession.

Butler, I. V., Charleston, S.C., to the author, November 23, 1999. Letter in author's possession.

Damon, Frank, A., Charleston, S.C., to the author, March 16, 2000. Letter in author's possession.

Hester, Albert, Historian, South Carolina Department of Parks, Recreation, and Tourism, Columbia, S.C., to the author, June 8, 2002. Letter in author's possession.

Taylor, William H., Aiken, S.C., to the author, November 1, 1999. Letter in author's possession.

South Carolina Newspapers

Aiken Standard and South Carolina Gazette
Charleston News and Courier
Charleston Post and Courier
Cheraw Chronicle
Clover Herald
Greenville Piedmont
Pickens Sentinel
Rock Hill Evening Herald
State
Sumter Daily Item
York Observer

Government Documents

Allen, Kevin. "Oconee State Park Historic District." National Register of Historic Places Registration Form, South Carolina Department of Archives and History, Columbia, 2004.

Berg, Shary Page. *The Civilian Conservation Corps: Shaping the Forests and Parks of Massachusetts.* Boston: Massachusetts Department of Environmental Management, Division of Resource Conservation, 1999.

Birnbaum, Charles A. "Protecting Cultural Landscapes:

Planning, Treatment and Management of Historic Landscapes." Preservation Brief 36. Washington, D.C.: National Park Service, 1994.

Blythe, Robert W., Maureen A. Carroll, and Steven H. Moffson. "Kings Mountain National Military Park." National Register of Historic Places Registration Form. South Carolina Department of Archives and History, Columbia, 1994.

———. *Kings Mountain National Military Park: Historic Resource Study.* Atlanta: Southeast Regional Office, National Park Service, 1995.

[Copp, Robin]. *The Civilian Conservation Corps in South Carolina, 1933–1942.* Public Programs Document Packet No. 4. Columbia: South Carolina Department of Archives and History, 1990.

Dunn, Kristina, and Al Hester. "Kings Mountain State Park Historic District." National Register of Historic Places Registration Form. South Carolina Department of Archives and History, Columbia, 2008.

Good, Albert H. *Park and Recreation Structures.* 3 vols. Washington, D.C.: National Park Service, 1938. Reprint, Boulder, Colo.: Graybooks, 1990.

———. *Park Structures and Facilities.* Washington, D.C.: National Park Service, 1935.

Hester, Albert. "Paris Mountain State Park Historic District." National Register of Historic Places Registration Form. South Carolina Department of Archives and History, Columbia, 1998.

Holland, Kenneth, and Frank Ernest Hill. *Youth in the CCC.* Washington, D.C.: American Council on Education, 1942. Reprint, New York: Arno Press, 1974.

Lee, Ronald F. *The Origin and Evolution of the National Military Park Idea.* Washington, D.C.: National Park Service, Office of Park Historic Preservation, 1973.

Lenhart, D. Y. *The South Carolina Civilian Conservation Corps Forester.* Columbia, S.C.: State Commission of Forestry, 1936.

Mastran, Shelley Smith, and Nan Lowere. *Mountaineers and Rangers: A History of Federal Forest Management in the Southern Appalachians, 1900–1981.* Washington, D.C.: U.S. Department of Agriculture, 1983.

McClelland, Linda Flint. *Presenting Nature: The Historic Landscape Design of the National Park Service, 1916–1942.* Washington, D.C.: National Register of Historic Places, 1993.

National Park Service. *A Study of the Park and Recreation Problem of the United States.* Washington, D.C.: GPO, 1941.

Otis, Alison T., et al. *The Forest Service and the Civilian Conservation Corps, 1933–1942.* Washington, D.C.: U. S. Forest Service, 1986.

Paige, John C. *The Civilian Conservation Corps and the National Park Service, 1933–1942: An Administrative History.* Washington, D.C.: National Park Service, 1985.

Sims, E. Thomas, and Julie Turner. "Table Rock Civilian Conservation Corps (CCC) Camp Site." National Register of Historic Places Registration Form. South Carolina Department of Archives and History, Columbia, 1989.

———. "Table Rock State Park Historic District." National Register of Historic Places Registration Form. South Carolina Department of Archives and History, Columbia, 1989.

Smith, Sandra Taylor. "The Civilian Conservation Corps in Arkansas, 1933–1942." Little Rock: Arkansas Historic Preservation Program, [1990?].

South Carolina Department of Archives and History. "Annual Report: State Forestry Commission." Columbia: Joint Committee on Printing, General Assembly of South Carolina, 1932–1942.

———. "Reports of State Officers, Boards, and Committees to the General Assembly of the State of South Carolina." Columbia: Joint Committee on Printing, General Assembly of South Carolina, 1933–1943.

South Carolina Department of Parks, Recreation, and Tourism. "An Historic Management Perspective of the South Carolina State Parks System." Columbia: South Carolina Department of Parks, Recreation, and Tourism, [1988?].

———. "History of South Carolina State Parks." Columbia: South Carolina Department of Parks, Recreation, and Tourism, 1992.

South Carolina Federal Writers' Project. *Palmetto Pioneers: Six Stories of Early South Carolinians.* Columbia: South Carolina Federal Writers' Project, 1938.

———. *South Carolina: A Guide to the Palmetto State.* American Guide Series, Works Projects Administration. Reprint, New York: Oxford University Press, 1963.

———. *South Carolina State Parks.* American Guide Series, Work Projects Administration. Columbia: South Carolina State Forest Service, 1940.

South Carolina State Historic Preservation Office. "Historic Resources of South Carolina State Parks." National Register of Historic Places Multiple Property Documentation Form. South Carolina Department of Archives and History, Columbia, 1989.

South Carolina State Planning Board. *Parks and Recreational Areas of South Carolina.* Bulletin No. 7. Columbia: South Carolina State Planning Board, 1941.

Stager, Claudette. "Pickett State Rustic Park Historic District." National Register of Historic Places Registration Form. Tennessee Historical Commission, 1986.

———. "Standing Stone State Rustic Park Historic District." National Register of Historic Places Registration Form. Tennessee Historical Commission, 1986.

Unrau, Harlan D., and G. Frank Williss, *Administrative History: Expansion of the National Park Service in the 1930s.* Denver: NPS Denver Service Center, 1983. http://www.cr.nps.gov/history/on-line__books/unrau-williss/adhi.htm. Accessed August 8, 2001.

Works Progress Administration of South Carolina. *Research and Records Work in South Carolina.* Columbia, S.C.: n.p., 1940.

Books

Alexander, Charles C. *Nationalism in American Thought.* Chicago: Rand McNally, 1969.

Badger, Anthony J. *The New Deal: The Depression Years, 1933–1940.* New York: Noonday Press, 1989.

Barton, Don. *The Clemson-Carolina Game, 1896–1966.* Columbia, S.C.: State Printing Company, 1966.

Belasco, Warren James. *Americans on the Road: From Autocamp to Motel, 1910–1945.* Cambridge, Mass.: MIT Press, 1981.

Biles, Roger. *The South and the New Deal.* Louisville: University Press of Kentucky, 1994.

Bland, Sidney R. *Preserving Charleston's Past, Shaping Its Future: The Life and Times of Susan Pringle Frost.* Columbia: University of South Carolina Press, 1999.

Brinkley, Alan. *Prosperity, Depression, and War: 1920–1945.* Washington, D.C.: American Historical Association, 1990.

Byrnes, James F. *All in One Lifetime.* New York: Harper & Brothers, 1958.

Campbell, Will D. *Brother to a Dragonfly.* New York: Continuum Publishing, 1971.

Carlton, David L. *Mill and Town in South Carolina, 1880–1920.* Baton Rouge: Louisiana State University Press, 1982.

Clark, Thomas D. *The Greening of the South: The Recovery of Land and Forest.* Lexington: University Press of Kentucky, 1984.

Cohen, Stan. *The Tree Army: A Pictorial History of the Civilian Conservation Corps, 1933–1942.* Missoula, Mont.: Pictorial Histories Publishing, 1980.

Cohodas, Nadine. *Strom Thurmond and the Politics of Southern Change.* New York: Simon and Schuster, 1993.

Cole, Olen, Jr. *The African-American Experience in the Civilian Conservation Corps.* Gainesville: University Press of Florida, 1999.

Conard, Rebecca. *Places of Quiet Beauty: Parks, Preserves, and Environmentalism.* Iowa City: University of Iowa Press, 1997.

Conkin, Paul K. *FDR and the Origins of the Welfare State.* New York: Thomas Y. Crowell, 1967.

———. *Tomorrow a New World: The New Deal Community Program.* Ithaca, N.Y.: Cornell University Press, 1959.

Cook, Blanche. *Eleanor Roosevelt,* Vol. 2, *1933–1938.* New York: Viking Press, 1982.

Cooney, Terry A. *Balancing Acts: American Thought and Culture in the 1930s.* New York: Twayne, 1995.

Cutler, Phoebe. *The Public Landscape of the New Deal.* New Haven, Conn.: Yale University Press, 1985.

Daniel, Pete. *Breaking the Land: The Transformation of the Cotton, Tobacco, and Rice Cultures since 1880.* Chicago: University of Illinois Press, 1985.

Daniels, Roger. *The Bonus March: An Episode of the Great Depression.* Westport, Conn.: Greenwood Press, 1971.

Davis, Kenneth S. *FDR: The New Deal Years, 1933–1937.* New York: Random House, 1986.

Dearborn, Ned H. *Once in a Lifetime: A Guide to the CCC Camp.* New York: Charles E. Merrill, 1936.

Draper, Lyman. *King's Mountain and Its Heroes: History of the Battle of King's Mountain, October 7th, 1780.* Cincinnati: Peter G. Thomson, 1881. Reprint, Nashville, Tenn.: Blue and Gray Press, 1971.

Edgar, Walter. *History of Santee-Cooper, 1934–1984.* Columbia, S.C.: R. L. Bryan, 1984.

———. *South Carolina: A History.* Columbia: University of South Carolina Press, 1998.

Ekirch, Arthur A., Jr. *Ideologies and Utopias: The Impact of the New Deal on American Thought.* Chicago: Quadrangle Books, 1969.

Fischer, David Hackett. *Albion's Seed: Four British Folkways in America.* New York: Oxford University Press, 1989.

Fite, Gilbert C. *Cotton Fields No More: Southern Agriculture, 1865–1980.* Lexington: University Press of Kentucky, 1984.

Fraser, Walter J., Jr. *Charleston! Charleston! The History of a Southern City.* Columbia: University of South Carolina Press, 1989.

Graebner, William. *A History of Retirement: The Meaning and Function of an American Institution, 1885–1978.* New Haven, Conn.: Yale University Press, 1980.

Grant, Nancy L. *TVA and Black Americans: Planning for the Status Quo.* Philadelphia: Temple University Press, 1990.

Hall, Jacquelyn Dowd, et al. *Like a Family: The Making of a Southern Cotton Mill World.* Chapel Hill: University of North Carolina Press, 1987.

Hayes, Jack Irby, Jr. *South Carolina and the New Deal.* Columbia: University of South Carolina Press, 2001.

Hodges, James. *New Deal Labor Policy and the Southern Cotton Textile Industry, 1933–1941.* Knoxville: University of Tennessee Press, 1986.

Howard, Donald. *The WPA and Federal Relief Policy.* New York: Russell Sage, 1942.

Huff, Archie Vernon, Jr. *Greenville: The History of the City and County in the South Carolina Piedmont.* Columbia: University of South Carolina Press, 1995.

Hurmence, Belinda, ed. *Before Freedom, When I Just Can Remember.* Winston-Salem, N.C.: John F. Blair, 1989.

Ickes, Harold L. *The First Thousand Days, 1933–1936.* New York: Simon and Schuster, 1955.

Irish, Ann B. *Joseph W. Byrns of Tennessee: A Political Biography.* Knoxville: University of Tennessee Press, 2001.

Irons, Janet Christine. *Testing the New Deal: The General Textile Strike of 1934 in the American South.* Chicago: University of Illinois Press, 2000.

Jakle, John A. *The Tourist: Travel in Twentieth-Century North America*. Lincoln: University of Nebraska Press, 1985.

Jolley, Harley E. *"That Magnificent Army of Youth and Peace": The Civilian Conservation Corps in North Carolina, 1933–1942*. Raleigh: North Carolina Department of Cultural Resources, Office of Archives and History, 2007.

Kennedy, David M. *Freedom from Fear: The American People in Depression and War, 1929–1945*. New York: Oxford University Press, 1999.

Kovacik, Charles F., and John J. Winberry. *South Carolina: The Making of a Landscape*. Columbia: University of South Carolina Press, 1987.

Lacy, Leslie Alexander. *The Soil Soldiers: The Civilian Conservation Corps in the Great Depression*. Radnor, Pa.: Chilton Book, 1976.

Leuchtenburg, William E. *The FDR Years: On Roosevelt and His Legacy*. New York: Columbia University Press, 1995.

———. *Franklin D. Roosevelt and the New Deal, 1932–1940*. New York: Harper Torchbooks, 1963.

Linenthal, Edward Tabor. *Sacred Ground: Americans and Their Battlefields*. Urbana: University of Illinois Press, 1993.

Lowitt, Richard, and Maurine Beasley, eds. *One Third of a Nation: Lorena Hickok Reports on the Great Depression*. Chicago: University of Illinois Press, 1981.

Maher, Neil. *Nature's New Deal: The Civilian Conservation Corps and the Roots of the American Environmental Movement*. New York: Oxford University Press, 2008.

McClelland, Linda. *Building the National Parks: Historic Landscape Design and Construction*. Baltimore: Johns Hopkins University Press, 1998.

McElvaine, Robert S. *The Great Depression: America 1929–1941*. New York: Times Books, 1984.

Merrill, Perry H. *Roosevelt's Forest Army: A History of the Civilian Conservation Corps, 1933–1942*. Montpelier, Vt.: by the author, 1981.

Moore, John Hammond. *Columbia and Richland County: A South Carolina Community, 1740–1990*. Columbia: University of South Carolina Press, 1993.

Newby, I. A. *Black Carolinians: A History of Blacks in South Carolina from 1895–1968*. Columbia: University of South Carolina Press, 1973.

Nixon, Edgar A., ed. *Franklin D. Roosevelt and Conservation, 1911–1945*. Vol. 1. New York: Arno Press, 1972.

Nolte, M. Chester, ed. *The Civilian Conservation Corps: The Way We Remember It*. Paducah, Ky.: Turner Publishing, 1990.

Oates, Joyce Carol, and Robert Atwan, eds. *The Best American Essays of the Century*. New York: Houghton Mifflin, 2001.

Owen, A. L. Riesch. *Conservation Under F.D.R.* New York: Praeger, 1983.

Parler, Josie Platt. *The Past Blows By: On the Road to Poinsett Park*. Sumter, S.C.: Knight Brothers, [1939].

Pasquill, Robert, Jr. *The Civilian Conservation Corps in Alabama, 1933–1942: A Great and Lasting Good*. Tuscaloosa: University of Alabama Press, 2008.

Patterson, James T. *The New Deal and the States: Federalism in Transition*. Princeton, N.J.: Princeton University Press, 1969.

Perkins, Frances. *The Roosevelt I Knew.* New York: Viking, 1946.

Perkins, Van L. *Crisis in Agriculture: The Agricultural Adjustment Administration and the New Deal, 1933.* Berkeley: University of California Press, 1969.

Reiman, Richard A. *The New Deal and American Youth: Ideas and Ideals in a Depression Decade.* Athens: University of Georgia Press, 1992.

Rettie, Dwight F. *Our National Park System: Caring for America's Greatest Natural and Historic Treasures.* Urbana: University of Illinois Press, 1995.

Robbins, William G. *American Forestry: A History of National, State, and Private Cooperation.* Lincoln: University of Nebraska Press, 1985.

Rothman, Hal. *America's National Monuments: The Politics of Preservation.* Lawrence: University Press of Kansas, 1994. Previously published as *Preserving Different.*

Pasts: The American National Monuments. Urbana: University of Illinois Press, 1989.

Salmond, John A. *The Civilian Conservation Corps, 1933–1942: A New Deal Case Study.* Durham, N.C.: Duke University Press, 1967.

———. *The General Textile Strike of 1934: From Maine to Alabama.* Columbia: University of Missouri Press, 2002.

Schwarz, Jordan A. *The New Dealers: Power Politics in the Age of Roosevelt.* New York: Knopf, 1993.

Schlesinger, Arthur. *The Age of Roosevelt.* 3 vols. Boston: Houghton Mifflin, 1957–1960, 2003.

———. *The Coming of the New Deal.* Boston: Houghton Mifflin, 1988.

Simon, Bryant. *A Fabric of Defeat: The Politics of South Carolina Millhands, 1910–1948.* Chapel Hill: University of North Carolina Press, 1998.

Simons, Jane K. *A Guide to Columbia: South Carolina's Capital City.* Columbia, S.C.: Columbia Sesquicentennial Commission, R. L. Bryan, 1939.

Sitkoff, Harvard. *A New Deal for Blacks: The Emergence of Civil Rights as a National Issue, The Depression Decade.* New York: Oxford University Press, 1978.

Steely, James Wright. *Parks for Texas: Enduring Landscapes of the New Deal.* Austin: University of Texas Press, 1999.

Steely, James Wright, and Joseph R. Monticone. *The Civilian Conservation Corps in Texas State Parks.* Austin: Texas Parks and Wildlife Department, 1986.

Stokes, Barbara F. *Myrtle Beach: A History, 1900–1980.* Columbia: University of South Carolina Press, 2007.

Sullivan, Patricia. *Days of Hope: Race and Democracy in the New Deal Era.* Chapel Hill: University of North Carolina Press, 1996.

Swensson, Lise C., and Nancy M. Higgins, eds. *New Deal Art in South Carolina.* Columbia: South Carolina State Museum, 1990.

Taylor, Nick. *American Made, The Enduring Legacy of the WPA: When FDR Put the Nation to Work.* New York: Bantam Books, 2008.

Tilden, Freeman. *The State Parks: Their Meaning in American Life.* New York: Alfred A. Knopf, 1962.

Tindall, George Brown. *The Emergence of the New South, 1913–1945.* Baton Rouge: Louisiana State University Press, 1967.

Utley, Dan K., and James W. Steely. *Guided with a Steady Hand: The Cultural Landscape of a Rural Texas Park.* Waco, Tex.: Baylor University Press, 1998.

Ware, Susan. *Beyond Suffrage: Women in the New Deal.* Cambridge, Mass.: Harvard University Press, 1981.

Watkins, T[om]. H. *The Hungry Years: A Narrative History of the Great Depression in America.* New York: Henry Holt, 1999.

West, Carroll Van. *Tennessee's New Deal Landscape: A Guidebook.* Knoxville: University of Tennessee Press, 2001.

Wirth, Conrad L. *Parks, Politics, and the People.* Oklahoma City: University of Oklahoma Press, 1980.

Articles and Chapters

Bates, James. "Long Cane/Enoree History." http://www.fs.fed.us/r8/fms/welcome/piedmont.htm. Accessed July 31, 2001.

Brown, D. Clayton, "Modernizing Rural Life: South Carolina's Push for Public Rural Electrification." *South Carolina Historical Magazine* 99 (January 1998): 66–85.

Bruggeman, Seth C. *Here, George Washington Was Born.* Athens: University of Georgia Press, 2008.

Cann, Marvin L. "Burnet Maybank and Charleston Politics in the New Deal Era." *Proceedings of the South Carolina Historical Association* (1979): 39–48.

Clancy, Patrick. "Conserving the Youth: The Civilian Conservation Corps Experience in the Shenandoah National Park." *Virginia Magazine of History and Biography* 105 (Autumn 1997): 439–72.

Coggins, Allen R. "The Early History of Tennessee's State Parks, 1919–1956." *Tennessee Historical Quarterly* 63 (Fall 1984): 295–315.

Conard, Rebecca, and Michael Carrier. "Integrating Cultural and Natural History in State Park Management." *George Wright Forum* 17, no. 3 (2000): 21–30.

Davidson, Lisa Pfueller, and James A. Jacobs. "Civilian Conservation Corps Activities in the National Capital Region of the National Park Service." *CRM: The Journal of Heritage Stewardship* 2 (Summer 2005): 90–95.

Davis, Ren. "Our Mark on This Land." *Georgia Journal* (March/April 1998): 20–29.

Fechner, Robert. "My Hopes for the CCC." *American Forests: The Magazine of the American Forestry Association* (January 1939). http://www.newdeal.feri.org/forests/af139.htm. Accessed May 2, 2000.

Fischer, David Hackett. "The Braided Narrative: Substance and Form in Social History." In *The Literature of Fact: Selected Papers from the English Institute*, ed. Angus Fletcher, 109–13. New York: Columbia University Press, 1976.

Flynt, J. Wayne. "The New Deal and Southern Labor." In *The New Deal and the South*, ed. James C. Cobb and Michael V. Namaroto, 63–95. Jackson: University Press of Mississippi, 1984.

[Foley, Mike.] "Your Parks for Fifty Years: South Carolina State Parks Celebrate Golden Anniversary." *Park Lites: State Parks Newsletter* (Spring 1984): 9–15.

Graham, Cole Blease Jr. "James Francis Byrnes." In *The South Carolina Encyclopedia*, ed. Walter Edgar, 114–15. Columbia: University of South Carolina Press for the Humanities Council, 2006.

Henneberger, John. "State Park Beginnings." *George Wright Forum* 17 (2000): 9–20.

Hiott, Susan G. "New Deal Art in South Carolina." http://people.clemson.edu/hiotts/pwap.html. Accessed December 14, 2001.

Hoffman, Edwin D. "The Genesis of the Modern Movement for Equal Rights in South Carolina, 1930–1939." *Journal of Negro History* 44 (October 1959): 346–69.

Holmes, Michael S. "The New Deal and Georgia's Black Youth." *Journal of Southern History* 38 (February 1972): 443–60.

Hogenauer, Alan K. "Gone, But Not Forgotten: The Delisted Units of the U.S. National Park System." *George Wright Forum* 7 (1991): 2–19.

———. "An Update to 'Gone But Not Forgotten: The Delisted Units of the U.S. National Park System.'" *George Wright Forum* 8 (1991): 26–28.

Jackson, Donald Dale. "They Were Poor, Hungry, and They Built to Last." *Smithsonian* (December 1994): 66–75.

Johnson, Charles W. "The Army, the Negro and the Civilian Conservation Corps, 1933–1942." *Military Affairs* 36 (October 1972): 82–88.

———. "The Army and the Civilian Conservation Corps, 1933–1942." *Prologue* (Fall 1972): 139–16.

Lofton, Paul. "The Columbia Black Community in the 1930s." *Proceedings of the South Carolina Historical Association* (1984): 86–95.

Lucas, Greg. "Field Trip: Oconee State Park." *South Carolina Wildlife* 40 (September–October 1993): 52–55.

Maher, Neil M. "A New Deal Body Politic: Landscape, Labor, and the Civilian Conservation Corps." *Environmental History* 7 (Summer 2002): 435–61.

McElvaine, Robert S. "The Works Progress Administration: Criticism and Praise." In *America's Decades: The 1930s*, ed. Louise I. Gerdes, 144–17. San Diego, Calif.: Greenhaven Press, 2000.

McIntosh, Phyllis. "The Corps of Conservation." *National Parks* 75 (September/October 2001): 23–27.

Moore, Winfred B., Jr. "'Soul of the South': James F. Byrnes and the Racial Issue in American Politics, 1911–1941." *Proceedings of the South Carolina Historical Association* (1978): 42–52.

Myers, Andrew H. *Black, White, and Olive Drab: Racial Integration at Fort Jackson, South Carolina, and the Civil Rights Movement* (Charlottesville: University of Virginia Press, 2006)

Nichols, Ruth D. "Civilian Conservation Corps." In *Tennessee Encyclopedia of History and Culture*, ed. Carroll Van West, 171–12. Nashville, Tenn.: Rutledge Hill Press, 1998.

———. "T. O. Fuller State Park." In *Tennessee Encyclopedia of History and Culture*, ed. Carroll Van West, 904. Nashville, Tenn.: Rutledge Hill Press, 1998.

Osterman, Tamar. "Historic Structures in National Parks." *Historic Preservation Forum* 10 (Summer 1996): 6–13.

Paige, John. "The CCC: It Gave a New Face to the NPS." *CRM Bulletin* 6 (September 1983): 1–3.

Paxton, Peggy J. *The National Forests and Purchase Units of Region Eight.* Atlanta: USDA Forest Service, 1950.

Reiter, Michael A., James P. Eagleman, and Jenna Luckenbaugh. "The Design and Value of Service Learning Partnerships in State Parks." *George Wright Forum* 17, no. 3 (2000): 47–54.

Saluoutos, Theodore. "New Deal Agricultural Policy: An Evaluation." *Journal of American History* 61 (September 1974): 394–416.

Shackleton, Robert. "A Battlefield That Is Seldom Visited—Kings Mountain." *Magazine of American History* 30 (July–August 1893): 38–46.

Shofner, Jerrell H. "Roosevelt's 'Tree Army': The Civilian Conservation Corps in Florida." *Florida Historical Quarterly* 65 (April 1987): 433–56.

Simon, Bryant. "'New Men in Body and Soul': The Civilian Conservation Corps and the Transformation of Male Bodies and the Body Politic." In *Gender and the Southern Body Politic,* ed. Nancy Bercaw, 131–10. Jackson: University Press of Mississippi, 2000.

Smith, Selden K. "'Cotton Ed' Smith's Response to Economic Adversity." *Proceedings of the South Carolina Historical Association* (1971): 16–23.

Speakman, Joseph. "Into the Woods: The First Year of the Civilian Conservation Corps." *Prologue* 38 (Fall 2006). http://www.archives.gov/publications/prologue/2006/fall/ccc.html. Accessed November 13, 2006.

———. "The New Deal Arrives in Penn's Woods: The Beginnings of the Civilian Conservation Corps in Pennsylvania." *Pennsylvania Magazine of History and Biography* 13 (April 2006). http://www.historycooperative.org/journals/pmh/130.2/speakman.html. Accessed May 23, 2006.

Stange, Maren. "Publicity, Husbandry, and Technocracy: Fact and Symbol in Civilian Conservation Corps Photography." In *Official Images: New Deal Photography,* ed. Pete Daniel et al., 66–71. Washington, D.C.: Smithsonian Institution Press, 1987.

Steely, James. "CCC in Texas." *Platform* (Fall 1999): 2–3, 10.

Swain, Martha H. "A New Deal for Southern Women: Gender and Race in Women's Work Relief." In *Women of the American South,* ed. Christie Anne Farnham, 241–57. New York: New York University Press, 1997.

Swing, Raymond Gram. "Take the Army Out of the CCC." *Nation* 141 (October 25, 1935): 459–60.

Waller, Robert. "The Civilian Conservation Corps and the Emergence of South Carolina's State Park System, 1933–1942." *South Carolina Historical Magazine* 104 (April 2003): 101–15.

———. "*Happy Days* and the CCC in South Carolina." *Historian* 64 (Fall 2001): 39–61.

Wandall, Luther C. "A Negro in the CCC." *Crisis* 42 (August 1935): 244, 253–54.

West, Carroll Van. "Chucalissa Village." In *Tennessee Encyclopedia of History and Culture,* ed. Carroll Van West, 157–18. Nashville, Tenn.: Rutledge Hill Press, 1998.

Woodward, Ellen. "Hot Lunches for a Million School Children," (1937?). Record Group 69, National Archives. http://newdeal.feri.org/texts/500.htm. Accessed December 12, 2002.

Wright, Marian Thompson. "Negro Youth and the Federal Emergency Programs: CCC and NYA." *Journal of Negro Education* 9 (July 1940): 397–407.

Zelinsky, Wilbur. "The Imprint of Central Authority." In *The Making of the American Landscape,* ed. Michael P. Conzen, 311–34. New York: Routledge, 1994.

Theses and Dissertations

Cann, Marvin L. "Burnet Rhett Maybank and the New Deal in South Carolina, 1931–1941." Ph.D. diss., University of North Carolina, 1967.

Copp, Roberta V. "South Carolina's Historic Records Survey, 1935–1942." M.A. thesis, University of South Carolina, 1988.

Cox, Stephen Lewis. "The History of Negro State Parks in South Carolina: 1940–1963." M.A. thesis, University of South Carolina, 1992.

Hamer, Fritz P. "A Southern City Enters the Twentieth Century: Charleston, Its Navy Yard, and World War II, 1940–1948." Ph.D. diss., University of South Carolina, 1998.

Hanson, Jill K. "'A Room of One's Own': Preserving Twentieth-Century Women's History in Columbia, South Carolina." M.A. thesis, University of South Carolina, 1994.

Hayes, Jack Irby, Jr. "South Carolina and the New Deal, 1932–1938." Ph.D. diss., University of South Carolina, 1972.

Hiott, William David. "New Deal Resettlement in South Carolina." M.A. thesis, University of South Carolina, 1986.

Kennerly, Edna. "The Civilian Conservation Corps as a Social Resource in South Carolina." M.S. W. thesis, University of South Carolina, 1940.

Kifer, Allen Francis. "The Negro Under the New Deal, 1933–1941." Ph.D. diss., University of Wisconsin, 1961.

Lesesne, Henry Herbert. "Opposition to the New Deal in South Carolina." M.A. thesis, University of South Carolina, 1995.

Maher, Neil S. "Planting More than Trees: The Civilian Conservation Corps and the Roots of the American Environmental Movement, 1929–1942." Ph.D. diss., New York University, 2001.

Nichols, Ruth D. "The Civilian Conservation Corps and Tennessee State Parks: 1933–1942." M.A. thesis, Middle Tennessee State University, 1994.

Ramsey, Ginger. "Cedars of Lebanon State Park: A Preservation Plan." M.A. thesis, Middle Tennessee State University, 1999.

Rich, Stephen O'Neal. "The Civilian Conservation Corps: A Life-Changing Experience." M.S. W. thesis, California State University, Long Beach, 2003.

Smith, W. S. "Rural Electrification in South Carolina." M.S. thesis, University of South Carolina, 1932.

Suzik, Jeffrey Ryan. "'Building Better Men': Education, Training, and Socialization of Working-Class Male Youth in the Civilian Conservation Corps, 1933–1942." Ph.D. diss., Carnegie Mellon University, 2005.

Weber, Stacy L. "Vision and Reality: TVA's Recreational Demonstration Program, 1933–1942." M.A. thesis, Middle Tennessee State University, 2002.

Unpublished Papers

Bernshouse, Wilbert. "Autobiography." Handwritten manuscript, [1996]. Photocopy.

Brown, Frank, Dan Elswick, and Tommy Sims. "The Establishment and Development of South Carolina State Parks." Unpublished report in research files. Historical

Services Division, South Carolina Department of Archives and History, Columbia, 1989. Photocopy.

Copp, Robin. "The Civilian Conservation Corps and South Carolina." Unpublished paper in research files. Historical Services Division, South Carolina Department of Archives and History, Columbia, 1985. Photocopy.

National Association of Civilian Conservation Corps Alumni, Chapter 36. "Fort Moultrie Chapter of the NACCCA," typewritten booklet, [1984]. Photocopy.

Skelton, Stephen W. "Poinsett State Park: National Register Nomination Preliminary Research." Unpublished paper in research files. Historical Services Division, South Carolina Department of Archives and History, Columbia, 1989. Photocopy.

Withrow, Scott. "The CCC Remembered in Upstate South Carolina: Bethany and Mountain Rest." Unpublished paper in Kings Mountain State Park files. South Carolina Department of Parks, Recreation, and Tourism, Columbia, 1985. Photocopy.